198

CONNOISSEURS
AND SECRET AGENTS

CONNOISSEURS
AND SECRET AGENTS

In Eighteenth Century Rome

LESLEY LEWIS

1961
CHATTO & WINDUS
LONDON

Published by
Chatto and Windus Ltd
42 William IV Street
London W.C.2

*

Clarke Irwin & Co. Ltd
Toronto

Printed in Great Britain
by Butler & Tanner Ltd
Frome and London

To David

Contents

	Preface	*page*	11
I	British Diplomatic Arrangements in the Ecclesiastical State		21
II	Alessandro Albani and Philip von Stosch		38
III	Stosch in Rome		63
IV	Diplomats and Spies		91
V	The War of the Austrian Succession and the Forty-Five Rebellion		117
VI	Between the Wars		144
VII	Albani's Concerns during the Seven Years War		176
VIII	Albani's Golden Age		204
	Notes		237
	Table of Principal Sources		263
	Bibliography		267
	Index		269

List of Illustrations

Plate   *Page*

1 CARDINAL ALESSANDRO ALBANI   48
   Engraving reproduced by courtesy of the British
   Museum

2 PRINCE JAMES STUART (THE OLD PRETEN-
   DER)   49
   Drawing by Pier Leone Ghezzi reproduced by
   courtesy of the Director of the Albertina, Vienna

3 THE MUTI PALACE, ROME (NOW PALAZZO
   BALESTRA)   64
   Photo Alinari

4 PHILIP VON STOSCH AND ROMAN ANTI-
   QUARIES   65
   Drawing by Pier Leone Ghezzi reproduced by
   courtesy of the Director of the Albertina, Vienna

5 THE PIAZZA NAVONA ON THE OCCASION OF
   A FETE GIVEN BY THE FRENCH AMBASSADOR
   IN 1729   112
   Detail of a painting by G. P. Pannini showing the
   Pretender and his sons in the middle distance, right.
   Reproduced by courtesy of the Director of the
   National Gallery of Ireland, Dublin

6 *a* PRINCE HENRY BENEDICT STUART   113
   b PRINCE CHARLES EDWARD STUART
   Paintings by Louis-Gabriel Blanchet reproduced by
   courtesy of Mrs Colin Davy (Exhibited Royal
   Academy 1960, "Italian Art and Britain")

7 A GROUP OF ENGLISHMEN IN ROME   128
   Painting of the English School, c. 1749–52, repro-
   duced by courtesy of the Hon. Mrs Ionides (Exhibited
   Royal Academy 1955–6, "English Taste in the
   Eighteenth Century")

LIST OF ILLUSTRATIONS

Plate   *Page*

8 BRANDENBURGH HOUSE   129
   *An engraving from Daniel Lysons, 'Environs of
   London, Vol. 2: Middlesex' (1795)*

9 CARICATURE GROUP, SHOWING HORACE
   MANN ON THE RIGHT   192
   *Painting by Thomas Patch, c. 1763, reproduced by
   courtesy of the Royal Albert Memorial Museum,
   Exeter (Exhibited Royal Academy 1960, "Italian
   Art and Britain")*

10 THE VILLA ALBANI   193
   *Reproduced by courtesy of Prince Torlonia from a
   photograph published by 'Connaissance des Arts',
   March 1960*

11 THE LOGGIA, VILLA ALBANI   208
   *Reproduced by courtesy of Prince Torlonia from a
   photograph published by 'Connaissance des Arts',
   March 1960*

12 THE GREAT GALLERY, VILLA ALBANI   209
   *Reproduced by courtesy of Prince Torlonia from a
   photograph published by 'Connaissance des Arts',
   March 1960*

Preface

THE curious story told in this book began to unfold itself when I was looking for material on the sojourn in Rome of Robert Strange the engraver. He had strong Jacobite connections, having himself fought at Culloden and married the sister of Andrew Lumsden, who became assistant secretary to the Old Pretender. Strange was acquainted in Rome with Cardinal Alessandro Albani, well known as an expert and dealer in Roman antiques and as the patron of the famous scholar Johann Joachim Winckelmann. A chance remark found in James Dennistoun's Memoirs of Sir Robert Strange and Andrew Lumsden,* to the effect that Alessandro Albani was a spy, led me to the Public Record Office in London where is deposited the Cardinal's official correspondence with Horace Mann, the British representative in Florence. The more I read the stranger it seemed that Albani, whose uncle Pope Clement XI had originally invited the Old Pretender to Rome, and whose nephew was Cardinal Stuart's close friend, should tell Mann so much about the doings of the Jacobite Court. He was Minister to Maria Theresa, who was Britain's ally, and as such "protected" British interests in Rome because, for religious reasons, Britain had no direct diplomatic representation there. Even so, however, his friendship towards the British and the nature of his correspondence with Mann seemed to go far beyond what his official position demanded and dead against what his family connections would lead one to expect. It dawned on me that the Jacobite reference to his being a spy might well have something in it.

Anyone who studies the affairs of the Jacobites in Rome

* See Bibliography.

or the work of Winckelmann comes very soon upon that strange and murky character, Philip von Stosch, a famous antiquarian collector, whom the British government paid for thirty-five years to report, under the pseudonym John Walton, on the doings of the Stuart Court. His despatches and other official correspondence suggested that not only were he and Albani closely associated as connoisseurs and dealers in objets d'art but that Stosch had probably drawn the Cardinal into his own political concerns as well, long before Albani's appointment as Maria Theresa's Minister during the War of the Austrian Succession gave him an official reason for passing information to Mann. Just as I was beginning to extract from documents in the Public Record Office in London exciting evidence of Albani's extra-official activities, Mr W. G. Constable drew my attention to an article by Friedrich Noack on Alessandro's relations with artists,* which revealed to me that Horace Mann's letters to the Cardinal, as well as his own drafts, must now be in the State Archives in Vienna. This was indeed the case, and I found nearly the whole of both sides of the Albani–Mann correspondence and was able to read it through chronologically and collate it with the corresponding material in the Public Record Office. The result was a remarkably clear picture of Albani's place in English politics and connoisseurship.

My book is based primarily on these two very ample sources, the relevant "State Papers Foreign" in the Public Record Office, London, and "Gesandtschaftsarchiv Rom/ Vatikan" in the Haus-, Hof- und Staatsarchiv, Vienna. The London papers, mainly in French and English, are divided into several sections but I have drawn only upon those called "General Correspondence" and "Archives". The former contains the main series of letters exchanged by British representatives abroad with the Secretary of State or

* See Bibliography.

officials in Whitehall, together with certain key communications from other persons, sent to London as being of special importance. Stosch's despatches, for instance, were forwarded in full, and certain letters from Albani were enclosed in Mann's own letters to the Secretary of State for the Southern Department, who dealt with Italian affairs. The Archives section contains supplementary material of all kinds, drafts, copies, extracts and letters exchanged between representatives abroad or received from foreign sources. The majority of Albani's own letters are in this section.

The two sections duplicate each other to some extent and there is also much duplication within each, for the complementary originals and drafts or copies may be in separate bundles. Wherever I have been able to trace it I have given a reference to an original in the General Correspondence, but I cannot claim that my examination of the papers has been sufficiently exhaustive to ensure the best source being invariably chosen. The systematic scheduling of the material would be a task for a team rather than an individual. Where I know there are originals and drafts of the same letters from Albani in London and Vienna respectively I have given both references purely for the convenience of the reader, but do not claim that the list of duplicates is complete. Mann's drafts in London appear to be so scarce during the early years of the correspondence, possibly because as he wrote in his own hand he made none, that I have not done the same in his case. Mere entries of dates of letters in the collections are not sufficient identification, because Albani often, and Mann sometimes, wrote more than one letter on the same day if dealing with different subjects. Undoubtedly the remaining sections of State Papers Foreign, which are of a more public nature, would provide additional information, but in the absence of any detailed list or index the labour of examining them appeared hardly justified. The repetition and duplication in General Correspondence and Archives make it unlikely that any major topic has been entirely missed. A reader who has the curiosity to follow up my references will find that in almost all cases the bundle contains further relevant material, and my list of bundles used may be regarded as the equivalent of a bibliography for much of the book. Index No. XIX in the Public Record Office gives a general description of contents but few names of individuals.

The Vienna papers are an easier proposition. The numerous "Faszicles" contain the correspondence carried on by Albani as Austrian Minister in Rome. The letters are in French, Italian and occasionally in German, but for my book I have relied almost entirely on those passing between Albani and Mann and written in French. The Englishman, incidentally, wrote far the better French, that of Alessandro or his secretary being marred by Italianisms such as the omission of personal pronouns. A few letters of a semi-private nature, such as those exchanged with the dealer Richard Gaven, have been used where relevant. Albani, who himself wrote a most villainous hand, appears to have dictated his letters both on official and private business to a team of secretaries and to have had much of it filed together. His clerical organisation was excellent, and year after year the letters answered in each week were placed with drafts of the replies in a neatly endorsed folder. The pages are not numbered, as is the case with most of the London papers, but any individual letter is fairly easy to find by date. It should be remembered, however, that the date of Albani's answer determines the position within a bundle of a letter received by him.

The London and Vienna documents could themselves be more exhaustively searched and also could certainly be much amplified from other contemporary sources such as the Rome and Turin archives. Three easily accessible

published ones are highly relevant: the Horace Walpole–
Horace Mann Correspondence in the Yale Edition* which
had appeared up to October 1748 at the time my book went
to press†; the Letters of Winckelmann with much interesting
supplementary material recently published in four volumes
in Berlin‡; and the Stuart Papers so far published by the
Historical Manuscripts Commission‡. I have used these
fairly extensively but by no means exhaustively and have
not sought access to the great bulk of the Stuart Papers in
Her Majesty's possession at Windsor which are still
unpublished.

A rather strange combination of circumstances has probably prevented the liaison between Stosch, Albani, the
Stuarts and Horace Mann from being explored hitherto as
thoroughly as might have been expected. Stosch's despatches
have been consistently discredited both by the much-
prejudiced Horace Walpole and, naturally enough, by
authors with partisan Jacobite sympathies. By far the most
interesting part of his career ended when he left Rome in
1731, and the liveliness of the despatches dating from the
nine years he was there has been obscured by the increasing
tedium of what he wrote during the succeeding twenty-six
years in Florence. The triviality of his later comments as
well as the bankruptcy of the Stuart cause can be gauged by
the small use he made of cypher. In his early letters he had
used it extensively, even though British representatives were
cautioned to be sparing, as nothing tended more to the discovery of cyphers than the quantity that might fall into the
hands of the decypherers.

As regards Albani, it so happened that Horace Walpole's
introduction to him failed to ripen into the closer friendship

* See Bibliography.
† The volumes covering the next period to March 1768 are referred
to in a few footnotes added subsequently.
‡ SP 98/69 f. 139 Halifax to Mann, St. James's 12. vi. 64.

which might have been expected in the circumstances. When Walpole was in Rome in 1740 a prolonged Conclave prevented his seeing the Cardinal more than momentarily. We may presume that we should have heard very much more of Alessandro Albani in England had he been a personal friend of Horace Walpole.

Another inhibiting factor was that Albani omitted to discuss with Mann Winckelmann's sensational death in 1768. A full account of the murder from the victim's patron would have been likely to focus more interest on the letters as a whole. Moreover had Winckelmann kept his promise to send a complete description of the Villa Albani to the Society of Antiquaries this might well have been more celebrated in England. In addition, that great scholar Karl Justi is in some respects misleading. He wrote on Stosch and Albani from a great number of obscure sources which are not all identifiable, and without access to the London and Vienna State Papers he could not have appreciated the extent of the connection with England. Had he read Albani's letters to Mann he would hardly have said that his true character would be sought in vain in his diplomatic despatches and that the only real trace of him remained in his Villa, in colour, line and composition and not in writing and opinions.*

In the references at the end of the book I have adopted the following plan:

Published works which have either been referred to more than once in the text or are indispensable for general background are listed alphabetically under the author's name in the bibliography, and specific references to them will be by that name only, with an abbreviated title where necessary. The index numbers of the bundles of papers in the Public Record Office are prefaced by the letters SP (i.e. State Papers) only; those in Vienna by the letter F. (for Faszicle

* Justi, *Preuss. Jahr.*, p. 259.

in the Gesandtschaftsarchiv Rom/Vatikan). As Albani's own letters in Vienna are necessarily all drafts they are not individually marked as such. Stosch and Mann can be assumed to be writing from Florence, and Albani and Giordani from Rome unless otherwise stated. As regards dating, letters written from England before the reform of the calendar in September 1752 are in Old Style, that is, eleven days behind that of the New Style in use on the continent and in all the foreign letters I have quoted. Old Style or both alternatives were used in letters from H.M. ships at sea and I have given the former. In all cases the modern dating of the New Year from January and not March has been adopted. All documents referred to are of the eighteenth century unless otherwise indicated.

L. L.

London, 1961

Acknowledgments

I HAVE received much help from many quarters in the preparation of this book and acknowledge it most gratefully. Mr W. G. Constable has throughout advised me both generally and specifically, and so has Mr Francis Watson, C.B.E. I have had the most courteous co-operation and attention from the staff of the Public Record Office, and Mr Noel Blakiston, O.B.E., has in addition given me much individual help, especially in the elucidation of Italian documents. Dr Richard Blaas and the staff of the Haus-, Hof- und Staatsarchiv were tireless in arranging for the two hundred or so bundles consulted to be readily available to me. Sir Anthony Blunt, K.C.V.O., and Dr Gertrude Bing advised me themselves and allowed me to make use of the excellent facilities of the Courtauld and Warburg Institutes, as did Lord Adrian, O.M., F.R.S., in the Library of Trinity College, Cambridge. In Rome the help of Mr J. B. Ward-Perkins, C.B.E., and the use of the libraries of the British School and the Hertziana were invaluable, as was the Geographical Section of the Nationalbibliothek in Vienna. I am particularly indebted to Prince Torlonia for allowing me to visit the Villa Albani and, with the co-operation of the proprietors of the *Connaissance des Arts*, to reproduce their excellent photographs of the Villa. I thank the Directors of the Albertina, the National Gallery of Ireland, the Royal Albert Memorial Museum, Exeter, the Trustees of the British Museum, the Hon. Mrs Ionides and Mrs Colin Davy for permission to reproduce pictures in their possession. The Duke of Northumberland, K.G., and Mr C. de Bestigui have kindly furnished information about paintings formerly at Northumberland House, and Earl Spencer about Albani's present of a vase to Georgiana,

Lady Spencer. Mr John Fleming, the author of a most
interesting article on Alessandro Albani, has given me
many useful hints, and Mr Richard Pommer has given me
some valuable details from his study of archives in Turin.
Mrs Stanley, who writes under the name of Nora K.
Strange, kindly lent me books and gave me supplementary
information about her Jacobite kinsmen. Mr Brinsley Ford
has allowed me to consult his valuable records of Englishmen in Rome, and Dr R. Kinauer to refer to his unpublished
thesis on Stosch's *Atlas*. Sir Kenneth Clark, K.C.B., C.H.,
the late Sir Marcus Cheke, K.C.V.O., C.M.G., Conte Nolfo
de Carpegna, Professor G. Baldini, Dr G. Spini, Dr Anna
von Spitzmüller, Messrs David Buxton, Henry Blunt, David
Evans; Basil Skinner, Dr Elizabeth Rosenbaum, Mrs
B. B. Parry, Miss Lilian Gurry and Mrs Wynyard Astell
helped me with introductions, translations and information
on specific points, while Mrs E. Jordan has saved me much
time in many ways. I owe a very special debt to the editors
of the Yale Edition of Horace Walpole's Correspondence,
especially Dr Warren H. Smith, for generosity and prompti-
tude in answering enquiries, and to Mr W. S. Lewis himself
for allowing me to refer to and quote from unpublished
letters in his possession from Mann to Bubb Dodington.
My husband has read typescripts and advised me most con-
structively throughout. I am particularly grateful to Miss
V. M. Dallas, M.B.E., for making the index.

Unpublished Crown copyright material in the Public
Record Office is reproduced by permission of the Con-
troller of Her Majesty's Stationery Office; material from the
Haus-, Hof- und Staatsarchiv, Vienna, by permission of the
Director; the Minute Books of the Society of Antiquaries
are referred to and quoted by courtesy of the Society, and
Dr Kinauer's unpublished thesis by that of the University of
Vienna.

CHAPTER I

British Diplomatic Arrangements in the Ecclesiastical State

THE collection of antique objets d'art from Europe and Asia Minor came into fashion among the English in the seventeenth century and, during the eighteenth, was enormously stimulated by the building and renovation of great houses with which members of the ruling class became so intensely preoccupied. Such collecting was at first royal or aristocratic, but the taste penetrated quickly through personal contacts and the fashion for the Grand Tour, to discerning or ambitious members of the middle class. Only men with considerable influence as well as wealth could at first indulge these tastes since there were few facilities for acquiring antiques except through consular, diplomatic and service channels, and it was therefore inevitable that connoisseurship should be intimately connected with the politics of the period. Italy, and more particularly Rome, were naturally the principal hunting-grounds for collectors, but the chronically strained Anglo-Roman relations were further bedevilled throughout a great part of the eighteenth century by the awkward presence of the exiled Stuarts under papal protection. This circumstance produced all kinds of complications for British travellers and would-be collectors, though certain advantages as well, and their affairs in Rome were influenced not only by the general political situation on the continent but by the intense diplomatic activity, including a great deal of espionage, which centred on the Old Pretender's Court.

In the Italian sovereign States Britain's interests were

normally represented by a Resident, Envoy Extraordinary or Minister Plenipotentiary who dealt with political affairs in general, and a Consul who was primarily concerned with trade but who sometimes deputised for a superior official and whose functions to some extent overlapped his. In Tuscany, for instance, a senior diplomat was always accredited to the Court in Florence and a Consul appointed for Leghorn, which was a great centre of British commerce. At the Pope's Court in Rome, however, a nation's political affairs might well be in the hands of a "Protector", who was a Cardinal paid for his services. Cardinal Gianfrancesco Albani, for instance, received 6000 crowns per annum when appointed Protector of Poland in 1751.[1] The great powers who had much business to transact in Rome might have a Minister or Ambassador in addition to a Protector either permanently or for some special business, but a Protector alone, with a Consul, seems to have been considered to provide adequate representation for British interests in the Ecclesiastical State when diplomatic relations more nearly approached the normal under the Catholic James II. A Cardinal Caprara held the former office and a certain Domenico Francesco Ricci or Rizzi the latter.[2a]

After the rebellion of 1688 in England, which resulted in the exile of James II and the accession of the Protestant sovereigns William III and Mary, no further official representatives were accredited by the Court in London to that of the Pope, and British interests in the Ecclesiastical State had to be looked after in a hole-and-corner manner by the Ministers of friendly powers, with papal connivance, and by private persons such as Richard Gaven and Thomas Chamberlayne, who, as we shall see, were ready enough to turn the situation to their own advantage. The shadow Court of the Stuarts, officially recognised by the Pope as that of England, continued to be represented in Rome by a Protector and, at the papal port of Civita Vecchia, by a so-called Consul, appointed, to the great disgust of the loyal English, by the Pope or the Pretender. Even as late as 1755, when feeling in Rome had softened towards the reigning King of England, there were still complaints on this head. Horace Mann, British Resident in Florence, then told Sir Thomas Robinson, Secretary of State, that he could not ascertain exactly when so-called British Consuls appointed by the Old Pretender had been first established in the Ecclesiastical Ports, but thought it must have been soon after James fixed his residence in Rome.[3] Certainly Rizzi was not confirmed or replaced in the appointment made by James II, because no officials for Rome, Civita Vecchia or Ancona were included in Lord Carteret's list for the notification of his appointment as Secretary of State for the Southern Department in 1721.[4]

In 1732 Brinley Skinner, British Consul at Leghorn, complained to London that the Pope had appointed a person who exacted not only the ordinary emoluments of the King's Consuls abroad but an additional two per cent duty on all English goods sold out of English bottoms into the Pope's dominions.[5] There then entered on the scene an Irish merchant, Richard Gaven, who later became Maria Theresa's agent to the British fleet in the Mediterranean[6] and also an international art dealer of some importance. The Government of Rome wanted to appoint him as Consul for the British at Civita Vecchia because his father owned eight ships and trade might thereby be attracted away from Leghorn to the advantage of the ecclesiastical port. The Inquisition, however, would not tolerate a heretic in the post, and Gaven, through the influence of a notable Jacobite, Sir Thomas Dereham, thereupon secured a grant to a nominee, Thomas Chamberlayne, on the understanding that he himself would take the profits. Gaven afterwards suspected that Chamberlayne would endeavour to supplant him altogether and, having been unsuccessful in further attempts to overcome the difficulty of his own religion, abandoned the post to him.[7]

Chamberlayne's relations with the British Government are obscure. He was British Consul at Messina for at least ten years up till 1731[8] but he then espoused the Jacobite cause in order presumably to take up the post granted him by the Government of Rome. In spite of this, several London merchants with business in Italy petitioned the Board of Trade in 1734 to establish a Consul in the Ecclesiastical States and recommended a certain Amos Pailfield for the post. The Board refused on the grounds that such an officer would be a public minister and as such could not properly be appointed in the Pope's dominions, but frugally suggested that the merchants should employ their own candidate and pay him themselves.[2b] Pailfield at about the same time applied to be made Consul at the other papal port, Ancona,[9] but nothing seems to have come of either of these proposals. Chamberlayne was reported in 1736 to have been sent by the Jacobites to Florence to kill a British spy, Dixon, and, although failing in this, to have wounded and scarred him so severely across the forehead that he would be of no further use to his previous employers.[10] Notwithstanding this episode Chamberlayne was, however, able to work himself back into the good graces of the loyalists, for during the War of the Austrian Succession he was said to have been "very serviceable" to British naval officers.[11a] Alessandro Albani, Protector for Maria Theresa, nevertheless regarded him with suspicion owing to his liaisons with the Pretender's household[12a] and in 1745 Mann warned Captain Long, R.N., not to put too much trust in him.[12b] Mann, however, corresponded with him and in 1747 received from him a report of the alleged discovery in Rome of a plot by a club of twelve persons who met in Holborn, had vowed vengeance on the Duke of Cumberland and used the password "Bloody Butcher".[11b] Chamberlayne reminded Mann that those who "worked in the British Vin-yard" were always considered according to their labour, a theme which recurred constantly in dealings with spies and cast doubt often enough on the truth of their reports. When Horace Mann complained in 1755 of Xavier Gilly, who was then claiming to exercise the consular functions at Civita Vecchia, the matter was at last regulated to everyone's satisfaction. Gilly was snubbed by the Vatican, told to abandon any title or patent which could offend George II and to conform in all respects to the practice of a certain nobleman, Storani, at Ancona, who styled himself Consul for England and all other Protestant powers and only had the Pope's arms over his door.[13]

In Rome itself British travellers who were loyal to the Protestant succession were from time to time embarrassed by the attempts of the Jacobite Court to help them diplomatically, and probably only those somewhat tainted with Stuart sympathies dared to accept these services. Such for instance was John Bouverie, Robert Wood's companion in the travels which resulted in the famous publication of the Ruins of Palmyra and Baalbec in 1753 and 1757. During the War of the Austrian Succession Bouverie and a friend, Phelps, got passports to Naples through the titular Lord Dunbar,[14a] a prominent member of the Old Pretender's circle, and in the Seven Years War the engraver Robert Strange, brother-in-law of the Pretender's secretary Andrew Lumsden, obtained a passport to France through the latter's interest.[15] Phelps, who vigorously protested his loyalty,[16] may have been believed at home to have been above suspicion, or later convinced the authorities of it, for he appears to have been the same man who discussed the Stuarts with the Duke of York (p. 204), was at one time Secretary at Turin and, for whatever that was worth, elected a member of the Society of Dilettanti in 1763.[17] Joshua Reynolds caricatured him in his large Parody of the

School of Athens, representing connoisseurs in Rome in 1750, and in a smaller group with the Earls of Charlemont and Cassilis and Mr Ward. (Both pictures are now in the National Gallery of Ireland.)

The more discreet travellers protested against the Roman irregularities,[14b] and Wood himself, who subsequently became an Under-Secretary of State, succeeded in getting a passport to Naples by legitimate means, while a certain Captain Clavering, threatened in 1751 with banishment from Rome after a fracas with a Swiss guard, indignantly rejected the good offices of the Pretender, offered him through a lady.[18a] It is evident that although the activities of bogus Consuls like Chamberlayne might be winked at to some extent in the unimportant business of the ecclesiastical ports "for the conveniency of trade" [3] the British Government was not disposed to be generally tolerant towards the Pretender's or the Pope's nominees and that the latter could be of no practical use to the majority of well-to-do travellers, who were therefore dependent on whatever friendly foreign Minister had for the time being undertaken to look after their interests.

Diplomatic inconveniences could be of little importance to English connoisseurs during the reigns of William III and Queen Anne. There were in any case few such travellers at this date, and the Court of James II and subsequently of his son at St Germain could hardly affect them although James III was punctilious in the exercise of his royal prerogatives. After his father's death he continued Cardinal Caprara in his post as Protector, writing his credential to Pope Clement XI in 1701[19a] and, when Caprara died in 1712, appointing Cardinal Gualterio (or Gualtieri) as his successor. This latter appointment was the subject of some embarrassment because Clement XI made the tempting suggestion that it should be given to his own nephew Annibale Albani. James had already promised it to Gualterio, and although it is obvious from his letter on the subject[19b] that he would have welcomed a release from his engagement, he most creditably kept his royal word to Gualterio and sacrificed the glittering prospect of having a papal nephew to look after his affairs in Rome at this crucial time. He continued throughout his life to appoint Protectors for the English, Scottish and Irish crowns, these posts at various times being filled by the Cardinals Davia, Pico della Mirandola, Lanti, Imperiali, Riviera, Spinelli and finally by Clement XI's great-nephew Gianfrancesco Albani.

Queen Anne's death in 1714 was the occasion for a great rise of Jacobite hopes, culminating in the unsuccessful rebellion of 1715 in Scotland. Its failure and James' discouraged return to France closely followed the death (in September 1715) of Louis XIV, and these events profoundly altered the Stuart position. James could still count on popular sentiment in France and the support of the old Court, but the Regent, the Duc d'Orléans, who ruled during the minority of Louis XIV's great-grandson Louis XV, reconsidered the position in regard to the Jacobites. Advised by his Minister, the formidable Abbé Dubois, he started to work for the Triple Alliance between England, France and Holland, which was signed in January 1717. A condition of its ratification was that the Pretender should be removed to the other side of the Alps. Although James had withdrawn in 1716 to the papal city of Avignon and the Pope was not of course a party to the treaty for the alliance, Clement XI could not undertake to protect him there against the wishes of Britain, ever ready as she was to bombard his ports and threaten reprisals on Catholics in England. The Pope, having previously offered the Pretender the choice of whatever place in the ecclesiastical dominions he thought most suitable and safe, expressed approval when he decided to move to Italy and somewhat guardedly promised him all the proofs of his special goodwill which were possible for him in those bad times.[19c]

James might now have reasonably expected to have the support of Victor Amadeus II, Duke of Savoy, Prince of Piedmont and for the time being King of Sicily, whose wife was a grandchild of Charles I through his daughter Henrietta and therefore next in succession to the bachelor Pretender if the latter's claim to the English throne were made good. She was indeed suspected of some ambitions in this direction, and in 1720 John Molesworth, Envoy Extraordinary to Turin, commented on her pleasure in having her hand kissed by English gentlemen "which piece of ceremony", he said, "might not be altogether so insignificant as most others were for the practice of it seemed to admit of Her Majesty's pretensions to the crown of Great Britain".[20] Victor Amadeus himself was, however, more realistically concerned for his own immediate advantage. His dukedom occupied a strategic position on the Alpine passes, but he was too formidable to have it annexed either by France or Austria. Consequently he was courted by the Bourbons as holding the key to Italy, and by England on behalf of the Hapsburgs, in support of her cherished doctrine of the balance of power. It was a situation to be exploited to good effect in the years to come, his successor, Charles Emanuel III, attacking Austria in the War of the Polish Succession, supporting her in the War of the Austrian Succession, profiting by both manœuvres and retaining throughout the friendship of England. By the Peace of Utrecht in 1713 Victor Amadeus had been allotted the Kingdom of Sicily in recognition of the great services of his House in the late War of the Spanish Succession, but in 1720 he was forced to cede it in exchange for the barren Kingdom of Sardinia. This was valuable for little more than its royal title, by which he was thenceforward known, and indeed a contemporary said of the island that one lost nothing by losing it and gained nothing by conquering it.[21a]

At the time of the Pretender's greatest need, therefore, Victor Amadeus, only precariously in possession of his rich prize of Sicily, was understandably reluctant to offend his powerful allies by any public support of his wife's embarrassing cousin. In 1716 the latter sent a certain George Bagnall to sound the Queen of Sicily on the possibility of settling somewhere in her husband's dominions and of getting exiled Jacobites taken into his service. She replied that Victor Amadeus' need of keeping in with King George made it impossible for him to consent and that if James passed that way he wished his stay to be as short as possible and not to see him himself.[19d] James therefore had little to hope for from the House of Savoy when he set out for Italy in February 1717 and that "dark, cunning gentleman",[19e] as a Stuart courtier called the King of Sicily, treated him only with conventional civilities. He sent one of his generals to meet him with servants and coaches at Norvallaise,[19f] had the snow swept from his path[22] and gave him a short and evidently constrained interview at Turin in which nothing passed but compliments and an intimation that he could do nothing for him. It was indeed suspected in Jacobite circles that the King intercepted a letter in which James himself described the meeting to a friend.[19g]

When the Pretender left France his supporters concentrated in the Netherlands where their presence was potentially dangerous in the light of the activities of Charles XII of Sweden. The latter openly supported Stuart claims and the Jacobites hoped, not perhaps without some foundation, that he would settle his differences with the Tsar of Russia and that both would then ally themselves with Spain to effect a Stuart restoration.[19h] It was therefore desirable for the British Government to detach the Emperor, Charles VI of Austria, from any participation in Jacobite interests and this was facilitated by the Emperor's fear of the Turk, his traditional foe on the eastern frontiers of his realm. In 1717 he told the Pretender's agent through Prince Eugene that he could not help him for fear of war with England, France and Holland,[19i] and in January 1718 the British bought him off with a secret subsidy.[21b] The consideration for this was an undertaking not to give shelter or passage to rebels or the person called the Pretender, thus neutralising as far as possible the threat from Jacobites in the Austrian Netherlands and Imperial territories adjacent to their northern sympathisers. The undertaking was publicly confirmed as one of the terms of the Quadruple Alliance formed shortly afterwards by England, France, Holland and the Emperor. By the time the Pretender first arrived in Rome early in 1717 his political isolation was therefore already foreshadowed, and in December 1718 he lost his redoubtable ally Charles XII, who was killed at the siege of Frederiksten. In the following June a Spanish-assisted rising in Scotland in the Jacobite interest was crushed at Glenshiel, putting to an end any immediate prospect of active help from Spain, which soon afterwards made peace with England. The Pope, who was impotent in the military and maritime sphere, was left as the Pretender's only overt ally of any consequence. Notwithstanding these events, however, and the solemn treaties with which George I's throne was buttressed, the Pretender remained a by no means negligible element in European politics, since any shift in alliances might result in an attempt being made to set him on his throne as a diversion in a larger enterprise. Britain had every reason to fear the intrigues which would inevitably surround him in Rome, and the possibility that the Catholic powers might compound secret agreements between themselves and the Pope, prejudicial to their treaty engagements with Protestant governments.

Meanwhile the Pope, privately quailing at the part his antecedents and his holy office compelled him to play, was irrevocably committed to befriending the Pretender in the

sight of the world. The bond between the exiled Stuarts and
the Albani family to which Clement XI belonged was a
close one, for he had from the very first espoused their
cause in no uncertain way. On his election to the papacy in
1700 James II and his wife Mary of Modena were said to
have wept with emotion and joy at the exaltation of one
whom they had so greatly esteemed as a Cardinal and now
regarded as a worthy successor of St Peter.[23] When James
II died in 1701 the Pope's eldest nephew, Annibale, was
selected to make his funeral oration in the papal chapel, a
favour which earned the lively gratitude of the widow. She
wrote of the repeated proofs of His Holiness' esteem for the
late King and compassion and kindness towards her son and
herself, and expressed a hope that Annibale's merit should
be rewarded with the highest dignities of the Church, as
indeed it was in due course. She also sent a personal message
to Abbé Albani and his parents, thanking them for such a
signal favour and expressing her esteem for persons so
closely connected with such a great and holy Pope.[19j]
Annibale, despite the political difficulties of friendship with
the Pretender, seems to have been substantially loyal to him
all his life and it was said to have been at his instances that
the cannon of the Castle of St Angelo was fired on the birth
Henry Stuart, James' second son.[24] In 1734 Roman gossip
reported a quarrel between them which put the Pretender
into so violent a fit of rage and grief that his wife had to be
called out of her bed to pacify him,[25] but it may be inferred
that he and Annibale afterwards reverted to their former
good relations. When in 1751 Annibale presented a large
sturgeon to Pope Benedict XIV the latter passed it on to the
Stuart household[18b] and when Annibale lay dying shortly
afterwards the Pope went to see him and immediately on his
death appointed the Pretender's son Arch-Priest and Prefect
of St Peter's, two benefices previously held by Annibale.[18c]
The latter was indeed a formidable ally for the Stuarts to

have in Rome, a contemporary describing him at the time
of the Conclave in 1740 as being highly esteemed for his
capacity although hated and feared; without faith or principles, an implacable enemy even when he appeared to be
reconciled; a genius in affairs, inexhaustibly resourceful in
intrigue, the best brain in the College and the wickedest man
in Rome.[26]

The Pope had three nephews, Annibale, Carlo and
Alessandro, the sons of his brother Orazio, and when the
Pretender arrived in Italy they played a leading part in his
affairs and were the channels through which Clement XI
conveyed his favours and his wishes and James made his own
requests. Don Carlo met him on the frontier of the papal
dominions, bearing the apostolic benediction and a letter of
welcome from Alessandro,[19k] at that time acting as Clement
XI's secretary. The Pretender then paid a brief visit to
Rome where he met the Pope and described him as a tall,
lusty, good-looking man who might indeed be wiser but
was sensible and kind and easy.[19l] At his invitation James
settled in the former Ducal Palace at Urbino, but after a few
months he and his followers were profoundly bored there.
The choice may have been influenced by the fact that
Urbino, a papal fief, was also the Albanis' native town with
which they still had connections and that Clement XI
wished to please the inhabitants by re-establishing a Court
which had lapsed on the death of the last Della Rovere.[27]
Quite apart from boredom, however, it was hardly a suitable place, for in 1727 Annibale Albani, who had an abbey
there, ran the risk of assassination after destroying the hide-
outs of bandits and had to have an armed guard.[28] Certainly
the Pope would have preferred for political reasons not to
have the Pretender living actually in Rome, and Carlo Albani
supervised alterations to a summer palace at Castel Gandolfo
to make it habitable for him all the year round.[19m] The
Spanish Cardinal Acquaviva, however, warned James that

Castel Gandolfo was not safe on account of Imperial soldiers in the vicinity, who might make him a prisoner,[19n] and in the end the Pope had little choice but to allow him to live permanently in the palazzo in Rome which he assigned to him early in 1718.

The question of the Pretender's marriage had for some time been in agitation, for he was in his late twenties when he left Avignon. The Jacobites earnestly desired it, hoping that the prospect of heirs would check the ebb in their fortunes, while the British Government, for this and other reasons, would probably have objected indiscriminately to any candidate, since one of suitable rank was bound to have influential connections. In 1716 a niece of the Emperor's was suggested and soon after the Pretender's arrival in Italy Annibale Albani was trying to arrange a match for him with a princess of Saxony, of which state he was Protector.[19o] At length, in the summer of 1718, James announced his betrothal to Clementina, daughter of Prince James Sobieski and a first cousin of the Emperor. Being not yet entirely satisfied as to the Catholic Charles VI's real intentions towards the Stuarts, the British Government protested against the match and exerted such diplomatic pressure that the Emperor was induced to order the arrest of Clementina at Innsbruck when she was on her way to meet the Pretender in the autumn of 1718. King George and his ministers took this, they said, as a strong proof of the sincere friendship of His Imperial Majesty,[29] but issued a stern warning that it was his business to guard her well since, if she escaped, everyone would believe he had connived at it, and the disadvantages to himself would be as great as if he had released her openly.[30a] St Saphorin, British Minister at Vienna, stressed the importance to the House of Austria of securing King George upon his throne, and suggested that certain of his Ministers and the Court in general did not sufficiently appreciate this point.[31a]

The Pope was furious but powerless to interfere effectually. Annibale Albani thought, however, that there had been unwise publicity about Clementina's journey and that the Emperor had thereby been obliged to take some step to placate his ally, England, and show official disapproval of the marriage.[19p] Carlo was James' confidant when the shattering news of Clementina's arrest arrived and altogether these two Albani brothers served and consoled him so well at this time that he regarded them both, he said, as his best friends.[19q] His dealings with the Pope's youngest nephew, Alessandro, were, however, neither so close nor so comfortable, and James seems to have felt a certain need of flattering or placating him. This is curious, because it is hardly credible that at this time the young Abbé, barely launched on his career, could have been expected to take a line independently of his uncle and to recognise that in the future the Emperor's side might have more to offer. The Pretender, however, may well have appreciated that the Pope's political dilemma made his sincerity suspect and have courted Alessandro as being the person most deeply in his confidence at this time.

James badly needed a subsidy from the Pope on the occasion of his marriage, and with this in view proposed to exercise in favour of Alessandro the nomination to the Sacred College which was one of the royal privileges he claimed. Prudence, he said, no less than conscience, prompted him to make this offer unconditionally to Alessandro.[19r] The latter's reply, which does not appear to have survived among the Stuart Papers at Windsor, was evidently unsatisfactory, for a letter of his was commented upon unfavourably[19s] and James warned his adherent, David Nairne, to be on his guard with Alessandro while still seeking his assistance over the marriage.[19t] It seems likely that Clement XI had confided to his youngest nephew the objections to siding with the Pretender and that the nomination was prudently refused for political reasons although it offered a tempting excuse for Alessandro's accelerated promotion to the cardinalate. James visited Rome in November 1718 against the wishes of the Pope, who feared to offend the Emperor, and had an interview with Alessandro who, he said, was a "most complete gentleman in his kind and could not easily conceal from him his master's apprehensions at his coming there".[19u]

The Pretender's matrimonial affairs were indeed acutely embarrassing both to the Pope and the Emperor. The latter, for religious and family reasons and indeed in common humanity, would no doubt have been willing to release Clementina in accordance with Clement XI's wishes but the British threatened him under cover of conveying messages through him to the Pope which left little doubt of their intentions towards himself. If the Pretender were allowed to live in Rome or create cardinals, they said, the Mediterranean Fleet would act against the Pope and had only so far been restrained from doing so out of consideration for the Emperor, in whose interests it was at present operating.[30b] Charles VI needed the help of British ships for hostilities against Sicily, and moreover the death of his infant son in 1716 had made it likely that he would some day need England's help to secure the succession to the female line in the person of his daughter Maria Theresa. He therefore had very good reasons for not conniving at Clementina's escape and when this took place in April 1719 St Saphorin at least absolved him from blame. The British Minister's version of the incident was more sensational, for he claimed to have discovered from an informant that the Ministers of Savoy had furnished money and a plan which was later found on a Jesuit in Prince Sobieski's service, together with letters containing promises of *"monts et merveilles"* from Victor Amadeus.[30c] Such gossip abounded in the diplomatic correspondence of the time and the information which could be bought for cash was often as unreliable as it was picturesque, but it must be admitted that public disavowal accompanied by private help to the Pretender was neither inconsistent with the practice of other Catholic sovereigns nor with the King of Sardinia's notoriously devious ways.

Meanwhile war had broken out between England and Spain, and the Pretender went to Madrid in 1718 to await the results of the attempted Scottish rising which failed at Glenshiel, as we have already seen. In his absence the Pope was left to welcome Clementina to Italy with all the warmth his engagements demanded, while observing the caution required in his dealings with his dreaded fellow-sovereigns in England and Austria. He sent Teresa Albani, Carlo's wife, to meet her and had a sumptuous apartment furnished for her in the Ursuline convent,[32] while it somehow got about nevertheless that when she arrived he pretended to be annoyed.[31b] He bowed to the wishes of the British by not sending Clementina off to join the Pretender in Spain but defied them to the extent of allowing the young couple in due course to settle in Rome, much as he would have preferred it otherwise, and recognising James' disputed royal right to nominate cardinals.

The Pretender, who was already in possession of a Dispensation signed by Annibale Albani allowing him to marry Clementina, without the publication of banns, wherever they thought proper,[19v] returned to Italy and celebrated his wedding at Montefiascone on 1st September 1719. From January 1718 the Muti Palace in the Piazza dei Santi Apostoli in Rome had been leased to the Apostolic Chamber for the residence of "the King of England" [19w] and there he settled with his bride, his elder son being born the year after his marriage. He only once again left Italy and that was in pursuit of the vain hopes raised by George I's death in 1727, which induced him to travel to France, Lorraine and

Avignon to try to rally support. The Old Pretender was therefore almost uninterruptedly at Rome or a summer palace not far distant for nearly the whole of the rest of his long and tragic life.

CHAPTER II

Alessandro Albani and Philip von Stosch

ALESSANDRO ALBANI was born at Urbino on
15th October 1692, the third and youngest son of
Orazio, a brother of Pope Clement XI.[1] His elder brothers,
as we have seen, were Annibale, who became a cardinal in
1711, and Carlo, who bore the princely title bestowed on
the family by the Emperor Joseph I in 1710. On Clement
XI's election the family moved to Rome to enjoy the traditional advantages of close relationship to the Pope but retained their palace at Urbino and their connections there,
although Alessandro for much of his life moved only between his palazzo in Rome, his mother's home at Soriano,
his villa at the Porta Salaria and various seaside retreats. He
does not seem at first to have been intended for an ecclesiastical career, since in 1708 he was commanding a regiment
of the Pope's cavalry in a minor engagement against the
Emperor's forces, which had occupied the small Adriatic
port of Comacchio, but he entered the Church in 1712 on
his father's death.

The highly cultured Clement XI had been prominent in
the brilliant circle of Queen Christina of Sweden in Rome,
and as Pope he became a notable collector and patron of the
arts. He fostered similar tastes in his two nephews, Annibale
and Alessandro, who came into contact with many scholars
and particularly with Marcantonio Sabatini, the papal antiquary. Thus encouraged, the young Alessandro developed
very early a passion for classical antiquities, and even a
youthful illness which weakened his sight for life was not
allowed to be a handicap. He had bronzes and medals

brought him in bed to handle and acquired a remarkable capacity for judging antiques by touch. A biographer, writing of him soon after his death, noted that when he grew blind in old age the sense of sight seemed to have migrated into his finger-tips. In 1714 Alessandro acquired from Clement XI Cassiano dal Pozzo's famous collection of drawings of antique remains, and in 1715, partly perhaps as a compliment to his uncle the Pope, was made an honorary member and director of studies in the Academy of San Luca. In the same year he met Philip von Stosch, his almost exact contemporary, a brilliant scholar, antiquarian and would-be diplomat, of doubtful morals, who was paying his first visit to Rome and was pensioned and befriended by Clement XI. He and Alessandro are said to have become inseparable, and undoubtedly the association was highly significant for them both. Together the two young men explored the buried treasures of Rome and laid the foundations of a friendship which, for better or worse, lasted till Stosch's death in 1757.

Alessandro has been described when young as being of delightful appearance, blond, blue-eyed, of athletic build, vivacious, intelligent and of singular charm. His complexion must have darkened later, because Benjamin West particularly noted his swarthiness, albeit in an account which does not otherwise sound very credible (p. 182). Another authority says he was short, keen-eyed, with a rather long hooked nose and a very cheerful expression, his conversation full of jokes and witty sayings.[2] The celebrated German scholar, Johann Joachim Winckelmann, who lived in his house for years, remarked on his impetuousness and called him a tempest or a roaring wind.[3] His kindness and generosity were proverbial, and were lavished on those who were poor and struggling as well as on the rich and influential. It is tantalising that no very satisfactory portrait of him appears at present to be known or available for study. A rather poor oil-painting by Lodovico Mazzanti in the Villa Albani and an engraving by Jerome Rossi after Pietro Nelli (Pl. I) appear somewhat tame renderings of a sitter so celebrated for his vivacity and strong personality. A marble bust in the Versailles Museum was not accessible at the time of going to press, and an excellent portrait by Ghezzi from the Castelbarco collection, recently exhibited in Rome,[4] must almost certainly represent Annibale and not Alessandro. Not only does the likeness fail to correspond with the younger brother's features, but Alessandro, in the lifetime of Annibale, was usually identified by his Christian name. A paper in the sitter's hand carries the title "Cardinal Albani" with Ghezzi's signature. Possibly, however, there still remains, somewhere in England, the portrait of himself by Catherine Read which Alessandro sent as a present to Bubb Dodington (p. 160).

Albani is said to have had sound health until extreme old age and it is noticeable that the gossips of Rome, harping on the apoplexies and intestinal troubles which seemed almost the occupational diseases of the Sacred College, seldom had anything to say about his health. Somebody remarked to the British Resident Francis Colman in 1727 that Alessandro had a fever and a melancholy so contrary to his lively character that it alarmed his doctors[5] and Mann sometimes condoled with him on an attack of gout, but this is about all. His voluminous and regular correspondence is in itself sufficient proof of his health and vitality, and the fact that he was able to keep his multifarious affairs under his own control perhaps had something to do with his capacity for managing intrigue and keeping secrets. He used a team of secretaries and indeed remonstrated with Horace Mann for fatiguing himself by writing always in his own hand,[6] but except for the Abbé Giordani, to whom we shall refer later, they must have been perfectly loyal to him. So essentially discreet was he, for all his impulsiveness and candour, that

the nature of some of his political activities seems to have
escaped the notice of all his biographers, even though the
Jacobite, Andrew Lumsden, suspected in 1766 that he was
"the private but known minister and spy of the Duke of
Hanover".[7]

The reports on Albani's eyesight are puzzling and it is
surprising that he did not complain of it to Horace Mann
in the course of their long correspondence. Possibly the
haemorrhage which is said to have damaged his eyes left
him with a limited vision which was more effective than it
appeared to those who did not know him well. Certainly
both Benjamin West (p. 182) and Casanova,[8] who met him in
1760 and 1761, thought he was blind or nearly so, and his
writing grew more and more indecipherable as he got
older. Yet it is impossible to believe, and Winckelmann does
not suggest, that the exquisitely idiosyncratic Villa Albani
could have been perfected through the eyes of others, or
that foreigners should over so long a period have relied on
a man severely handicapped both for the art-dealing and
subtle political, manœuvre in which he helped them. It is,
however, possible that a deterioration in his sight was a
contributing factor to the sudden cessation of his correspondence with Mann in 1774 (p. 233), for he does seem to
have been blind at his death.

In 1718 Alessandro became domestic chaplain to his
uncle the Pope, and later in the same year replaced his
brother Annibale as Secretary of the Memorials. He was
evidently being groomed for high political office, because
Horace Mann, writing at a much later date of this post,
when the future of the Jesuit Order presented equally
serious international problems, spoke of the appointment as
being one of the most delicate and always given by the
Popes to those in whom they placed the greatest confidence.[9]
On 16th November 1719 St Saphorin, British Minister at
Vienna, commented to Lord Stanhope, then Secretary of

State in England, on the cabals and intrigues which beset
Roman affairs at the Emperor's Court and said that the Pope
did not wish them to be dealt with by his Nuncio there
because he wanted to send his nephew Albani as "*homme de
confiance*".[10a] A few days later he reported an intimation from
the Emperor's Minister, the Comte de Sinzendorff, that the
Pope wished to send his nephew to Vienna to act in concert
with the Spanish faction and that this implied sinister and
dangerous designs against the Alliance. St Saphorin went on
to say that he could not oppose Albani's appointment
openly for fear of betraying his informants, but had spoken
forcibly about it to de Sinzendorff, who he thought would
say something to the Emperor.[10b] A month afterwards he
reported what he called the unconcealed intention of the
Spanish faction to make mischief between the King of
England and the Emperor, so as to dispose the latter to
turn to Spain.[10c] Notwithstanding British hostility, however, Alessandro Albani arrived in Vienna in March 1720.
The Pope's motives in appointing him may have been somewhat mixed, and in view of his difficulties over the Pretender
and Alessandro's apparent recent refusal of his nomination
for the cardinalate (p. 35), British apprehensions were probably exaggerated. It may even have been that the specially
confidential side of Alessandro's mission was not Spanish
intrigue at all but the propitiation of the British, as will pres-
ently appear. Ostensibly, however, his task was to negotiate on specific matters at issue between the Pope and the
Emperor, which included the former's recognition of the
Sicilian monarchy, hitherto denied, rights of ecclesiastical
presentation and investitures in Naples and the much-dis-
puted possession of Comacchio which the Emperor needed
for the landing of troops for Naples.[11a]

Clement XI was by now in a desperate position as a result
of his own vacillations and of the rivalries of Bourbons and
Hapsburgs. In 1700, the year of his election as Pope, the

last Hapsburg King of Spain had died, bequeathing his kingdom to Philip of Anjou, grandson of Louis XIV of France. Regardless of treaty obligations towards England and the Dutch, Louis accepted the crown on Philip's behalf, and the latter in due course became Philip V of Spain. Clement XI, whose sympathies were strongly French, at first supported Philip's claim but had to climb down when the Emperor Leopold I of Austria sent troops into Italy to secure the Spanish possessions there for his own son the Archduke Charles. The ensuing War of the Spanish Succession, in which England also played a leading part, was ended in 1713 by the Peace of Utrecht, which gave Spain and Spanish America to Philip V, the Netherlands, Milan, Naples, Mantua, Sardinia, and the Spanish ports in Tuscany to the Emperor, and Sicily, for a few years only, to the Duke of Savoy. One result of this Peace was that Clement XI, whose actions had pleased neither the King of France nor the Emperor, lost valuable papal fiefs and for years suffered the rapacious presence of Imperial troops in his own State. In the same year, 1713, he still further alienated France by promulgating the Bull Unigenitus condemning the Jansenist teaching so popular there. Clement XI himself appreciated only too well the extent to which the temporal power of Rome had declined during his pontificate. He was said to have observed: "*si la foi se perd en France, il reviendra mille apôtres pour le reprêcher; mais, quand la soldatesque aura ruiné notre pays tous les apôtres du monde n'y feront pas revenir un chou*".[12] His difficulties were accentuated by his championing of the Stuart cause, and the British Government feared that he might be driven to some desperate expedient which would not only disturb the delicately balanced peace of Europe but bring the Pretender again into dangerous prominence. The Jacobite threat remained by no means negligible, with rebels still living in considerable numbers in the Netherlands[13] and herding in the seaport towns of

France,[14a] and every Prince and State in Italy except the
Duke of Modena was Jacobite in sympathy and hostile to
the existing alliance of great powers, or so at least said St
Saphorin.[10d] Moreover George I, as Elector of Hanover,
was concerned for the welfare of his Protestant subjects on
the continent and feared that, to draw the hated Imperial
troops out of Italy, the Pope would settle his differences
with the Emperor and persuade him to launch a Holy War,
with the "new improvement", as Molesworth pointed out
from Turin, that it was to be employed against Protestants
instead of Saracens.[15a] Against this menacing background
Alessandro Albani's appearance on the scene at Vienna
could only be regarded as sinister.

The British understanding with France had been largely
achieved through the good offices of the Abbé Dubois, the
Regent's confidential Minister. Disguised as a connoisseur
of books and paintings, he had gone to The Hague in 1716
to negotiate the Triple Alliance between England, France
and Holland[16a] which in 1718 was converted into the
Quadruple Alliance by the adherence of the Emperor,
Charles VI. British Ministers probably never quite trusted
Dubois, for they noticed in 1721 a certain variation in his
conduct and discourse from what he used formerly to
hold,[14b] suspected him of intrigues with Spain and suggested that he cannily avoided officially accrediting the
French representative at Vienna so that any communications distasteful to the Emperor should seem to come from
England, which had a Minister qualified to transmit them.[14c]
To attach Dubois more firmly to their side for the future,
under cover of rewarding him for past services, they resolved to further his heart's desire of becoming a cardinal,
St Saphorin remarking that if he could be thus secured it
would be most salutary for the interests of all the parties
composing the Grand Alliance.[17] Dubois tried himself to
obtain this promotion through French influence but was

frustrated by the hostility of Clement XI, who made Alessandro Albani write from Rome to say that if the Regent would consent to the decardinalisation of de Noailles (who had defied the Pope in the matter of Unigenitus) Dubois could have the vacancy.[16b] As he knew the French would never consent to this it was in effect a refusal and the British now sought a nomination from the Emperor instead. The latter agreed in principle but nominations to the Sacred College were powerful bargaining counters in the hands of the great Catholic powers and the Emperor was in no hurry to spend one of his on the common interests of the Allies without some substantial quid pro quo for himself.[18a] While he procrastinated Dubois grew frantic and tried to ingratiate himself simultaneously with the Pope and with Alessandro Albani by promising the Regent's support to Alessandro's appointment as Nuncio at the coming Congress of Cambrai, at which the final peace terms were to be regulated. As a last startling resort he even obtained the promise of a nomination from the impecunious Pretender in return for a French subsidy.[16c] Cardinal Annibale Albani had much to do with the latter transaction and was said to have offered his services to Dubois for 30,000 Roman crowns of which he stood in urgent need.[16d] Finally the Pretender's request on behalf of Dubois was presented two days after the Emperor's Minister in Rome had obtained the Pope's unwilling consent to the future promotion and, from pure indiscretion or from a belief it was common knowledge or from some deep political motive, Alessandro let out Dubois' dark secret in Vienna. St Saphorin, adding however that he did not know what to believe, said that Dubois threw "*feu et flame*" against Alessandro and that the latter had been obliged to eat his words and say that a false rumour had been spread from Rome just to make mischief.[11b] Whatever actually happened, neither Dubois nor Alessandro was harmed by it in Rome for both were to be made cardinals by Innocent XIII in July 1721 in accordance with Clement XI's promises.

This curious episode was linked with another in which the young Albani attracted the surprised attention of Lord Cadogan and St Saphorin, the two British representatives then in Vienna. England had little or nothing to gain from the Congress of Cambrai, then being organised, and Ministers, fearing that disputes about Italian territories might even start a new war, had actually sounded Dubois on the possibility of not holding it at all.[14d] The matters to be settled between the Pope and the Emperor included the rights to the Investitures of Parma, Piacenza, Comacchio, Ferrara and Castro,[18b] and although these were of no direct concern to the British the latter preferred the claims of their ally the Emperor, on which depended those of the Dukes of Parma and Modena. They also, as we have seen, feared some secret attempt on Clement XI's part to upset the existing alliances for his own ends. The holding of the Congress appearing inevitable, it was therefore with considerable apprehension that the British Ministers heard of the Pope's desire to send his own nephew Alessandro as his representative there. The Emperor thought the Pope had the right to send whomsoever he wished but promised he would do nothing to help Alessandro.[18c] The French, on the other hand, favoured the plan, which seemed likely to secure the red hat for Dubois, and the latter continued to make strenuous efforts to ingratiate himself as much as possible with Alessandro Albani.

Cadogan and St Saphorin reported the matter at length in a joint letter to Lord Stanhope, the Secretary of State. Albani, the Pope's nephew, they wrote, was urgently trying to get admitted to the Peace Congress. To surmount the objections which he rightly supposed His Majesty would make he had been trying for a long time to have an interview with St Saphorin, and had since appeared to wish to speak also to Cadogan. He was, however, so new that he had not known how to find an opportunity to speak to either. Failing in that he had revealed his plan to a third person, who had spoken of it to St Saphorin and reported the latter's objections to Albani. Alessandro had insinuated to this third party that if the King of England refrained from making difficulties his uncle would in exchange, so far as he could without compromising the decorum of the Papacy, behave towards the Pretender in the way His Majesty would wish, and he expressed himself as though the Pope was already tired and disgusted with this subject. The Pope, according to the customs of Rome, continued the British Ministers, was not entitled to make two of his nephews cardinals unless the second had acquired some particular merit, so that he would be promoted as a man who had rendered great services to the Church rather than in the capacity of the Pope's relative. Clement XI, who tenderly loved the young Albani, had therefore sent him to Vienna to acquire merit in his own right, and for the same reason wanted him to go to the Congress, to justify his receiving the hat which was being kept for him "*in peto*" or "*in pectore*", that was to say, secretly reserved by the Pope for the next promotion of cardinals. St Saphorin had sounded the Comte de Sinzendorff as to whether Albani had communicated to the Emperor's Ministers his intention of going to the Congress and found he had. De Sinzendorff had been surprised at Albani's attempt at negotiation with the British since he thought the Pope only had to send him in the same way as he had sent a Nuncio to the Peace of Nimwegen and all other such conferences. St Saphorin had pointed out to the Austrian Minister all the inconveniences which would result from Alessandro's appointment and how much it was to be feared that the Papal Nuncio would work to unite France and Spain against the Emperor and His Majesty.[18d]

Notwithstanding the protest from Vienna, Dubois did,

however, secure the unwilling consent of the British Government to Albani's appointment to the Congress, given only on condition that the British Ministers would have no direct relations with him.[16e] This was probably not good enough for Alessandro, who by September 1720 was reported as having no further intention of going to the Congress.[18e] The interesting point in all this is the one de Sinzendorff noticed, the apparently unnecessary sounding of the British Ministers, which suggests that either Alessandro or his uncle set a high value on their approval. In any case, whatever advantages the appointment might have brought him, it would probably not have really affected his promotion, for which he had already qualified by established convention. It was a jealously guarded privilege of the great Catholic powers that a Nuncio to their Courts should be made a cardinal after the close of his mission, as Horace Mann remarked when at a later date the King of Sardinia presumptuously demanded the right.[19]

Alessandro's whole mission to Vienna seems on the face of it to have been a failure, both officially and personally, and he had little chance to improve on his bad start there. On 19th March 1721 a timely death released the unfortunate Clement XI from his desperate political tangle, and his nephew returned to Rome a few days later with his business uncompleted. Lord Townshend, then Secretary of State, wrote that as by the death of the Pope all Albani's negotiations had apparently fallen to the ground, the Duke of Modena was out of danger for the present, at least from the wrong that might have been done to him in relation to Comacchio. Alessandro was duly made Cardinal, of the church of St Adriano, the following July, but to lose the advantage of being the Pope's favourite nephew when on the threshold of his career could not fail to check him, even with so powerful a brother as Annibale to watch his interests, and little is heard of him for a few years after this.

Alexander Albanus Cameræ Apoſtolicæ Clericus, Vrbinas, S.R.E. Diaconus Cardinalis creatus à SSmo D.N. INNOCENTIO PAPA XIII. in Consiſto. rio secreto die 16. Iulij 1721.

Petrus Nelli delin.   Hieron. Rossi incid.

British Museum

CARDINAL ALESSANDRO ALBANI

PRINCE JAMES STUART (THE OLD PRETENDER)
Drawing by Pier Leone Ghezzi

The Albanis' friend Philip von Stosch was born at Küstrin, Brandenburg, on 2nd March 1691, one of the five children of a doctor, a member of a noble family which, on account of poverty, had abandoned the baronial title later reassumed by Philip.[20] He was first educated at the Lutheran school at Küstrin and then sent to Frankfurt-an-der-Oder to read theology. Once there, he took up instead the study of coins, receiving encouragement both from his father and from the Imperial Antiquarian, Carl Schott. In 1708 he started on a series of travels to collections in Germany and Holland, and arrived in Amsterdam in the autumn of 1709. Here he made friends with a group of scholars, notably Ludolf Küster, whose contacts with Dr Richard Bentley in England were probably of some importance for Stosch. The highly individual talents, which made him an antiquary of outstanding quality and precocious fame, led him to reject the idea of a formal education at the University of Leyden in favour of travelling about Europe to examine coins, medals and engraved gems. He does not appear to have been particularly learned either in ancient or modern tongues, for he said himself on one occasion that he was not a good enough scholar to judge of collations from Vatican manuscripts in Greek,[21] and he evidently knew little English. Horace Mann, who in after years saw the Baron constantly in Florence, when he was a British secret agent, always quoted in French such amusing remarks as the one Stosch made to himself about his health: "*Mais quoique vous avez un tempérament délicat, vous n'êtes point sujet pourtant à des apoplexies ni maladies pareilles*".[22]

Stosch obviously had the excellent memory and much reading which, according to him, the profession of anti-quary required, but the real inspiration of his studies appears to have been the actual objects fabricated by ancient peoples, which he could see and handle. Through these he hoped to compile something like a universal history, but the means gained rapidly upon the ends and it was as a collector and art expert that he found the greatest scope for his talents as well as inexhaustible opportunities for getting into debt. The result was that when he died in 1757 he left marvellous collections of gems, coins, medals, books, maps, manuscripts, drawings and objets d'art of all kinds but, to the embarrassment of his nephew and heir, William Muzell, nothing else at all. Stosch also left little autobiographical material and appears to have been reticent and mysterious about his own affairs, which is hardly surprising, since by profession he was a spy, and by reputation a homosexual, an atheist, a blasphemer, a liar and a thief. Nevertheless he could not have gained the entrée, as he did, to some of the best company in Europe in his youth had he not been a man of great intelligence, enterprise and wit, and even in the period when he seems to have been pretty far gone in debt and general depravity he remained entertaining and irrepressible.

Horace Mann, from the evidence of his letters, quite obviously found him good company, regarded him with a certain tolerant and rather shocked amusement and saw more of him than their official relations would appear to have required, though he lost no opportunity of entertaining Horace Walpole most scurrilously at his expense. There were, however, limits to Mann's complaisance and his ordinarily urbane tones rose almost to a note of panic in a letter to the Duke of Newcastle written in November 1742. He was under the necessity, he said, of acquainting His Grace with the applications that had been made to him by Mr Langlois, an English merchant at Leghorn, for permission to sequester Stosch's effects on the personal obligation the latter had always given, for a security of the money he had been furnished with. Mann had told Mr Langlois that he could by no means permit any steps to be taken like those he proposed, and had for the present quieted him by undertaking to represent to the Duke the inconvenience that might ensue unless His Grace would be pleased to order a regulation in this affair. The person in question, Mann continued, had frequently made complaints to him and at the same time given him to understand that on the least molestation on his personal obligations, or difficulty of being supplied with money for the future, he would take protection in the British Resident's house, to prevent which inconvenience Mann could not help taking the liberty of being more importunate with His Grace than he would dare to be about his own affairs.[23]

It is difficult not to suspect that there was something equivocal about Stosch's impressive friendships, and indeed Alessandro Albani's, but one must recognise that bright young men played a part in the lives, hearts and often in the households of older protectors, which their contemporaries are not heard to condemn and which it is wise to regard at least with an open mind. In 1710 Stosch went to The Hague, where his brother-in-law, Baron von Schmettau, was Prussian Ambassador, and met Franz Fagel, then fifty-one years of age and the universally esteemed Greffier or Secretary of the Assembly of the States-General. He became his friend and benefactor for the rest of his own life. Fagel was himself a notable collector of coins and gave Stosch some antique ones to keep and deal with for himself in return for buying Fagel new silver coins on his travels. The Greffier also appears to have employed Stosch on minor diplomatic missions abroad, but in the absence of further evidence it is impossible to say whether these were a cover for antiquarian researches or vice versa. The cloak of real or simulated scholarship was a convenient and not unusual disguise for secret agents and was used both by Dubois when he went to The Hague in 1716, as we have already seen, and by a certain Eusébe Renaudot, an orientalist and theological writer, who for years was the secret agent of the

French Court with the English Jacobite party.[24] Cardinal Alberoni who, as a Minister in Madrid, had helped to pre-cipitate the Anglo-Spanish War of 1718, also made use of the device when he had returned to Rome in disgrace. An interest in reading and belles-lettres was his cover for meet-ings with Stosch during which he tried to ingratiate himself by informing on the Pretender.[25]

Stosch went to England in 1712, probably under Fagel's protection, at the same time as Prince Eugene, but there is no evidence of diplomatic duties and he seems to have spent his time in the company of scholars, notably Richard Bentley at Cambridge, and in visiting famous collections. In his *Gemmae Antiquae Caelatae*, published in Amsterdam in 1724, he illustrated examples from the cabinets of Lord Morpeth, Lord Arundel and the Duke of Devonshire which he must have seen at this time. He made the acquaintance of the Earls of Pembroke and Winchilsea, and Sir Andrew Fountaine, who were also collectors. In June 1712 Ludolf Küster wrote from London to Richard Bentley, "Mr Whiston giveth his service to you, as also Mr Stoshius",[26] and it seems certain that the last-named was Philip von Stosch. William Whiston, who had been Lucasian Professor of Mathematics at Cambridge, had been expelled from the University in 1710 for the publication of heretical views and had since lived in London. He had influential friends, in-cluding Addison and Steele, who encouraged him to give lectures in astronomy at Button's coffee-house in Covent Garden, which attracted good audiences and helped him to support himself.[27] His varied learning and interest in ancient civilisations was likely to commend Stosch to him, and if they were acquainted in London Stosch himself prob-ably kept good company there as everywhere else.

Stosch is reputed to have spent six months with Bentley at Cambridge but so far no record of his stay has been found there. He was perhaps one of the Master's many private guests who helped to provoke the complaints that he used College stores for boarders and let for his own profit chambers in Trinity to which Fellows were entitled.[28] For many years Bentley was gathering materials for an edition of Homer, to be dedicated to Lord Carteret, and for a new translation of the Greek Testament, neither of which was in fact ever published. Although ignorant of modern languages he corresponded freely in Latin with many European savants and attracted some to Cambridge, Küster being one of them. Stosch and Bentley had reciprocal interests, for Stosch learned from him to study ancient remains through the ancient authors, and the Master went to the remains for the purposes of his text. In the Preface to his *Life of Horace*, published in 1711, he had followed "the Orthography as it was in the Augustan Age which abundantly appears from Inscriptions, Medals and Ancient Manuscripts".[29]

At a somewhat later date Bentley was a close friend of Lord Carteret, but it seems unlikely that Stosch owed to this circumstance his own acquaintanceship with the future Secretary of State for the latter was only twenty-two at the time and had been at Oxford, not Cambridge. Probably Stosch met him first over antiquarian matters, for Carteret's father had been the owner of an outstanding collection of coins and medals. It was sold during the son's minority, but the latter may have inherited the taste, for Molesworth, although not knowing, he said, whether Carteret would be interested, told him in 1722 of a collection for sale in Florence.[30] However mysterious its details, Stosch's visit, from his own point of view, was a great success. It brought him considerable additions to his own learning and probably to his collections, profitable contacts with English connoisseurs and, through his friendship with Carteret, employment later on as a secret agent of the British Government.

Stosch returned to the continent and in 1714 started out

with von Schmettau on a journey to Italy, passing through France in the same year. A curious story relating to this visit is told by Charles de Brosses, whose published *Lettres d'Italie* describe a journey he made in 1739–40. Stosch with a party, he said, was being shown the royal collection of gems at Versailles, when a very famous one was found to be missing, even after everyone had been searched to the skin. The custodian then said to Stosch: "Sir, I know all the party except you and besides that I fear for your health; you seem to have a very yellow complexion which denotes repletion. I think that a little dose of emetic, taken on the spot, is absolutely necessary for you." The remedy, taken immediately, was said to have had a wonderful effect and to have cured the poor man of the illness of the stone he had swallowed.[31] This unedifying story, told from hearsay so many years after the alleged event, is not necessarily true, but it is an example of the kind of thing contemporaries said, or were ready to believe, about Stosch, who in his later years had a very bad press and appears to have developed into a recognised butt for jokes in the very worst of taste, many of them cracked by Mann and Horace Walpole, who often referred to him as "Cyclops". In fact their spiteful anecdotes, though probably not without foundation, tend to obscure Stosch's very considerable position in Florence as a collector, scholar and art expert of international renown, his vices notwithstanding.

Stosch seems to have parted from his brother-in-law fairly early in the trip and arrived by himself in Rome at the time of the Carnival in 1715. As usual he had at least one introduction which proved of great value. Bernard de Montfaucon, celebrated scholar and antiquary, recommended him to the Papal Chamberlain, Justus Fontanini, through whom presumably he got to know Clement XI. The latter received him warmly as a great scholar, gave him a pension which continued till the Pope's death in 1721 and, when he left Rome, a present of rare books and introductions to his Nuncios at all the Courts. Stosch resisted the Pope's efforts to convert him to Catholicism but, in spite of this, remained on close and affectionate terms with him. He also got to know the young Alessandro Albani, his nephew, who lived then in the Quirinal and was "turning up the whole soil of Rome for antiquities", an activity in which Stosch no doubt was only too happy to join him.

He left Rome two years later, summoned home by his father to attend to family affairs on the death of his brother Ludwig, Royal Physician-in-Ordinary in Paris. He does not appear to have hurried unduly for to this journey belongs a fairly long stay in Florence. Here, at the Court of the Medici Grand Duke Cosimo III, he met many notable scholars and an Englishman, Thomas Dereham, who represented the Medici interests in London during the negotiations leading to the Quadruple Alliance and whom Stosch was to meet again in Rome as a prominent Jacobite. He went also to Vienna where his assistance with the Emperor's and Prince Eugene's collections helped to lay the foundations for considerable patronage from the Hapsburg Court. Charles VI, together with Clement XI, was mentioned as one of the Baron's benefactors in an inscription prepared after Stosch's death by the Academy of Cortona for its tercentenary celebrations in 1758 and Stosch dedicated his *Gemmae Antiquae Caelatae* to him, being rewarded with a gold chain and the Imperial portrait. Possibly at some time or another he had some secret employment under the Court of Vienna. In 1739, when complaining to Prince Craon, Imperial Minister in Florence, that the latter did not receive him at his parties and that the Grand Duke was cold to him, Stosch referred to the convincing proofs of his attachment to the House of Austria given, he said, in Vienna, The Hague, Rome and Florence.[32] It sounds as though he meant more than services as an antiquary and he also reported once from Rome that the Emperor had offered him a post with money and dignity but that he did not wish to leave the service of the King of England.[33]

Passing through Dresden Stosch met Count Flemming, Prime Minister of Augustus II, Elector of Saxony and King of Poland, and was appointed, in October 1718, Royal Antiquarian to Augustus and substitute at The Hague for Baron von Gersdorf, a Saxon Minister incapacitated by illness. The post may have included something in the nature of intelligence service, because in letters to Flemming he mentioned enclosed extracts of secret letters and said that he had heard nothing in the conversations of Ministers which was worth the trouble of writing about. In 1719 Stosch received an invitation from "Monsignor Albani" to accompany him to the Congress of Cambrai, and Karl Justi, a great authority on Albani and Stosch, associates this with Annibale. In view, however, of Alessandro's attempts to get to the Congress it seems far more likely that it was he who invited Stosch, particularly as in a letter to Flemming of March 1721 he said that Albani's coming to the Congress had been his reason for extending his own stay away from Dresden, but that from his last letters he thought he would shortly be returning to Rome. Annibale himself appears to have been in Rome at the time, holding various appointments there, whereas Alessandro was certainly at Vienna. King Augustus would have given Stosch leave of absence to go to Cambrai but at one time he refused. The sad state of his finances, he wrote to Flemming in November 1719, not allowing him to leave The Hague for a town where a Congress was being held and therefore very expensive to live in, His Excellency would well believe that he would try to get out of this journey. He would not wish to make it at Monsignor Albani's expense and would not be able to at his own. Otherwise, he concluded, he would have been curious enough to see the Congress where he would witness the last scene of a tragedy which he had seen composed and acted, and in which he knew personally all the principal actors.

Although Stosch complained of the state of his finances, due, as he said, to his habit *"de manger mon blé en herbe"*, he should at this time have been relatively prosperous. He was receiving the salary of his diplomatic post, his 600 thaler a year as Royal Antiquarian as well as Clement XI's pension and was living in the house of the Greffier Fagel, his most consistent benefactor. This potentially favourable state of affairs did not, however, last long, since his pension from the Pope ceased when the latter died and von Gersdorf died at about the same time. The result of this was that Stosch lost his post as substitute, was not appointed as von Gersdorf's successor and was left with only his salary as Antiquarian, in which capacity he travelled about Holland and made acquisitions for the royal collections. He anticipated being recalled to Dresden and hoped that in the palace where the King intended to keep his collections there might be some space over to accommodate himself and his library, which was composed, he said, of nearly all the authors necessary for the knowledge of all sorts of antiques and modern curiosities as well as for that of books and manuscripts.

This setback in his diplomatic career was evidently mortifying to Stosch and, in view of his impressive connections and the good start in life they had procured him, it seems probable that his failure to obtain promotion at this critical stage was due to personal shortcomings as well as to the lack of means to which he himself attributed it. Although so passionate an antiquarian he viewed without enthusiasm the prospect of devoting himself to his studies alone. He wrote to Flemming in April 1721, saying that since the death of Clement XI he had been obliged to cut his expenditure by more than half and found himself reduced to not having a penny more than the King's pension. This had made him, he said, resolve much against his will to resume the study of antiquities "like a man who in despair made himself a Capucin", hoping that it would cost him less trouble to pass in time for one of the leading antiquaries than it would have to pass for a mediocre politician. The changes of situation to which a political career was subject on the death of a Prince, which might make a man lose the fruit of many years' work and reduce him to nothing, often without resources, were too sudden, he said, and too many people were in that profession. Everyone, however, was not suitable for that of an antiquarian as it required a very good memory and much reading, and not everyone wished to give themselves the trouble so that there were few rivals to fear. "It is true", observed Stosch,* "that in politics one can become great and have the pleasure of governing, which men regard as the greatest advantage in the world, as indeed it is. But as an antiquary I shall rule with little danger over Caesars and Scipios, Greeks and Romans, and I shall place them where I like and fear them much less than a politician his cook. I am not fitted to govern the living and only with much difficulty can manage my household, which merely consists of a servant and a dog, and yet they enrage me. I shall live truly in obscurity and without grandeur. But if I can be fortunate enough to enjoy Your Excellency's company, I will do without the rest of humanity. Because the pleasure of seeing you happy will give me as much satisfaction as grandeur would. . . ."

Flemming replied somewhat coldly to this effusion, saying that the knowledge of antiquities not being a science in which he concerned himself, he could not judge of the parallel Stosch made between it and politics but, observing from his letter that he was going to resume this study with pleasure, he congratulated him just as he had when he gave it up. Flemming's disclaimer of antiquarian interests shows

* In French in the original.

that these were not the basis of their friendship and Flemming may have seen reasons other than his protégé's financial demands at this time for a marked cooling-off when the Baron's arrival in Dresden seemed imminent. Unabashed, however, by what seems a distinct rebuff, Stosch wrote again in May saying that the congratulations with which His Excellency had honoured him, coming from the person who was in the position to procure him that happiness, consoled him infinitely. "Antiquary or not antiquary", he added,* "I shall always hold myself fortunate as long as I can enjoy the honour of your friendship. My fate depends always on your will. I will rule my passions so that the strongest shall always be destined for your service." Stosch, however, seems eventually to have taken the hint and he remarked rather plaintively in June 1721 that he had observed that nothing in the world so alienated the heart of a Minister from his creature as too frequent demands. It being impossible in a government to satisfy everyone, there were circumstances which obliged a Minister to advance the interests of his enemies, to win them over, rather than those of the friends who were most attached to him.

What with his debts and his estrangement from Flemming, Stosch was now in a most awkward predicament, because apart from all other considerations his debts always made it extremely difficult for him to get away from any place where he happened to be. He was rescued providentially and somewhat sensationally by the Greffier Fagel and by his old acquaintance Lord Carteret, now Secretary of State in England for the Southern Department. In October 1721 Stosch wrote to Flemming acknowledging orders transmitted through the Royal Polish Antiquarian, Count Manteuffel, to add to the King's collections however possible, and saying that he would now have a much more favourable opportunity of doing so than before. One of his

* In French in the original.

friends, he said, had offered to pay his expenses for a journey over all Italy. As it was the country of antiquities where there were the most opportunities for getting them cheap, and as besides that he would have through his friends the advantage of being able to export all he wished out of the country, it seemed that he ought not to neglect such a chance of serving the King, and at the same time perfecting and making himself more fit for his service. This was why with all possible humility he took the liberty of entreating His Excellency to add this benefit to many others for which he was already indebted to him, and begged King Augustus to do him the favour of allowing him to make this journey. His present salary and the advantage of getting the journey for nothing would, he said, enable him to live in Italy much better than where he was, and besides that he would rejoice in the satisfaction of being more useful to His Majesty. He went on to say that as he could not leave Holland without paying his debts he did not doubt but that his friend would undertake to pay them without claiming any return, provided that he accepted the proposed post. This would be a considerable advantage to his finances, which were greatly involved as usual and could not be re-established without powerful help from outside.

The friend to whom Stosch referred was Fagel, who continued to pay his debts from time to time,[34a] looked after his books at The Hague until he was able to send them to him in Italy[34b] and corresponded regularly with him until he himself died. Having helped him initially in the study of coins and allied subjects, the Greffier had also inspired Stosch, during one of his visits to The Hague, with the idea of compiling his so-called *Atlas*, which was really a kind of giant scrap-book. The basis for the work was Blaeu's great atlas, published in Amsterdam 1662–5, around which were to be assembled more detailed maps, together with plans, drawings and engravings of buildings, natural features, battles and other celebrated events, so as to make a world history based on topography. The material acquired in this pursuit included some of great rarity and value, so that Stosch's *Atlas* eventually rivalled in reputation his collection of ancient engraved gems. His ambitions regarding the latter were no less comprehensive. He aimed to collect all that were in existence in the form either of originals, contemporary or modern copies or, failing both, sulphur and wax impressions. A charitable interpretation of de Brosses' story might be that Stosch was in the habit of abducting gems temporarily for the purpose of copying them.

Stosch cannot always be believed, but there seems no reason to doubt what he said of his relations with Fagel, for he was to refer to them in 1751 when seeking the Earl of Holdernesse's help to recover arrears of pay from the British Government.[35a] Holdernesse must have known the circumstances, because he had been Minister Plenipotentiary at The Hague and had married Fagel's niece. Moreover, the application was successful, Stosch remarking that it was a great happiness for him to see live again in the "*Illustre Epoux de la Nièce de feu Mr Fagel*" a protector of whom the death of this great man had deprived him.[35b] Indeed, the Greffier's death when it came seems to have plunged Stosch into as great financial embarrassment as had that of Clement XI a quarter-century before.

It is probable enough that Fagel protected Stosch quite genuinely for the sake both of friendship and of adding to his own collections, but the commission he gave him in 1721 was also a cloak for the far more important secret assignment which he received at the same time from the British Government and held for the rest of his life.[34b] Stosch was appointed to live in Rome and report to the Secretary of State in England on the doings of the Stuarts, their adherents, and British travellers, and from the tone of his despatches he was evidently on the most friendly terms with

Carteret. The background to Stosch's appointment was the political situation already outlined in relation to Alessandro Albani's mission to Vienna, and England's deep distrust of papal intentions. In February 1721 Molesworth at Turin stressed the importance of fixing up a correspondence with a spy in Rome which, he said, would cost in all £400 a year,[15b] and this matter was still under consideration when Clement XI died in March. His death did little to reassure the British Ministers since the situation created during his reign would be inherited by his successor, and to Molesworth it seemed vital to obtain intelligence from the Conclave as to the probable policy of whatever Pope might be elected. The affair, however, was being handled by Lord Townshend, Secretary of State for the Northern Department, who does not appear to have had his heart in it. He told St Saphorin at Vienna that the Government had no interest in the election of a new Pope,[36] in reply to his communication that during the Conclave the Cardinals d'Althan and Davia had fought with their fists, Annibale Albani had made to throw an inkstand at Cardinal Pamphili's head and the latter had kicked him in return.[11c] He quibbled over the expense of the Roman correspondent and Molesworth had to look for someone else, finding a person who, he said, only wanted £200 a year and might be reduced to £150, which was as little as a man could live on if he were to keep good company and not have his attention diverted by the needs of mere subsistence.[15c] The result of the Conclave was the election of Cardinal Conti as Innocent XIII and Molesworth's fears of his intentions must at last have been taken seriously. The question of the Roman spy was taken up by the Secretary of State for the Southern Department, to whose province it would henceforward belong. This, of course, was Stosch's old acquaintance Lord Carteret, who threw economy to the winds to the extent at least of appointing Stosch at Molesworth's original figure of £400 sterling a year.

CHAPTER III

Stosch in Rome

STOSCH was delighted with his new appointment, but his very first letter from Rome written 31st January 1722 under the pseudonym "John Walton", which he always used in his despatches to the Secretary of State, reported trouble about the payment of his salary such as would recur for the rest of his life. He hoped Carteret would remedy his financial difficulties as soon as possible so that he could the better satisfy His Lordship's noble taste for antiquities and belles-lettres.[1a] The arrangement was that Stosch's salary, raised in 1723 to £520,[1b] was to be paid to him quarterly by a Leghorn merchant, Langlois, who would be reimbursed by the British Government through Sir Theodore Jansen.[2a] He also claimed for properly incurred disbursements, but there was often a dispute about these because it was maintained from Whitehall that the £120 rise had been meant to cover extraordinary expenses.[3a] According to Stosch, Langlois frequently refused to pay him because he himself had not received the money from England, and at a later date, in Florence, Stosch had to give a personal undertaking, underwritten by his brother Henry in case of his death, to repay to Langlois any instalment not refunded by the British Government.[2b] Even allowing for the fact that Stosch's claims had to be taken with a pinch of salt, he undoubtedly suffered, as did even properly accredited and acknowledged British representatives abroad, from the dilatoriness and niggardliness of his employers. Lord Essex indeed believed that Stosch was hardly used and wrote to the Duke of Newcastle from Turin in 1733 saying that although he hated the character of a spy yet he really thought the poor man did his duty by the King and was in great want, which made his intelligence trifling and low.[4a] The unfortunate Stosch's financial difficulties have a peculiar interest today in that most of the rather scanty autobiographical material to be gleaned from his correspondence occurs in letters in which he was raking up his grievances in order to obtain payment.

Stosch's position in Rome was, however, not at first too unfavourable. He still had the Saxon pension, which was continued till about 1727[5] and which, he said, enabled him to work on a "cosmographical" map of the whole of Rome which would be one of the rarest works of the century.[6] This, of course, was part of his *Atlas* (p. 60). He had been given, or continued to receive, money from Fagel with which he bought objets d'art and no doubt financed himself as a dealer.[5] He had many friends remaining from his previous visit and could count on the protection of the Imperial Minister in Rome, Cardinal Cienfuegos who, he said, showed himself very partial to the interests of the King of Great Britain.[1c] He was well acquainted with the Cardinals Polignac, Imperiali and Alberoni, who were of the inner councils of the Pretender, and through them could obtain or be expected to obtain the secret political information required by the British Government. He also had minor spies who collected such items as the news that a picture had fallen on the Pretender's head in his palace and obliged him to keep to his room for several days.[1a] Stosch's relations with the influential Albanis, whom he already knew well, are obscure. On his arrival in Rome he was, he said, well received at the houses of Colonna and Albani. Alessandro had offered him a house and the necessary furniture but he had preferred to return to an old apartnment so as to be free and not a burden on His Eminence, to whom he already owed so many obligations over many years.[1a] He spoke once of accompanying "Cardinal Albani" to Nettuno for a few days[1d]

Photo Alinari

THE MUTI PALACE, ROME
(Now Palazzo Balestra)

PHILIP VON STOSCH AND ROMAN ANTIQUARIES

Drawing by Pier Leone Ghezzi

but he may have meant Annibale, also a considerable connoisseur, and does not seem to have been conspicuously associated with the younger brother in antiquarian matters. There is no evidence that Alessandro knew from the first of Stosch's highly secret assignment, but in view of their former friendship and later collaboration it is hard to resist the conclusion that any reserve in public was a deliberate policy. The Colonnas' house might have covered their meetings. The widow of the Constable Colonna was at one time Alessandro Albani's mistress and herself a collector of engraved gems, one of which Stosch illustrated in his book on this subject.

Immediately on his arrival in Rome Stosch started his weekly despatches in French, which were put into cypher when this appeared desirable. His practice was to make a rough draft from which he prepared the cyphered version sent to the Secretary of State in England, and as the great majority of his drafts have survived, his despatches for the most part are duplicated in the Public Record Office. In theory the drafts should be a more reliable source than the copies deciphered in London, but in practice there appear to be few discrepancies.

In a long despatch to Carteret of 28th February 1722[1e] Stosch reported in cypher the activities of a Jacobite agent in Russia called Gordon, the secret support given to the Pretender by the Catholic powers in Rome and other political matters. Quite as much of the letter, however, was not in cypher and consisted of a racy account of his own adventures and plans which suggested a considerable intimacy with Carteret. He told him that he had since his last letter continued to see his old friends of both sexes and all ranks and to frequent all the big and small receptions, all he lacked being time to profit at his ease from the wise and witty things he heard said every day. His household, he continued, was composed of two servants, one of whom went round the town with him and was the greatest "*maquereau*" [7] in Rome, while the other was a German he had brought with him, who was the stupidest man possible and hardly understood his own mother tongue but had a wonderful talent for copying all living and dead languages in whatever characters they were written and however badly, who stayed in the house night and day and was indefatigable and faithful to the last degree. To complete his team there must be added a carriage and two horses, with a coachman, more phlegmatic than his horses, who without saying a word remained firm and motionless while waiting for him entire nights and did not stir from his place any more than a stone. In short, his establishment was suitable for a man like himself whose movements were necessarily influenced by circumstances favourable to the conjunction of time and place and of the people with whom he should converse. This household, he said, did not fail to exhaust the whole of his income, and he thought that after his return from Rome he would be able to render an account to his superiors like that which Sancho Panza gave to his Government of the Island of Barataria, that he arrived without a penny and departed with less.

Stosch went on to describe a meeting with Cardinal Alberoni. He was outside the Porta Pia, he said, copying some antique inscriptions found recently at the Cardinal's villa, and while thus engaged he saw him. Alberoni overwhelmed him with courtesies, walked about for some time with him, and conversed on a hundred different matters. Stosch could from his own experience, he wrote, say truthfully that he was a great genius who had all the talents necessary for a great Minister except knowing how to hold his tongue. It proved an eventful outing for Stosch for, as he was returning to the town, he met Princess Clementina, the Pretender's wife, who was on foot and greeted him most graciously. If he were as much of a courtier as he was an antiquary, he remarked, he ought to go and call on her, but he thought this time he would conform to the requirements of honesty and decency and not furnish a news item which would make reporters in Rome waste ink and paper.

Stosch went on to talk of inanimate things having, he said, spoken enough about the living. Draughtsmen had been pestering him to give them work under the impression that he could train them to be as clever at drawing from the antique as Ghezzi and Odam had become under his direction. He had therefore begun to have drawings made of all the marbles, bas-reliefs, statues, bronzes, engraved gems and medals which illustrated the dissipations of the Ancients, their Bacchanals, Priapic Games and sacrifices. He had found many fine things, he said, which proved clearly that the Ancient Europeans and Asiatics knew how to amuse themselves as well as any of the Chinese and Christian peoples of the present day.* He would, he continued, add drawings composed by himself and the Chevaliers Ghezzi and Odam, illustrating passages from ancient authors, such as the feast of Tigellinus from Tacitus, and all other festivals of debauch celebrated by the best pens of antiquity, Greek and Roman. All this, he said, was being done "*sub rosa*" and after drinking, therefore with all possible liveliness and naturalness. The expense would be moderate, as he would direct the work himself and had a reputation for paying his workers half in soft words. No one would make any objection because it was in the interests of those who were doing the work to say nothing. Nevertheless all this was being done, he pointed out, at Carteret's expense, and he begged him to warn his banker, Béranger, that he, Stosch, might be drawing on him directly for £30 or £40 sterling. It was only fair, he added, that if necessary he should draw in this way

* Obscene drawings and prints, both Chinese and others, were bought by the King of Prussia from Stosch's collection after his death. Walpole V. p. 202. Mann to H. Walpole 13. v. 58 and note 14.

for a trifle such as the one he was undertaking, which would adorn Carteret's library in so unique and inimitable a manner. It would console the Republic of Letters for the loss of the works of the Greek Elephantis so praised by Pliny and others for learning in feminine matters. This choice piece of pornography was evidently thought up by Stosch as a lucrative by-product in the preparation of his beautiful folio *Gemmae Antiquae Caelatae*,[8] for which Jerome Odam and Pier Leone Ghezzi provided illustrations, but there is no evidence that it ever actually found its way into Carteret's hands. A contemporary scholar, Bottari, suggested that Stosch was in the habit of promising books which never materialised,[9] and this probably was one of them.

Soon after this the British Envoy Extraordinary to Tuscany, Henry Davenant, arrived in Rome. He can only have been paying an unofficial visit, since the diplomatic situation in the Holy See would have precluded any other, but British representatives and Ministers did make such visits from time to time, on more or less flimsy excuses. Davenant called on Stosch under the guise of a student of engraved gems, and Stosch concealed from him his own liaison with England, some people thinking, he said, that he was employed by the Tsar, some by the King of Prussia, but none as yet suspecting the truth.[1f] Davenant, according to Stosch, was at a disadvantage with Italians in holding his wine, as strangers were apt to be, and talked too much when in drink.[1g] His remarks about the Pretender, whom devout Catholics now regarded as a martyr to his faith,[1h] caused the British envoy to be closely watched. Stosch, who saw much of him, was therefore also treated *"en prince"*, as he called it, having more spies round him than hairs on his head. To put them off he called only on Cardinal Gualterio, the Princesse des Ursins and other persons notoriously attached to the Pretender.[1i] Davenant, who according to Stosch was better pleased by the antiquities of Rome than by most of its modern inhabitants,[1j] does not seem to have guessed the Baron's assignment and had Cardinal Cienfuegos warned that he was an untrustworthy emissary of the Dutch Republic, plotting in favour of the Pretender. Stosch indeed was anxious lest the steps he had taken to deceive Davenant should lead to Carteret's getting adverse reports of himself.[1k] The Secretaries of State seem indeed to have been very careful to conceal even from their own officials the fact that Stosch and Walton were the same person, and Brinley Skinner, Consul at Leghorn, did not at one time know the connection.[10a]

For all his precautions Stosch was anxious lest his mail should be tampered with and the cypher in which it was written make people suspect that his correspondence was not merely commercial. He therefore pressed for arrangements for his own safety to be thought out in advance. It was impossible, he said, that a man could well serve in Rome without employing spies, as he did every day, and the circumstance could not be avoided that the persons employed were often paid by both sides. Experience had, however, taught him that these people often served better than others a man who knew how to manage them and hide his hand, for when they reported things about others they might be used to introduce into the mind of the enemy whatever it was desirable for him to think. Nevertheless a man was bound in the end to be betrayed by his own instruments, Stosch said, and pressed for more money to compensate his spies for the risks they ran.[1i]

By August 1722 he was even more anxious and asked Carteret to try to procure him, through St Saphorin, the title of "Conseiller de l'Empereur", which had been given, he said, to Protestants as well as Catholics and which would put him out of range of pursuit and yet not betray his liaison with England.[1l] He never obtained this but wrote in October saying that he had made his own approach through his friends in Vienna and as the Emperor knew him personally he had ordered a letter to be written to his Minister, Cienfuegos, so that the latter should protect Stosch as a person much esteemed by His Imperial Majesty for his knowledge and erudition.[1m] In December his main anxieties were again financial and he pressed for repayment of his expenses, enclosing a receipt in blank which he asked Carteret to fill up as he thought fit, according to what his services in a highly equivocal and thorny post had deserved in the past year, not forgetting, he said, one item which was that of having made love to an old woman of eighty-four, a fact of which all Rome was witness.[1n] The old woman referred to was evidently the Princesse des Ursins, whose death he announced in the same letter. She was a Frenchwoman who had had great influence at the Court of Spain during Alberoni's ministry there, and it is possible that she had turned spy on the Pretender when she got to Rome. It seems more probable, however, that she made use of her intimacy with Stosch to pump him and to stuff him up with whatever she wanted him to think. She appeared to be devoted to the Pretender and bequeathed him a dressing set worth 50,000 crowns, which Molesworth thought was too piquant a commentary on his character to please his friends.[11] It is difficult to believe that she was disloyal and her apparently equivocal behaviour was paralleled by that of John Hay, titular Earl of Inverness and the Pretender's close confidant, who, Stosch thought, tried to trap him into disclosing his liaison with England by insinuating that he, Hay, was tired of the Stuarts and seeking a pardon. Stosch did not, he said, fall into Hay's trap, and after talking as long as he could about books, drawings, entertainments and antiquities, gave a non-committal answer.[10]

Probably it was through such channels that Stosch's secret began to leak out very soon after his arrival in Rome. In 1722 a jeweller called William Dugood, Ducat or Duckett, who had served the Pretender and knew all the Englishmen who came to Rome, was imprisoned by the Inquisition on the usual pretext of impiety and Stosch used his influence to get him released. He had not treated the affair as a political one, he said, but had represented to certain cardinals who were friends of his how adversely such treatment of Protestants affected possible converts to Catholicism. Certain free expressions on the subject of religion must, he had pointed out, be tolerated from the Dutch and the English, who were accustomed to speak thus from their childhood.[1b] It had been necessary, Stosch wrote on another occasion, to stop the mouth of this man at the outset because he was the only person who was aware from the time of his first visit to Rome that he knew Lord Carteret, and it had therefore been impossible entirely to hide his liaison from him.[1q] Duckett was always a highly suspicious character and was imprisoned in 1733 by the Government of Rome on the orders of the Pretender, so it was said.[12a] Brinley Skinner, then acting Resident at Florence, recalled a complicated story told him by Stosch. Duckett, he said, had informed the Pretender's wife that Hay was communicating with the Baron, and as she refused to meddle in the matter Duckett had told his confessor, who had reported the matter to the Pretender. The latter had demanded an explanation from Duckett, who had subsequently been persecuted by Hay.[12b] Probably he was of the select company of spies for both sides and in 1731 Francis Colman put his own agent Denys Wright on to him to find out about his liaisons with the Pretender's people.[13] In 1734 Duckett's persecution was said to be over and he was to be allowed to stay in Rome, to the great mortification of the Jacobites.[14]

Stosch continued to complain about his lack of funds and of having had to pawn his medals and rings to pay for information. Since the Pretender, he said, had ceased to receive funds from England, the tapestries of his room spoke and he himself found more spies on his hands than he knew how to pay. Either King George must allow the Jacobites to send money from England to the Pretender or must increase his, Stosch's, pay, because unless he did the one or the other either James or he would certainly go bankrupt.[1r] He also asked for an extra £10 a month to keep open a certain channel of information. Having noticed, he said, that the Pretender's adherents went often to a certain house belonging to a friend of his own, he had provided this person with the best wines and other ingredients to attract them there even more, and that would have its effect provided he was in a position to support his man in the expenses of his house.[1s] Stosch always had considerable faith in the effect of wine on potential informants and called it "*la clef universelle des mystères humains*".[1t]

He himself continued to keep exalted company and was discussing the new British Government one day with Cardinal Gualterio. "I replied jokingly," wrote Stosch,* "that Plato had said the world could not be well governed except by philosophers; that I myself was of the opinion that to the word 'philosophers' one should join antiquaries, because at present the greater part of Europe was governed either by Princes or Ministers who were antiquaries, the Emperor, the Regent, Your Excellency [Carteret], Fagell, Prince Eugene and His Eminence himself." [1u] Stosch had, or believed he had, considerable influence in high places and when some cardinals thought the Pretender should move to Urbino because Rome was losing more than 400,000 crowns a year through no Englishmen coming there, he asked to have King George's opinion as to whether he should seek to get him moved. Stosch himself thought that although James could intrigue in Rome with the Ministers of all the crowned heads he was better where he could be watched, since, as he observed, to betray the greatest secrets passed

* In French in the original.

for a heroic virtue in persons of sublime rank.[1v] He had few illusions about the dignitaries of Rome, experience having taught him, he said, that once an ecclesiastic had been made to pass the Rubicon of Orthodoxy the fear of losing his spiritual reputation, which was all his patrimony, made him remain faithful, just as love of her good name kept a pious woman constant to a lover who had once passed with her the limits prescribed by the laws of chastity.[1w]

The first months of 1724 found Stosch still agitating about the title of Counsellor of the Emperor and alarmed because the Bishop of Rochester, *"Primat du Royaume imaginaire du Prétendant"*, had told Hay his name and pseudonym and said he had heard in England that Stosch was the author of all the Pretender's misfortunes. He could protect himself against the Romans, he said, by leading them by the nose, and if his liaisons with the King of Great Britain were ever discovered the Secretary of State must attribute the fault to London and not to Rome, where he played his part in such a way that it was impossible to do more and he could render an account of it to all who understood the profession.[15a] Temporarily, however, he was relieved of, or distracted from, his anxieties by the death of Innocent XIII and hoped to arrange for good correspondents in the Conclave itself, who would warn him of any prejudices to the King's interests in favour of the Pretender.[15b] It would cost him more than double his usual expenses, he said, for he must pay an *"espion de qualité"* (by which presumably he meant a high-ranking ecclesiastic), within the Conclave and two others outside.[16a]

According to Stosch's reports, the Conclave was distinguished by frantic intrigue on the part of the two Albani cardinals, Annibale and Alessandro, who made themselves so unpopular in Rome by trying to procure the election of one of their creatures that the family palace was nearly burnt by the mob.[15c] Stosch himself, if he can be believed, used his influence to try to prevent the election of an extremist, for, as he very rightly said, every man of intelligence would be in the interests of the King and every bigot would favour the Pretender.[15d] He said he had been used as a sort of mediator to induce the Albanis to yield, and added that he thought he was the first Protestant who by his personal credit had entered into and operated in the election of a Pope with as much authority, indirectly, as any Minister of a crowned head could have directly.[15e] Unfortunately for his boast Cardinal Orsini, who was elected a fortnight later as Benedict XIII, appeared likely to be more devoted to the Pretender's interests than ever, though in the end this was not the case.

Alessandro Albani's conduct in the Conclave is mysterious, in view of the manœuvres we have already noted at Vienna, but he had as yet no political appointment, was probably, as always, pressed for money, and on this occasion perhaps merely sought the immediate advantage of securing the election of a Pope who sympathised with the Albani family interests and would give him the good start in Rome of which Clement XI's death appeared to have robbed him. Whatever his aims were he pursued them with his usual gusto, according to Stosch. Cardinal Spada reproached him for his intrigues and Alessandro fell into such a rage that he replied with appalling insults, not at all proper in the mouth of a cardinal. The dispute went so far that Orsini, crucifix in hand, and the Cardinals Saterno and Tolomei with papal Bulls, had great difficulty in calming the irritation of their Eminences. Some cardinals wanted to come out of the Conclave and the Marshal was called to restore order while Cardinal Pamphili, a character given to jesting, ran up with a great jug full of water in his hand, reported Stosch.[15f]

After it was all over Stosch told how his friends among

the cardinals had recounted in detail the intrigues of the Conclave, rather like soldiers describing the success of a battle, that was to say, each different from the other according to what he had seen.[15g] Alessandro Albani received his reward in the shape of the Abbey of Nonantola, worth 6000 crowns a year; the Pretender with his wife and young son had an audience with Benedict XIII and was said to have asked for a more convenient palace and an increase in his pension; his son, aged four, scandalised the faithful by refusing to kiss the Pope's feet[15h] and, in the interests of their studies, the prelates of the Judicature were forbidden to go in the evenings to assemblies of ladies. "I think", said Stosch,* "that Hannibal before the gates gave no more alarm to the soldiers of ancient Rome than this order to the officers of the Spiritual Militia in the modern City."[15i]

Stosch had to realign his policy, find a new set of informants and at the same time serve a new Secretary of State, for Carteret had in May 1724 been replaced by the Duke of Newcastle, who begged Stosch to continue sending his interesting reports on the same terms.[15j] Newcastle also had antiquarian tastes, for in 1728 he arranged for the Chargé d'Affaires, Edward Allen, in Turin, to have an index prepared of the manuscripts of the Renaissance architect Pirro Ligorio which were kept there.[17] Stosch used in his official despatches to inform him about matters of artistic interest, such as the sale to Philip V of Spain of statues, bas-reliefs and busts formerly belonging to Queen Christina of Sweden, but the old ease of intercourse with Carteret had gone.

In July 1724 Stosch reported a strange development. The Ministers of France and of the Emperor had, he said, received specific orders from their Courts to convey to the Cardinals Albani their disapproval of their conduct in the Conclave. These cardinals, seeing the estrangement of the crowned heads and thinking it necessary to keep Stosch's

* In French in the original.

friendship at all costs, had made an approach to Cardinal Paulucci, the Pope's Secretary of State. By means of a third person who was in his confidence Paulucci had assured Stosch that he had need of the protection of no other Prince in order to live entirely at his ease in Rome, and if indeed it were true that he had liaisons with England Paulucci would be pleased to communicate with him direct every time he had need of him, the Pope having no other desire than to keep the peace in the world and to be on good terms with all the Princes who tolerated the peaceful practice of the Roman Catholic religion in their states. Stosch was much surprised at this approach, and as he feared that it was just a device for embarrassing him with the Imperial party, or for alienating him from the confidence of several cardinals who were powerful enemies of the Pope, he made an ambiguous reply "*à la Normande*" as he called it, from which he defied them to gather any reasonable sense. Meanwhile he resolved to have Paulucci sounded and would refrain from paying him the visit he seemed so earnestly to desire on the pretext of their old friendship until he had taken all precautions, for good or evil, to protect himself against the intrigues of others. "I think meanwhile", added Stosch, "I shall find a way to keep the friendship of my friends, as well as that of the Papal and Imperial Courts, and if during this manœuvre I am obliged to commit some sin against the Canons I hope that Your Excellency on my return will use your good offices with the King so that in his capacity as Supreme Bishop of the Anglican Church he will give me his pontifical Absolution, jointly with a pension proportionate to the services I shall have rendered to His Majesty." *[151]

Alberoni, either to ingratiate himself with England for the restoration of his own fortunes, or for the sake of counter-espionage on behalf of the Pretender, had been closely associated with Stosch since the latter's arrival in Rome and,

* In French in the original.

as long as he had need of him, said Stosch, served the King's interests very faithfully.[15m] He had even been one of those who pressed Stosch to obtain the title of Counsellor of the Emperor, although the Baron thought that this was because his papers, if seized, would be very prejudicial to Alberoni and his associates in a country governed by priests.[16b] Since then, however, Alberoni had become reconciled to his great enemies the Cardinals Albani and Imperiali, was closely associated with Cardinal Polignac, who served the French Court, and to curry favour with the Pope had constituted himself Protector for the Pretender.[15m] Stosch therefore had to look for other confidants and he found them, or thought he had, in the persons of the Prince of Montemileto, who had been the bearer of Paulucci's proposal,[16c] and a protégé of Benedict XIII, the Prelate Coscia. As sweeteners Stosch proposed that pressure should be applied in Vienna to get the order of the Golden Fleece for Montemileto[15n] and that Coscia should have a present of some trifles from England.[15o] Montemileto was to prove a disappointment, for three years later he returned to his own estates having despaired of influencing the Pope.[18] Meanwhile Stosch thought it wise, on the pretext of the heat of the season, to withdraw little by little from the confidence of the Cardinals Albani, who were those "*les plus menacés de tempêtes*", as he put it.[15p] In his despatches he represented them as being at this time wholly on the side of the Pretender and urged that the King should keep himself armed by sea and land rather than rely on the most sacred promises of a Pope entirely dominated by the House of Albani.[15q] Although it agrees with his later policy, Alessandro therefore seems unlikely to have been the cardinal who was said to have made the following forthright reply to a suggestion made in a Congregation that the treasure of Sixtus V should be used to recover England for the Catholic Church: "Your Eminence", said this individual, "will ruin both at once, the Church by taking away the only money reserved as her last resource, and King James by sacrificing to the hands of the executioner himself, without any probability of the success of the enterprise, those few adherents of consequence who remain to him in England, with the result that during the troubles of England the House of Bourbon will become Master of Italy." * [15q]

Under the new papacy and assisted by Montemileto's partiality to England, Stosch seems to have started the year 1725 rather more reassured about his own safety, although his employment was no longer a secret. While he was passing the Palazzo Borghese one evening his coachman was wounded in the face by a footman in livery who followed the carriage sword in hand. Although it turned out to be only a quarrel between servants the Government of Rome acted energetically on Stosch's behalf and he spoke with satisfaction of the surprise of the Pretender and his adherents at the vigorous steps taken in his favour, as it was publicly known that he served the King of England.[15r] He was broke as usual, having, he said, spend 3000 crowns of his own money and not been paid his extraordinary expenses for two years,[15s] but nevertheless he still seemed to be enjoying himself in his own peculiar way. "I always let people find me idle in my house",* he wrote, "and amusing myself with two nocturnal birds, a sort of owls called here 'Barbagianni', teaching them to keep awake in the day and sleep at night, while the Pretender and his Ministers have been perpetually active." [15t] One of these owls is to be seen in Ghezzi's drawing of Stosch with a group of connoisseurs (Pl. 4), and the Baron, who on one occasion complained of the mice having eaten his books at The Hague,[4b] may have had a good reason for keeping these pets as well as the cats of which he was so fond.

Towards the end of January 1725 Stosch was disturbed by

* In French in the original.

a curious incident. A Captain Bacon Morrice, Governor of
Landguard Point Fort, a regular soldier and said to be a
cousin of the Walpoles, had arrived in Rome late in 1724
and was suspected by the Jacobites of having a liaison with
Horatio Walpole, British Ambassador in Paris, and of having been sent to spy on them.[15u] It is quite possible that he
had been. In a note in English to Stosch in which he complained of being too tired to visit him, he said that they
both served the same master and that he would be willing
to co-operate with him. He went on to ask Stosch not to
neglect having the drawings copied "in such a manner as
Mr Walpole may have an Idea of the Originals",[16d] but his
note has a certain conspiratorial undertone which suggests
the approach of one spy to another on the pretext of an
artistic commission. Whether as a blind or not he did, however, order drawings which he failed to pay for and for
which Stosch was afterwards dunned.[15v] The Jacobites intercepted Morrice's mail, which however only contained
literary matter, and interfered with his credit. Consequently
Stosch, who said he showed much zeal for the King's service, felt obliged to protect him, drive about openly with
him and take him to see Alberoni as he earnestly desired.[15w]
Notwithstanding Stosch's protection, which was evidently
worth something at this time, a dangerous attempt was
made upon Morrice's life[15x] and an order of banishment
passed upon him by the Government of Rome. He afterwards deposed to Francis Colman at Florence that he had
avoided going to public places, so as not to give offence
when he found himself unpopular, but the Pretender's
fears were not to be calmed. A severe fit of illness, he said,
obliged him to go to Frascati for some country air in
Stosch's company and on returning to his lodgings in Rome
they unluckily met the Pretender and his wife in so narrow
a street that he and the Baron had to draw up to let them
pass. By chance, Morrice added, he had a gun with him in

the chaise and this gave the Pretender such strange apprehensions that he prevailed on the Pope that very night to
order his banishment.[19a] After protests this order was withdrawn but Bacon Morrice thought it more prudent to place
himself under Francis Colman's protection in Florence and
thereafter to pursue his remedies from a distance. He was
championed by the British Government, for the Duke of
Newcastle instructed Colman to make appropriate representations in Rome,[20] but whether because he was a secret
agent or just because he was a British officer and subject it is
hard to say. If he was a spy he was a very inept one, and the
rest of his career does not seem to have been very prosperous. In the Army List of 1740 he figured as a Captain of
Invalids, having been first commissioned in 1709. Interesting
features of the incident in Rome are the Pretender's personal
timorousness, alleged on other occasions as well, and the
fact that Stosch had at this time sufficiently powerful protection to maintain himself against the fierce hostility of
the Jacobites.

At the end of 1725 Stosch began to report rumours of an
estrangement between the Pretender and his wife. He attributed this to an affair between James and the titular Countess
of Inverness,[15y] but the better opinion seems to be that this
was slander, the true causes being Clementina's objection
to Protestant tutors for her sons, incompatibility and a
neurotic tendency which this spirited and charming princess
developed under the stresses of life in Rome with the rigid
and melancholy Pretender. He was evidently jealous and
difficult to live with, as his younger son was to discover later,
and Skinner had a story in 1733 that one of the sons, presumably the elder, who was then thirteen, had threatened to
draw his sword on his father if he used his mother ill.[12c]
Certainly in the early days of her marriage she was very
different and James Edgar, the Pretender's secretary, was
charmed by her vivacity. He recounted how the Pope had

once lent her his litter for her return from her *villegiatura*
and how, as His Holiness often went about with little ceremony, many people thought it was he who was in it and
knelt down for a blessing. Some, Edgar said, laughed at
their mistake, while others were much out of countenance,
and he told how on getting home Clementina had described
with much liveliness and good humour the diversion she
had had.[21a] Whatever the reasons for them, the differences
between the Pretender and his wife were highly prejudicial
to their cause, and Brinley Skinner wrote of the discontent
of the Roman nobility at having to yield precedence to him,
the complaints of the poor at the burden he was to the
State and the grumbling of the middle class at the reduction
in numbers of British visitors with consequent damage to
the trade in medals, pictures and statues. Skinner believed
that the Government itself felt the same.[10b]

Among the allegedly rare English visitors was one who
brought Stosch news of an old friend. This was Thomas
Bentley, nephew of the great Richard Bentley, who came
at the end of 1725 to collate Greek manuscripts in the Vatican for his uncle. He wrote to the latter saying that the
Princess Sobieski was reported to have gone into a nunnery,
some said upon a quarrel about the Lady Inverness, who
lived in the family with them, and others that her husband
had put a Protestant tutor to her son and that she could not
bear that. The Baron was very civil to him, he continued,
and he had dined with him often. He loved to talk of
Richard Bentley and was very grateful for all his kindness.
He said he would come into England soon, would of all
things in the world like to retire to Cambridge and study,
and should be happy if he were but Professor of Modern
History. He had, continued Bentley, made prodigious collections indeed and would do fine things in that way.[22a] He
wrote about him again, rather less warmly, a month later
saying that Stosch was discontented, wanted to come to

England and that they did not pay him. The Baron had written to the Duke of Newcastle but there was no great occasion for his services now, Bentley thought, as he could only write word to the Government about what Englishmen came to Rome and how they behaved themselves and that the cause was low.[22b] Thomas Bentley was a loyal subject of King George and collected for Colman the interesting information that the Pretender had given fifty guineas to "one Willoughby an English man to go to Muscovy".[19b]

A traveller with other sympathies was the Duke of Beaufort, who must have given great satisfaction in Rome as he spent more than 3000 crowns on pictures and statues[23a] and lavishly entertained such of the English as were not frequenters of Stosch's house. The latter had to try to find out "little by little, according as the heat of the wine made the Duke's people talk" * what had passed at his audience with the Pretender.[23b] Stosch told the Governor of Rome, who tried to sound him on the subject of the Duke, that he had no special orders about him, but the King's service obliged him to watch his movements as he did those of all other English travellers in Rome.[23c]

Although Stosch had attributed to the influence of the Albani brothers the conciliatory approach which Paulucci had made to him, they were both still ostensibly of the Pretender's party, and Alessandro went in June 1726 with the Cardinals Alberoni, Polignac and others to Frascati, on the pretext, Stosch said, of seeing the festivities of the fair there but really to condole with the Pretender on the death of his great friend the Duke of Ripperda.[23d] Whether or not there had been a previous political liaison between Alessandro and Stosch their relationship entered on a fresh phase soon after this. In October 1726 the Baron wrote to the Duke of Newcastle saying that he had just been informed by the Cardinal Alessandro Albani, who had even

* In French in the original.

allowed him to mention his name in a despatch, that certainly the Pretender would return the next month from Bologna.[23e] This apparent volte-face on the part of Alessandro appears to have been connected with the manner in which his own career was progressing. He had for some years been taking an increasingly prominent part in the affairs of Sardinia, being a member of a minority of ecclesiastics who espoused the cause of the King against the Pope in the negotiations following on Victor Amadeus' assumption of the crown of Sardinia and his claim to royal prerogatives.[23f] In 1727 these negotiations, which had already been frustrated on two occasions by the death of a Pope, were brought to a temporary settlement under which the King was to enjoy in his realm the same rights of ecclesiastical presentation vis-à-vis the Pope as did the King of France in his. This result was unpleasing to Benedict XIII and to many influential clerics, and Alessandro Albani had to look for his reward to the King of Sardinia who gave him immediately the rich abbey of Staffarda[24] and in 1730 made him his Protector.[25]

Alessandro was therefore already by 1726 persona non grata to a powerful group in Rome, even though the Pope was reputed to have started his reign as an Albani puppet, and the rejection of Alessandro's application for the post of Prefect of the Signature, alleged by Stosch,[23g] may well have decided him to turn to external politics for a career rather than to seek Roman appointments. The precocious disillusionment with the Jacobite cause which he had shown in Vienna may have been confirmed or revived by the rift in the Pretender's household and by the emergence in the Sacred College of a party hostile to Stuart ambitions, while his far-sighted policy in regard to Sardinia would tend to throw him on to the side of the British. However many times the Kings of Sardinia turned their coats on the continent the mutual desire of the British Government and the

House of Savoy to stand well with each other remained pretty constant, and was to do so even under the strain of the reported near-success of the Forty-Five Rebellion. The Marquis d'Orméa, Sardinian Minister in Rome in 1725, was careful to address the Old Pretender only as King without appending the name of Great Britain.[15z] Whatever lay behind it all, however, Stosch was no longer avoiding Alessandro, and in May 1727 passed a week with him at Nettuno having drawings made of a quay built by Innocent XII on part of the mole of the ancient Roman fort at Antium, the modern architects, said Stosch, having made such a bad job of it that the Pope's galleys could only shelter there with difficulty and danger.[23h] It may be conjectured that the two friends discussed other matters besides the antiquarian ones so congenial to them both.

The death of George I in June 1727 found the Pretender, with his usual bad luck or bad management, in no condition to take the best advantage of a possible opportunity for another rally of his followers. When the news came he was at Bologna, as yet unreconciled with his wife, and from there made an abortive journey to France and then to Avignon. The Pope, however, being highly apprehensive of disobliging the King of England on the subject of the Pretender's residence at a time when there was so powerful a squadron of ships in the Mediterranean, prudently and precipitately recalled him to Italy, or so at least wrote Brinley Skinner.[10c]

In spite of the apparent bankruptcy of the Jacobite cause, Stosch's anxieties were by no means diminishing and he began to exhibit a certain loss of nerve. In August 1729 he thought it would be better for the King's interests if the Pretender could live at Bologna or in some other town in the Ecclesiastical States and that this could be arranged if money were spent secretly among those all-powerful at Court. In Rome, he said, the Stuart followers seduced most of the young men who travelled and drew them imperceptibly into the interests of the elder son of the Pretender, and all his own vigilance could not prevent this evil while his hands were tied in regard to extraordinary expenses, and the Pretender's people, sustained by the Spaniards, put spies on him while he was not in a state to do the same by them.[23i] In 1730 another papal election took place, that of Lorenzo Corsini as Clement XII, and in pressing for his arrears of extraordinary expenses Stosch remarked that his post while the Pope's throne was vacant was already sufficiently dangerous in itself without joining to the other unavoidable anxieties that of thinking how to find money.[3b] He knew, he said, that in writing truthfully what he learned regarding the conduct of great lords and other rich and powerful persons he made himself powerful enemies, who one day or another would destroy him as he was poor and without support.[23j]

The attitude of the new Pope was a disappointment because, although he had not previously appeared very friendly to the Jacobites and had kept open house for English travellers,[3c] he and his family started immediately after his election to show the Pretender particular marks of favour.[3d] Spinola, Governor of Rome, had destroyed Stosch's credit, he said, by falsely accusing him of a debt although he knew the great punctuality with which he had always paid his servants, against the accustomed style of Rome.[23k] The British Secretary of State had asked the Court of France to procure for Stosch the protection of the French Ambassador, Cardinal Polignac, but this was quite ineffectual.[21b] In March 1730 Stosch reported that the Pretender himself had presented a memorial to the cardinals in authority at the time of the Conclave, asking them to clear him out of Rome as a dangerous man who hatched dangerous plots against him, did unbelievable harm to members of his party as well as to the Catholics of Great Britain and

Ireland, and that he feared neither God nor man, having atheistic and machiavellian principles.[3e]

There seems good reason for suspecting that the revival of Jacobite arrogance and of Stosch's apprehensions were due less to the new papacy and to political changes than to the presence in Rome of Charles Radcliffe, brother of that young Earl of Derwentwater who had been executed for his part in the 1715 rebellion. Charles, also implicated, had escaped from Newgate in 1716 and thereafter lived on the continent with his wife,[26a] who was Countess of Newburgh in her own right. He was in Turin in 1727[27] and it was probably shortly afterwards that he came to Rome to join his rather shady Uncle William, who was already living there and under whose will he subsequently benefited.[26b] Stosch had remarked in 1722 that the Jacobite Court was "*une rapsodie de gens de fort mèdiocre portée*"[1d] and, with the Pretender lacking as he was in the gift of leadership, the advent of such a character as Radcliffe could hardly fail to have an effect. His house became the meeting-place of English travellers attracted there by the beauty of the Lady Newburgh's daughters[3f] by a previous marriage and in 1734 the "*désordres parmis la jeunesse de Rome*" provoked by his assemblies induced the Pope to order their cessation and to segregate the young women for a time in the Convent of St Silvester.[28] Visitors mingled so freely with the Pretender's people during these highly attractive parties that in 1731 it was said to be impossible to distinguish who was loyal, even some whose principles were known to be entirely Whig being thus enticed.[3g] Stosch insisted later that if this furious and headstrong enthusiast, as he called Radcliffe, were not removed from Rome, it would be impossible for anyone serving the King of England to remain there.[3h] In addition to Radcliffe Stosch had a dangerous enemy in Sir Thomas Dereham, whom he had known in Florence but who had turned against him in Rome on learning of his liaisons with England.[29]

On 21st January 1731 the long-expected blow fell. "The enemies of the King's Government," Stosch wrote,* "after having used threats and all sorts of tricks during the nine years of my sojourn here to get me out of Rome, have finally reached the last extremities. On Sunday, two hours before midnight and in full moonlight, when I was returning home from Cardinal Bentivoglio's, my carriage was surrounded near Prince Ruspoli's palace, by three men with muskets in their hands, supported at a distance by other evil-looking men with cloaks up to their faces. The first, taking the horses by the bridle, threatened to kill the coachman if he moved, the second did the same to the footman and the third broke the windows with the butt of his musket so that the pieces wounded me, and put the muzzle of the weapon against my chest. I tried to throw myself out on the other side but another musket-barrel was presented at me. After holding me in this position for a few minutes one said to me loudly in Italian: 'If you do not leave Rome within eight days you are a dead man'. After that they allowed the carriage to go on and disappeared in different directions. . . . [Such] threats would have been enough to make a more apprehensive man die of fright and I assure Your Excellency that I have never seen an uglier face than the muzzles of two muskets propped on the doors of my carriage." [3i]

Stosch protested to the Governor of Rome, Cardinal Corsini, and to the French Ambassador, Cardinal Polignac, but they gave him so little satisfaction that he resolved to leave as soon as possible, obtained a loan from a Roman merchant,[3j] advertised for creditors and started to pack up. His departure was delayed because the roads were impassable with snow, but on 18th February he arrived in Florence to place himself under the protection of Francis Colman, who, he said, was affectionately disposed towards him and recalled in much detail conversations they had

* In French in the original.

had together in Leghorn in 1717.[3k] He also tried to work himself into the good graces of the Grand Duke of Tuscany and, characteristically enough, presented him with "a pocket thermometer invented by Fahrenheit which he had been very impatient to see".* [3l]

The true facts about, and the authors of, the attack upon Stosch have never been established and it was suspected even at the time that he might have made the story up. It would have got him out of an intolerable situation in Rome without his resigning his post and losing the English salary which was his only regular income since the Saxon pension had ceased. The earlier correspondence, however, suggests a gradual building up of hostility to Stosch, which seems inevitable in a city where the Pretender's Court and the Inquisition were potent forces and to both of which he was abhorrent, as well, no doubt, as to many private individuals. According to the testimony of his nephew at his death many years later in Florence he was happy-go-lucky and optimistic by nature and although threatened by expulsion from Tuscany was awaiting it philosophically and passively. A systematic setting of the scene for a fictitious attack and the staging of the attack itself therefore seem out of character even for the mysterious, dingy Stosch, as Horace Walpole called him, and probably the incident itself may be accepted as genuine, with reservations as to its perpetrators. Stosch himself would of course have a natural bias towards blaming the Jacobites so as to extort as much compensation as possible from the British, but he was corroborated by one contemporary at least. Count Wackerbarth-Salmour, the Saxon Minister in Rome at the time, thought the incident more characteristic of English than of Roman customs. Italy, he observed, killed without saying anything, but the more humane Englishman spared life provided he could attain his object.[30]

* In French in the original.

Amidst a mass of correspondence subsequent to the attack nothing much more conclusive emerged than the views expressed by Colman immediately after he had seen Stosch and received various other initial reports from Rome. Most people, he said, were of opinion that the stroke could come from no other party but that of the Government. Others thought it came from some of the Pretender's party and there were even some who carried their suspicions so far as to fancy the Duchess of Buckingham was concerned in it. Others accused the Baron of contriving secretly to have himself attacked in the hope of getting rid of so uneasy a post with advantage. Those, however, of the best sense and experience in Florence were firmly persuaded that the affair could not have happened in Rome without the knowledge and order of the Government, which would try any means it could safely employ to get rid of a person disagreeable to them on many accounts and particularly for being too well acquainted with its secret ways of acting. This manner of proceeding had besides been customary in like cases in Italy, where sometimes a person was given a fright when the Prince of the country dared not, for some other considerations, openly order him to depart. As to the second report, Colman continued, the known avowed and inveterate hatred of the Pretender's party to Baron Stosch, and the sudden and private departure of Hay soon after the thing happened might have given occasion for that suspicion which, if true, might naturally lead to another, namely, that probably there were some secret projects now carrying on in Rome which the Jacobites were afraid the Baron might discover and so came to the desperate resolution of forcing him from thence. Concerning the third point, said Colman, his correspondent would judge how ill-founded or highly improbable such a suggestion was and how much more likely it was to be an invention made use of in Rome the better to conceal the true authors of the fact.

As to the fourth and last suggestion, since the Baron had escaped without harm he might now safely laugh at all the malice of his enemies and particularly at their charging him with a plot against himself which, if he might be allowed the levity, reminded him "of the old Iricism of Teague's being run away with by his own legs".[31] The Duchess of Buckingham's alleged knowledge of or connivance in the plot was not altogether unlikely, for she always claimed, rightly or wrongly, that she was James II's natural daughter.[32a] Stosch said that on the day after the attack she sent a servant to his house on the pretext of enquiring if he would sell her an engraved stone for £10, and that the man changed colour twenty times in a quarter of an hour on finding him in bed surrounded by firearms of all calibres.[3k]

Stosch now departs from the Roman scene if not from our story. He was to remain in Florence until his death in 1757, writing weekly despatches to the Secretary of State in England and regularly claiming money for the continued payment of spies in Rome. A great part of his letters consisted of a dull journal of the Old Pretender's minutest comings and goings and, as Stosch increasingly lost touch with his personal acquaintances, of information from more or less public news reports. In the end perhaps his despatches were only of use for checking items from other sources or, as Horace Walpole suggested in 1743, to amuse George II.[32b] This much must, however, be said for the British Government, that although appallingly dilatory in paying Stosch it was no less dilatory in paying other far more important representatives abroad and, having rendered him quite unemployable by other powers and helped to encompass his financial ruin, it did go on paying him for the rest of his deplorable life, long after his information had ceased to be of any real value.

CHAPTER IV

Diplomats and Spies

IT was not immediately apparent that Stosch's career in Rome was finished and he said that until the British Government gave him fresh orders he would keep up a correspondence with his friends there, and so far as he could rely on the good faith of Italian Roman Catholics he would do his best to provide reliable information by comparing the reports of different people unknown to each other. He added, however, that his friends were so appalled at what had happened to him that he had had great difficulty in rallying the more courageous of them, and that if a cardinal of authority, an old friend of his and naturally well disposed to His Majesty, had not taken it upon himself to protect certain of them provisionally he would not have been able to engage anyone to involve himself in the Pretender's affairs and correspond with him during his absence. The British Government were considering sending him back to Rome but he was not enthusiastic. Rome, he said, was a place governed by influence and not by law like other civilised towns. If he had had the salary of a Minister, and the means of paying his spies as well as the others did, no one would have dared to touch him and the Government would not have been able to do so without one of the officials giving him warning beforehand. In Rome, he said, Ministers were respected more according to their appearance and conduct than in relation to their master. Thus Bentivoglio, fierce and resolute, attended by two bravoes with big moustaches, made himself feared and respected, whereas Cienfuegos, who was wise and good, could hardly protect his own servants from insults.[1a] Bentivoglio's bravoes do indeed seem to have been notorious, because a few years before this they had attacked and mortally wounded Alessandro Albani's coachman.[2]

It is irresistible to identify Stosch's helpful cardinal with Alessandro Albani, who was again seriously involved with the disputes between Rome and Turin which reopened when the new king, Charles Emmanuel III, demanded homage from papal fiefs in Piedmont.[1b] Alessandro boldly championed the interests of Savoy, of which he was now Protector, to the detriment of those of the Pope whom he openly defied, and Stosch's informants told him that he had in consequence been suspended from all Congregations and ran a risk of something worse. It would be a great loss for His Majesty's interests, remarked Stosch, if this cardinal were oppressed, for he was the only member of the Sacred College who was sincerely attached to the interests of Great Britain and who not only during his stay in Rome had helped him with good advice and protection, but after his departure had always kept up a correspondence with him in cypher. Stosch felt it necessary, he said, to tell Newcastle this in the greatest secrecy, because if Alessandro's papers were seized they would be found to contain enough material to make of this correspondence a crime of the first order and he would be in danger unless, through the Court of Vienna, the King of England protected him secretly and effectually. The protection of the King of Sardinia alone would not be enough to keep him safe under the Government of a Pope who, Stosch said, was in his dotage or dominated by the advice of madmen who had lost all respect, human and divine.[1c]

In the following month, June 1731, Stosch wrote again on the same subject. Alessandro Albani, he said, had written twice, strongly pressing him to get his antique marble statues sold in England as he needed money for his niece's dower. Stosch thought that by this means the British could buy the sympathy of this Cardinal who, he said, was the most suitable member of the Sacred College to serve His Majesty's interest, being a man of superior character, one of the best brains in the College and naturally friendly to the English nation.[1d] No specific result of this proposal is revealed in the official correspondence, but on 31st July 1731 Stosch wrote to Colman at Parma that Brigadier Churchill seemed very pleased with Cardinal Albani who had made him a present of two magnificent antique busts and two very beautiful vases of oriental alabaster.[3a] The Brigadier was apparently Charles Churchill, whose son married Walpole's legitimated daughter by his second wife, and busts of Septimius Severus and Commodus are recorded as having been "given to General Churchill by Cardinal Alexander Albani and by him to Sir Robert Walpole".[4] It seems probable that these were the busts Stosch referred to, and evidently the gift was related to other transactions. In October 1731 Stosch wrote to Brigadier Churchill about works of art which the latter wanted to buy, complained that his own medals and other belongings had been sequestered by his creditors and said that if the Cardinal ever decided to sell his bust of Caligula he felt sure he would give him, Stosch, the preference. Stosch himself sent a present the following month to Sir Robert Walpole, a vase of green porphyry which he said he had asked Mr Skinner, an officer on Admiral Wager's ship, to present to Sir Robert. This vase had been found several years before, quite complete as it now was, in the ruins of the ancient Atella in the Kingdom of Naples, and had come into his hands through the good offices of the Neapolitan scholar, Matteo Egizzio. He accompanied this gift by a letter to Walpole, asking to be allowed to return to Holland and keep up a correspondence with Rome from there, and for money to prevent all his possessions being sold by his creditors to pay his debts.[3b]

Notwithstanding his desire to arrange a high-level correspondence in Rome to fill the gap left by Stosch, the Duke of Newcastle does not appear to have followed up the Baron's suggestion by any immediate official approach to Albani, but in August 1732 Bubb Dodington, a Lord of the Treasury, arrived in Rome and had a look round the most remarkable things in the town.[1e]

Dodington, as George Bubb, had been Envoy Extraordinary in Spain from 1715 to 1717 and his acquaintance with Cardinal Alberoni's politics may have left him very well informed about intrigues surrounding the Pretender. His visit to Rome was of course unofficial, but Cardinal Giudice, who had been employed by the House of Austria and in 1735 was made Imperial Protector,[5a] excused himself from receiving James Stuart at his palace to see the annual flooding of the Piazza Navona, on account of what Stosch thought was a diplomatic illness provoked by Dodington's presence.[1e] There seems no doubt that it was during this visit of a month or so, because they never met again, that the two connoisseurs struck up the warm personal friendship which they were to keep alive by means of letters, art-dealing, presents and mutual introductions until Dodington's death, as Lord Melcombe, in 1762. The Englishman indeed acquired a nostalgia for Italy which he never lost. If only the Pope were a great temporal Prince, he wrote in 1754, he would prefer the Roman ambassadorship to everything else.[6] Stosch's affair was evidently discussed with him both in Rome and Florence, and in March of the year following his visit the Baron laid down the conditions on which he would return to Rome and said he would be content to leave Dodington to put his case to the Duke of Newcastle.[1f] Dodington seems then to have consulted Albani, the evidence for this being two draft or copy letters in a bundle of papers in the Public Record Office in London relating to Rome and Florence.[3c] They are unsigned but one in French, dated from Eastbury (Dodington's country house) 9th July 1733 has a pencil note in the margin saying that it is from Dodington to Albani. The other, in Italian, is dated from Rome 30th August 1733 and is similarly marked as being Albani's reply to Dodington. The first letter was to the effect that the writer wanted their friend in Florence to return to Rome and it seemed to him that things were at present so favourable that nearly all the difficulties came from him. Dodington did not know why but the friend was not giving him all the facilities he would have expected from him, to make this affair succeed, and he had written to him about it by the same post. Albani's reply is rather obscure but seems to suggest Stosch returning under the cover of Portuguese affairs. Their common friend in Florence, he said, was intelligent enough to fall in with Dodington's counsels very quickly, especially as it was much to his reputation and to that of the British Ministry and Court to come back, and he had written to tell him so very forcibly. The interest which the King of Portugal was taking in the affairs of Rome, concerning Castro and Ronciglione, about which the Portuguese Ambassador would have made strong representations in England, would furnish a favourable occasion to the said friend to come back, and by simply showing himself aware of this treaty he would exact much respect. Stosch, however, did not return and probably never really meant to. He is not referred to by name in these letters but the subject matter, the dates and the fact that they are bound up in a volume of Stosch's draft despatches seem to leave no doubt that they concern his case.

Meanwhile the Secretary of State was getting a good deal of information about the Pretender's movements through the Ministers at Turin, the seat of the King of Sardinia's Court. The Earl of Essex went there as special Envoy in 1731 with the object, principally, of mediating in a treaty much desired by the British between the Emperor and the

King of Sardinia. His mission was unsuccessful in that Charles Emmanuel III, complaining of the coldness of the Court of Vienna and being promised quicker rewards by the French, concluded an alliance with the latter in 1733 and fought on their side against Austria in the War of the Polish Succession. Essex, though deeply mortified by the King of Sardinia's underhand methods, managed to remain on good terms with the Marquis d'Orméa, principal Sardinian Minister, who himself seems to have disliked and distrusted his master's new alliance, and as Walpole resolutely kept England out of this war Anglo-French relations were not in theory disturbed. There were, however, signs of fresh developments in European politics generally, and Essex wrote to the Duke of Newcastle in April 1733 saying that the perfect concert France and Spain had doubtless entered into for promoting the Pretender's interests seemed to require some person at each of these Courts who by his intimacy with the Jacobites and his dexterity might give underhand intelligence of their transactions with these crowns.[7a] Essex's instructions from Whitehall bound him to find out the doings of the Jacobites in Rome as best he could and if possible to fix up a correspondence with someone there. The person at first selected for this purpose had been the Abbé Antonio Rota,[8a] the Pope's Auditor, who was Internuncio in Paris in 1730 and 1732 while Lord Waldegrave was Ambassador there. The Duke of Newcastle had asked Lord Waldegrave to lodge a protest in Rome through the Abbé about the assault on Stosch and certain proceedings taken at apparently about the same time against another spy, Denys Wright,[9] who, Stosch said, had been chased out of Rome by Radcliffe and his cabal of monks.[1a] In November 1732 Essex suggested that when the Abbé returned to Rome he should particularly watch the dealings of the Pretender with the French Ambassador there and correspond with His Majesty's Ministers in foreign Courts.[8b]

Rota, however, seems not to have co-operated, because in November 1733 Newcastle said he had heard nothing of him for twelve months.[10a] Essex saw him at Pesaro in 1735, but as he did not own to having been in secret communication with some of the British Ministers Essex could not refer to that, he said. He thought nevertheless that he had succeeded in fixing up a correspondence with him,[11a] but nothing seems to have come of it. When he was back in Rome the Abbé Rota was perhaps unwilling to cross what Stosch had called the "Rubicon of Orthodoxy" (p. 73), by which he apparently meant the fine line between helpful mediation and downright spying. Meanwhile Arthur Villettes, Secretary at Turin, had in 1734 arranged for a Piedmontese, the Abbé Lampo, Secretary to Count Lagnasco at Rome, to communicate information by means of a friend of his who was a priest at Turin.[12a]

The Marquis d'Orméa himself had in April 1734 expressed surprise at the British still having no regular correspondent in Rome. The present circumstances, he said, required the utmost vigilance and the Duke of Liria's[13] long and repeated conferences with the French Ambassador and the Pretender, to which several Irish officers in the Spanish service had been called, had filled the Jacobite party with hopes which they did not conceal. Their least motions should now be narrowly watched by some trusty servant of His Majesty, and it would not be very difficult, he continued, to find means of keeping one at Rome under the protection of some of the cardinals of the Imperial faction, who might by way of Vienna send constant accounts of all the Jacobites' activities. Essex thought this advice, coming from d'Orméa at the present juncture, was extraordinary but weighty enough to be transmitted to London.[12b] Stosch in fact had said in 1731 that the Imperial Ministers in Rome were always against the Pretender, even when the Courts of London and Vienna were not on good terms, but the French Ministers supported him when France and England were supposed to be closely allied.[1a]

Alessandro Albani, having become Protector of Sardinia in 1730, used to send d'Orméa "a general communication of all Letters and Despatches which the Court of Rome write to and receive from the Pope's Nuncios in the Several Courts of Europe",[11b] from which d'Orméa relayed information to Lord Essex. In 1731, when out of favour with the Pope over Sardinian affairs, Albani sent Caffignoli, his doctor and confidant, to Turin by way of Florence,[1g] and as this man was later well known to English travellers and suspected of anti-Jacobite correspondence,[14] there may have been some liaison. Albani in 1732 sent particulars, which were forwarded to England, of the Roman banker, Belloni's, questionable conduct in the case of a certain Thomson who fled from London when the "Charitable Corporation" failed. Belloni was said to have got Thomson imprisoned and then made him give up £30,000 sterling in return for being left to enjoy the remainder.[8c] Again, in 1737, d'Orméa showed Villettes a letter in which Alessandro intimated the Pretender's request, which was not granted, that his elder son should be received at Turin during a proposed tour of Italy.[15]

There is no certainty that Albani knew or intended that his official reports to d'Orméa would be of use to the British, and his political activities at this time seem particularly equivocal. As Protector for Sardinia, which was now allied to France, he naturally had a great deal of official business with the Duc de St Aignan, French Ambassador in Rome, and as France and England were still bound together by treaty this was not necessarily incompatible with the friendliness he had begun to show towards the latter. His presence at functions so public as the great parties given by the French Ambassador (Pl. 5) on the Festival of St Louis[16] or after the spectacle of flooding the Piazza Navona, which were attended by the Pretender,[17a] was to be expected, but according to the accounts from Rome he seems to have seen more of the Stuarts than the affairs of Sardinia alone could require. Stosch indeed grouped him with the Pretender's adherents when reporting a visit paid in 1734,[17b] but without further evidence it is impossible to say whether he associated with Jacobites for the sake of information or was genuinely contemplating a return to the old family allegiance. His contacts with the Stuarts included a conference with the Pretender and the French Ambassador in December 1733[1h] and a visit on the same evening as the French and Spanish representatives in 1734[17c]; walking with James Stuart on two occasions in 1735[17d] and complimentary Christmas or Easter visits with other cardinals in 1736, 1738, 1739[18a] and 1740;[19a] a talk with him at the Villa Strozzi in 1737[18b] and a meeting with Murray, of the Pretender's household, in the same year,[18c] evidently connected with Prince Charles Edward's proposed visit to Turin; other interviews with Murray in 1738; various dinner engagements at which well-known Jacobite sympathisers were present in 1738 and 1739 and a call on himself by the Pretender and his sons.[18d] The dinners seem to have taken place during *villegiaturas* at Castel Gandolfo where the smaller community, more informal conditions and family ties would have perhaps made such meetings unavoidable. Annibale Albani was at the same time suspected of being the intermediary in some design carrying on by Spain in favour of the Pretender jointly with the Court of Rome.[20a] He was, however, Protector of Saxony, whose Minister, Count Lagnasco, had in 1735 been instructed by his own Government to correspond with Charles Fane, British Minister at Florence, on all the discoveries he could make relating to the Pretender and his adherents.[5b] Alessandro himself also appears to have been on good terms with Saxony, for in April 1739 he was having made a table of oriental alabaster which he was going to present to the Prince Electoral together

with two fine landscapes out of the palaces at Nettuno.[21a]
By this is probably meant antique mosaics or paintings from
the remains there. He had already sold a collection of thirty
statues to Augustus III of Poland and Saxony in 1728.[22]

Alessandro Albani's politics are therefore at this time excessively difficult to follow, but certainly the British Ministers at Turin seem to have placed less reliance on him than
on his colleague Count Rivera. The latter was in 1738 appointed Sardinian Plenipotentiary jointly with Albani to
arrange a final reconciliation between the Pope and the
Court of Turin, a "sensible, shrewd man" for whose dispositions Villettes said he was prepared to answer. Rivera's
Court promised to give him special instructions to watch the
Pretender and the Jacobite party at Rome and to pass news
on to Villettes, who thought this would meet the need for
a regular correspondent in Rome.[20b] Whatever Alessandro's
intentions may have been he did not apparently persist for
long in any flirtation with the Jacobite cause and was not
named in 1740 as being present at conferences held between
the Pretender, the Duc de St Aignan, Murray and the Cardinals
Tencin and Acquaviva, at which it was suspected the question of the Young Pretender's going to Spain was discussed.[23a] After 1740 his meetings with the Stuarts ceased,
or at least were not reported by Stosch, and it is perhaps significant that Horace Walpole had an introduction to him
when he came to Rome that year. To the regret of both they
only met momentarily, because the six-month-long Conclave of Benedict XIV was in session. Taking the opportunity of the gates being unlocked for the entry of two
cardinals, Walpole went to meet Alessandro from whom he
had received "great civilities",[24] but in the end was obliged
to leave Rome before the Pope was elected.

The British representatives at Florence and Leghorn were
even more concerned than those at Turin to learn the movements of the Jacobites and had employed spies even while

Stosch was still living in Rome. They were apt to be imposed on by people who made up stories to sell them, such as a man describing himself as Ladislas Clocer, a German painter,[25a] who pretended to discover a plot in Rome and was never heard of again after the Consul sent him money.[26] This Consul, Brinley Skinner, even suspected that the Jacobites ran an office in Rome to disseminate false letters about the Pretender's affairs, in the hopes either of gaining information by the answers they received or of putting off spies by constant disappointments.[25a] The Consul's accounts for the years 1726 to 1729 included an item of 270 dollars for reports about the Pretender, twenty-two of which had been spent on a snuff-box, presented to the postmaster to get the post officers to inform. After many attempts to get the money refunded by the Government Skinner had eventually received a sharp snub for leaving his accounts running for more than a year and not sending vouchers.[25b] It says much for the loyalty of British representatives in Italy that some collected information assiduously while never being certain that their expenses in doing so would be allowed. Their posts can only have been tenable on the footing that they made what they could out of them, and Essex's complaint to Newcastle, made in 1733, is readily comprehensible. There was not, he said, in all Italy a person whose advice could be relied on, the Consuls, Skinner excepted, being much more taken up with their private concerns than with those of the nation.[7b]

While the Consul at Leghorn dealt with minor spies who would report on the day-to-day activities of the Jacobites and pry into their mail, the higher officials accredited to the Court of Florence tried to fathom the political motives behind such details and hunted much bigger game. In October 1726 the Resident, Francis Colman, wrote to the Duke of Newcastle saying that whatever he could learn either of the Pretender or of any of his adherents he would be sure faithfully to transmit at the first opportunity. He heartily wished it lay in his power to send better reports, though he did not doubt His Grace had the best from other hands. He believed very good ones were to be had by means of Cardinal Polignac who, as he had been told by a certain Minister, had the entire confidence of the Pretendress and might "know many things as a Lover or humble Admirer which would perhaps be kept hid from the Ministers".[27] Polignac, a Frenchman who had once been friendly with Stosch and had later become French Ambassador in Rome, might not too improbably have helped the British Minister, whose country was technically an ally of France. It was, however, a demonstration of the extraordinary conditions in Rome that any of the Stuarts should have dared to make a close confidant of a cleric with ostensibly hostile political affiliations. Their trust was not apparently misplaced because Polignac, when asked to protect Stosch, seems to have done very little for him either before or after the assault, even though Colman naïvely believed that he would exert himself to the utmost because of the firm alliance which happily subsisted between England and France.[28a] Horace Mann very rightly said a few years later: "We despise the Court of Rome, in England, very justly in one respect, but too much in another. One should consider what weight its opinions have all over Italy and in most parts of Europe. The very subjects of princes in alliance with us, of which numbers reside at Rome, are by the maxims of that Court, taught publicly to confess what they might not [dare] to own in their own countries, and must do it to advance their fortunes at Rome, till it becomes habitual to them, and so the poison spreads everywhere. The very ambassadors of those princes in alliance with the King . . . are forced to adore another in that quality."[29]

Although it had always been thought desirable to supplement Stosch's reports, his expulsion from Rome in 1731 had made it imperative. The incubation of the War of the Polish Succession was certainly accompanied by increased Jacobite activity and there were grounds for Colman's suspicion that the Stosch incident was connected with a larger scheme, although the personal enthusiasm of Radcliffe (p. 86) and the Duke of Liria probably outran that of the latter's kinsman, the Pretender. John Hay's sudden departure from Rome just afterwards lent colour to the notion that something important was afoot and Colman sent his spy Denys Wright to find out something about Hay's intentions from the Carmelite monks with whom he had lodged at Pisa.[1i] Wright was a Scotsman, formerly a Jacobite, and being a "man of very insinuating address'[30a] and an "inquisitive traveller",[31a] well acquainted with some English and Irish friars,[28b] was evidently very useful. Unfortunately for the British representatives he got himself killed in a drunken brawl with one Fotheringham in 1737.[32a]

In March 1732 the Duke of Newcastle hoped soon to establish a good correspondence but the difficulty, he said, would be how to receive advices from Rome without their falling into such hands as should by all means be avoided. The best way, he thought, would be to have there a trustworthy person to receive the letters from the correspondent at Rome and carry them directly to Consul Skinner to be forwarded either by British homebound ships or by way of Holland. The latter would also be the safest way for Colman and Skinner to write anything of importance rather than to let their letters pass through France. Newcastle further instructed Colman particularly to live upon such a foot of friendship and intimacy with all the Imperial Ministers as might enable him to get from them the information of their correspondents in Rome about whatever was "stirring or projecting in favour of the Pretender".[30b] At about the same time Skinner received an offer from "Mr Semple, Lord Semple's brother", to act as a spy in Rome[33a] but

nothing more seems to have come of this and shortly afterwards he was disappointed again. He went to Rome himself
to meet a Mrs Wescombe, who had cast doubt somewhat
sensationally on the loyalty of certain Ministers in England.
It was concluded, however, that she was either mad or had
some special motive for making mischief in the Government.[30c] In August of that year Dodington passed through
Florence, bringing leave for Colman to go to Rome with
him but Colman, mortally ill with consumption, was unable
to undertake what he said would have been to him the most
agreeable journey in the world with so particular and intimate a friend.[30d] We have already seen that Dodington
looked into Stosch's affair and that the Baron's return to
Rome was at that time contemplated.

Colman died in April 1733 and Skinner, who had gone
to Florence to take over the work during his illness, risking
his own health, he said, in being with him, asked to be
appointed Resident in his stead. He complained of having
been paid nothing for filling Colman's place nor for the
expense of keeping up two establishments,[31b] but he seems
to have received little satisfaction. In October 1734 he had
to hand over the post to Charles Fane who, unlucky as he
was always to be in Italy, instantly took to his bed with a
violent cold.[34] Fane's official instructions were supplemented
by a letter marked "Most Private" which defined his duties
in relation to Jacobite activities. His intended station, he
was told, being nearer Rome than that of any other of the
King's Ministers in Italy, he would have a better opportunity of getting early intelligence of the motives and designs of the Pretender and his adherents and of sending
home constant and perfect accounts of them. Upon his
arrival in Florence he was to endeavour to get into the acquaintance and friendship of the family of Corsini and dispose them to use their interest with their relation the Cardinal Corsini at Rome to favour His Majesty's interests,

and in order to achieve this he might insinuate to them that
the Cardinal would be rewarded for it. If Fane should receive such encouragement from the Corsinis as gave him
reason to hope that, if he were to take a journey to Rome
for his own pleasure and diversion, he might have an opportunity of engaging the Cardinal to give him such lights
as to the motions and designs of the Pretender and his adherents as he could very well do if he were so disposed,
His Majesty would not only like him to undertake that
journey but was willing that he should make the Cardinal
an offer of such a sum of money in present or yearly allowance as the importance of his discoveries might deserve. In
case he went thus to Rome Fane was told to wait upon
Cardinal Cienfuegos, the Emperor's Minister, and, after having made himself known to him, to desire his protection
and assistance in whatever might occur for the King's service, which it was not to be doubted he would grant him
very willingly. He might get from him some lights that
might be of use to him in accomplishing his business and
might in general converse with Cienfuegos in a free and
open manner. If, however, he was successful in fixing up a
particular correspondence about the Pretender he was on no
account to acquaint the Cardinal with it, since however well
disposed he was a secret of such a nature could not be too
strictly kept.[33b]

On enquiry in Florence Fane found that the only member
of the Corsini family who was in the Pope's confidence
and had not moved with him to Rome was the Chevalier
Ginori, and as the latter had declared himself devoted to the
French interest he did not think he could trust him.[35a]
However, Lady Essex, wife of that Ambassador to Turin
with whom Fane had already been instructed to concert
his plans,[10b] was going to Rome in 1735 and he proposed
to escort her there as a pretext for his own visit which must,
of course, be unofficial. Some accident prevented their

starting together,[35b] but he set out on 3rd March, a few days after her,[35c] and duly recounted his adventures to the Duke of Newcastle.[35d] Immediately on his arrival in Rome he had, he said, received a message of compliment from Cardinal Cienfuegos whom he had afterwards called on to desire his protection and assistance in whatever might occur for His Majesty's service. The Cardinal, Fane said, very readily assured him of both, out of inclination as well as in obedience to the orders he had received from his Court.

In their conversations the British Minister told Cienfuegos that as the Pretender had of late been so very active in doing mischief to the Emperor by carrying messages and managing interviews between His Imperial Majesty's enemies and such of the nobility at Rome as had influence in the Kingdom of Naples, it was not to be doubted that His Eminence had kept a very watchful eye over him and his party. In consequence he must be able, if he wished, to inform him of several circumstances in which His Majesty's interests were concerned and extremely proper for the Government of England to be acquainted with at such a juncture. Cienfuegos told Fane that he actually had three people in his pay in the Pretender's house and did not think it possible for anyone to be more attentive than he was to all the motions of the Jacobites at Rome, but nevertheless he could not hear the least thing that gave him reason to suspect their having any particular schemes in view at the present time. From what he could observe, however, Fane said he had to admit candidly that he thought Cienfuegos very apt to be deceived by those on whom he depended for intelligence, in those matters as well as in his own Court's affairs, and he was therefore the more desirous of finding a proper person to be employed for the King's service at Rome. He was, however, forced to go about it with great caution, having soon found himself surrounded by spies, one of whom, on the pretence of being a correspondent of

Stosch's, was never out of his house when he was in it or there when he was not.

Fane then spoke of an arrangement he had made with a Swiss Abbé then going by the name of Bentivoglio, who had assured him of his best endeavours and would be paid by results. After making this agreement with the Abbé, Fane had, he said, asked Cienfuegos to put him in the way of letting the Court of Rome know that the King was not at all satisfied with the treatment that several of his subjects had lately met with there, and His Eminence had assured him that he had spoken to Cardinal Corsini. The latter, Fane continued, immediately appointed him a time at which he went and represented to him the substance of what he had been directed to say on the subject, upon which Corsini protested that he was extremely surprised at any such complaints having been made in England since to his knowledge there had not been the least grounds for them. When Fane mentioned the affair of Stosch he said he knew very well the *"ménagements qu'ils avoient à garder avec l'Angleterre"* as well as abhorring any act of that nature, but that Stosch himself would not give them the least assistance towards making a discovery of the persons concerned in that attempt, saying it was the business of the Government and not his to find them. Corsini then pointed out that Fane knew very well how difficult it must be for them, since Rome was not like London, where people were continually passing in the streets, to which he replied that he had always heard that the Government had as many ways of coming to the knowledge of things which they really had a mind to know as any other upon earth. Moreover, he added, if the fewness or people at Rome was allowed as a reason for the persons not having been seized on the spot it proved also how much more easily they might have been found afterwards than in a more populous place. Had a like outrage been offered to the agent of a great King, even though he was not in direct correspondence with the Court of England, the Government, said Fane, would have found means to detect them even among the multitudes of London and by their punishment have given satisfaction to the Prince whose servant had been so cruelly insulted. The Cardinal replied that he could not have done more than he had if the like had happened to his own nephew, and hinted that he suspected the authors of it to have been Englishmen desirous of getting rid of Stosch, whom they looked on as a constraint and spy upon their conduct.

Corsini pointed out that his family had not deserved reproaches for their behaviour to the English, since the Pope when he was a cardinal had always received them with perticular distinctions at his house, which was ever open to them. It was not to be supposed that he was changed so entirely by becoming a ruling Prince that he would allow any ill-treatment to be offered them in his dominions. It was true, he continued, that there had been two instances during the Pope's reign of Englishmen being imprisoned in Rome, but both of them were robbers and the things they had stolen found upon them so he could not imagine that their arrest would have given offence. Fane replied that he was not informed of all these particulars but had the King's orders to let the Government of Rome know that His Majesty could not suffer any of his subjects to be arrested or sent out of Rome at the instances of any person, on pretence of their having an authority over them, without such notice being taken of it in England as would not perhaps be agreeable to them. Corsini assured Fane upon his word that nothing of that sort would happen, though he hoped no one expected that Englishmen would be allowed to behave indecently to the Pretender when they met him. Fane thereupon told Corsini that Cardinal Cienfuegos, under whose protection most of the English placed themselves on arrival in Rome, would whenever he was informed of anything of that nature immediately put a stop to it. Corsini then repeated his promise to Fane and said that all manner of regard would be paid to the representations of Cardinal Cienfuegos.

Although the absence of encouragement from Corsini relatives in Florence had given Fane small hopes of any help from that family, he took the opportunity of letting the Cardinal know on this occasion that it might have been much more to his advantage had he chosen to favour the King of England's interests rather than shown any unusual mark of distinction to the Pretender and that, even still, he had it in his power to make the King his friend. As the Cardinal did not respond to this overture by giving an opening for further offers Fane felt he could not "condescend further in His Majesty's name" and took his leave.

In the same very long letter Fane described also how he saw Sir Thomas Dereham, who represented to him how he befriended and protected his own countrymen and did not know what they would have done without him as the Ministers neither of the Emperor nor of France nor of any other power had troubled at all about protecting them of late. Fane added, however, that Dereham had a great correspondence in England and by means of the French Ambassador made a very regular report of it to the Pretender. Conversations with Count Lagnasco, the Minister in Rome of the Elector of Saxony, appeared more promising and Fane suggested that his Court might order him to correspond with British Ministers, which he believed Lagnasco would very willingly do as he was extremely exasperated with the Pretender for having meddled with his country's affairs at the Court of Rome.

After his return to Florence Fane was still trying to find out how he could fix up a good and permanent Roman correspondence, but his supply of information does seem to have improved as a result of his journey. His efforts were not, however, entirely approved of in London and he suspected Stosch of making mischief. "The abstaining from having any communication with people habituated like him", he wrote, "is I believe the safest method and greatest security against their treachery and false reports." [35e] He added a request for the payment of his expenses which he repeated a few months later, saying he had nothing of his own and what money his father had been able to supply him with had gone towards equipage and furnishing his house, and he therefore humbly begged the Duke of Newcastle's leave to charge whatever he had laid out in extraordinary expenses for His Majesty's service, which amounted to nearly £300.[35f] Fane in due course was allowed to recoup himself at the expense of his successor, Horace Mann, who was not paid the salary of £1086 he claimed for the first eighteen months of his own appointment,[36] in spite of his repeated complaints and the submission of a formal Memorial on the subject to Whitehall.[23b]

By July 1736 Fane was in favour again and Newcastle wrote approving his conduct and enclosing an open letter for him to pass on to Stosch should the latter give him any more cause for complaint. The Roman correspondence was, however, not yet fully satisfactory and Fane was told to try to secure, through the Abbé, presumably Bentivoglio, the services of a certain valet-de-chambre in the Pretender's household.[33c] Information was essential since Jacobite affairs were entering on a new and more menacing phase. The Pretender's two sons were now attractive and promising boys of eleven and sixteen years of age, and French designs to use Stuart ambitions in the interests of France against England began to have a new meaning when seen in conjunction with the enterprising character of the elder Prince. His temperament, according to Stosch, was very different to that of his father, for he was bold and proud[17e] and consequently likely to be a much more formidable enemy.

In May 1737 preparations were being made at the Corsini palace in Florence for the reception of the Pretender's son and by July he was staying there, going to the Opera in the Prince Corsini's box and being entertained by him at a state ball.[32b] The Imperial officials in Tuscany, susceptible to pressure from England, behaved on the whole correctly, and Newcastle said he would report favourably to Vienna on the conduct of von Wachtendonck and Braitwitz.[37] The Dowager Duchess of Parma, however, distinguished the Stuart Prince particularly, and Prince Lobkowitz, commanding the Imperial troops in that Duchy, followed her example, unnecessarily, Fane thought, by paying him assiduous attention.[32c] The Dowager Duchess' partiality might have been expected. A marriage treaty between herself and the Old Pretender had been rumoured[17f] soon after Clementina Sobieski's death and he commissioned for her in 1737 two charming portraits of his sons by Louis-Gabriel Blanchet (Pl. 6).

The visit seems to have more or less coincided with a determined attempt to get Stosch removed from Florence at the instances of the Inquisition on the pretext that he encouraged meetings of Freemasons, a Society which was to be officially condemned by the Pope in 1738 and of which the Old Pretender himself was extremely apprehensive. Amidst all these complications the unlucky Fane somehow contrived to do the wrong thing and wrote that he was very sorry that every particular of his conduct during the stay of the Pretender's son in Florence had not been such as to merit the King's gracious approval, and if he had thought he could have acted for His Majesty's service in any better manner than he had he would certainly have chosen to do so.[32d] Newcastle had reprimanded him for consenting to the Grand Duke's admitting the Young Pretender to a private interview in his own room,[33d] which he had done, he said, solely on account of the Grand Duke's state of health and his pleasure at seeing young visitors.[32e] The visit did not in fact take place and Gian Gastone, the last of the Medici dynasty, died in July 1737, being succeeded by Maria Theresa's husband, afterwards Emperor Francis I.

In the following March Fane asked permission to go to England to settle his private affairs and never returned. He wrote on this occasion that he believed it certain that the King's business would not suffer if he might be allowed to leave Mr Mann to carry it on as well as the correspondence with His Majesty's Ministers during his absence, for he was well known and esteemed by the Ministers there as indeed he was by everybody in the country.[32f] Horace Mann saw Fane off from Leghorn in April 1738[32g] and, having applied in the following August to succeed him should he not return,[32h] was in April 1740 appointed "with the Character of Resident to the Great Duke of Tuscany".[23c]

Horace Mann was born in 1701 and took up his diplomatic post under Fane in 1738. He appears to have come out from England in order to do so, but a few years before that he almost certainly paid a visit to Rome as a private person. The writer Joseph Spence, who himself travelled considerably on the continent, noted that in 1732 he met someone called "Man" at Naples.[38] The spelling was not unusual for the time and this person is thought to have been Horace Mann, several close friends of whom are known to have been in Italy then. As Spence's acquaintance returned by way of Venice and Paris he would almost certainly have followed the usual Grand Tourist route from Naples through Rome. Moreover, in 1747, when commenting to Alessandro Albani on the execution of Charles Radcliffe for participation in the Forty-Five Rebellion, Mann said he had known him when at Rome,[39] which as we know could have been in the early 'thirties. The fact that Mann, with his many acquaintances and interests there, never followed the example of his predecessors in office and paid it

THE PIAZZA NAVONA ON THE OCCASION
OF A FETE GIVEN BY THE FRENCH
AMBASSADOR IN 1729
Detail of a painting by G. P. Pannini showing the Pretender and
his sons in the middle distance, right

PRINCE CHARLES EDWARD STUART

PRINCE HENRY BENEDICT STUART

an unofficial visit is some sort of evidence that he had already been. If this were the case he may have had some idea of the difficulties of Roman intelligence before his arrival in Florence as a diplomat. The warm terms in which he referred to Dodington in later correspondence and his own letters to him suggest that they were personally acquainted and if Mann really was in Italy in 1732 his visit may have coincided with that of Dodington, who also met Spence. This is speculation, but certainly Mann tackled Roman affairs energetically when they fell to his task and wrote to Newcastle in June 1738 saying that he would think himself unfortunate if some of the methods he had adopted to obtain information about the Jacobites at Rome did not succeed.[32i] Stosch's intelligence was still highly valued, even though Essex already suspected that it was but "the common talk of Ordinaries and eating-houses in Rome and Florence",[7c] and Mann made the strongest representations as to the King of England's interest in him when the Grand Duke threatened to expel him, and defended him staunchly against all who threatened him however varied their complaints and great their justification.

In accordance with instructions from their Court the Austrian ministers in Florence were furnishing what information they could, Braitwitz assuring Mann that he had laid a foundation for a correspondence which he hoped might be of great service, and though the person concerned was in low life he was in a situation to give very good intelligence.[21b] Unfortunately, as Mann remarked a month later, it was difficult for people in low life to be properly informed and they were continually inventing stories in order to be thought diligent, and he felt it necessary, he said, to "procure the assistance of some Foreign Minister residing at Rome, who could protect the low People employed".[21c] Jacobites in Rome were said to be seducing the young English travellers by various civilities and engaging the most indiscreet of them in parties of pleasure with the Pretender's son, while the dangerous rumour was being spread that the latter was very far from being as much attached to his religion as his father was, made very light of it and would at least allow liberty of conscience.[21d] Moreover the Old Pretender, according to Stosch, received de Tencin, nephew of the cardinal of that name and commander of Maltese ships *"en forme publique"*. Up till now, said the Baron, the Pope, the cardinals, Princes and Ambassadors had only treated him on the footing of incognito.[18e] James was also said to have had medals struck for his elder son, the reverse to represent "the City of London with a Rising Sun".[23d]

In October 1740 the Emperor Charles VI died, leaving no male heir. The title to the Holy Roman Empire was elective and only open to males, but as far as his own dominions went Charles had done his utmost to ensure that they passed intact to his daughter Maria Theresa. By force of arms and hard bargaining over many years he had secured recognition of her claims from most of the European powers and it had been agreed that she should rule over the Hapsburg inheritance while her husband, Francis Stephen of Lorraine, should be elected Emperor in succession to Charles VI. Meanwhile increasing strains had developed within the existing system of alliances and the temptation to dismember Maria Theresa's patrimony was great. The ambitious Elizabeth Farnese, second wife of Philip V of Spain, was determined to secure establishments in Italy for her own sons, whose claims on their father's domains appeared to be defeated by the existence of an heir by his first marriage. The Prince of Bavaria was intent on his own election as Holy Roman Emperor and France, jettisoning her engagements to the late Charles VI, pledged herself to secure it for him together with such pickings from Maria Theresa's possessions as would adequately support the Imperial title. He

was in fact elected as Charles VII in 1742. Sardinia meanwhile saw a chance of gaining a long-coveted part of the
Austrian Duchy of Milan, and the King of Prussia wanted
Maria Theresa's rich province of Silesia. There were here
all the makings of a major European war and Frederick
the Great duly initiated it by invading Silesia in 1740.

The British Government stood by Maria Theresa and
contrived to negotiate an agreement in 1743 between her
and the King of Sardinia, whose armies then fought beside
hers in Italy. England did not at once declare war on France
but as an auxiliary of Maria Theresa's sent troops to join
the Hanoverian and Austrian armies in Germany, scoring a
success against the French at Dettingen. France formally
declared war on England in 1744 in fulfilment of pledges to
her ally, Spain, which was also at war with her. There followed immediately preparations for a French expedition to
land the Young Pretender in England, and in the Mediterranean the peppery Admiral Matthews[40] and his squadron
harried the French and Spanish fleets which were supporting land operations in Italy.

In Rome the Jacobite party was in triumphant resurgence.
To his sterner qualities the young Prince Charles Edward
added an engaging inclination towards women and dancing, and startled the connoisseurs by the beauty of the jewels
he wore at a ball with his *"Habit de Montagnard d'Ecosse"*.[19b]
It is small wonder that the romantic appeal of this new
leader blinded his followers to the sorry fact that he was only
a tool for the purposes of France. With his country engaged
in naval warfare on the Italian coasts the British Resident in
Tuscany necessarily entered upon a new and closer relationship with his opposite numbers, the Ministers of the
allied powers of Austria and Sardinia. Among these the
leading figure as far as Mann was concerned was Alessandro
Albani himself. Alessandro, now a middle-aged man of experience and discretion, had at last got into smoother water,

for his long struggle with the papacy on behalf of Sardinia had just ended on terms most favourable for Charles Emmanuel III. Cardinal Lambertini, who with Annibale Albani's backing had become Pope as Benedict XIV in 1740, had served the King of Sardinia in the negotiations of Benedict XIII's reign and agreement was reached a few months after his own election. The reconciliation effected by England between Austria and Sardinia made an honest man of Albani for these powers were now all on the same side and Alessandro could serve all three without equivocation. In 1743 he was made Protector for Maria Theresa (known as the Queen of Hungary until her husband became Emperor in 1745) and continued to hold his original post for Sardinia. The Courts of Vienna and Turin had been consistently loyal to George II and when hostilities began in Italy Alessandro found himself with excellent official reasons for friendship with British Ministers and coldness to the Pretender and his adherents. In the stimulating atmosphere of naval activity in the Mediterranean and a threatened Jacobite invasion of England Alessandro Albani and Horace Mann started the immense correspondence which they were to keep up through three decades of peace and war and which, as a by-product, assisted Albani's emergence as a kind of Duveen of the eighteenth century. The Cardinal, to his own great advantage, had noticed in good time that the Romans had the antiques and English gentlemen the money with which to buy them.

CHAPTER V

The War of the Austrian Succession and the Forty-Five Rebellion

ALESSANDRO ALBANI'S official connection with the affairs of Austria appears to have begun some time in 1742, because in February 1743 Stosch reported the recent death of Cardinal Giudice and said that Alessandro had been entrusted with the duties of his Protectorate for the last few months of the Cardinal's life. It was much to be hoped, wrote Stosch, that the office would be left with Albani, because he had on all occasions shown himself very favourable to His Majesty's interests, and English travellers had at that time no other protection in Rome save that of the cardinals who looked after the interests of the Queen of Hungary.[1a] These hopes were realised, for in April 1743 Stosch was able to report that Alessandro had been made Protector of all the States subject to the Queen of Hungary and Bohemia, adding shortly afterwards that the appointment had been made by permission of the King of Sardinia and that Albani would continue to hold the Protectorate of the latter State for the time being until the Prelate Millo, a subject of the House of Savoy, was made a cardinal.[1b] In fact Millo did not get his red hat until 1753 and Alessandro appears to have been employed by the Court of Turin until his own death in 1779.[2] He inaugurated his office characteristically enough by arranging a magnificent Roman Te Deum to celebrate the coronation, in Prague, of Maria Theresa, and following it up with a splendid dinner for the prelates and nobles who attended.[1c]

In his new appointment Albani was still in the opposite

camp to the Pope, even though the Sardinian dispute had been settled. The Roman people favoured the House of Austria, as they had shown by their acclamations of Albani when he appeared in the procession at his coronation Te Deum. The Pope, however, was so buffeted by both sides that even though, according to Mann, he was Austrian at heart,[3a] the misunderstandings between the Courts of Rome and Vienna were said in 1742 to be increasing daily and tending to an open rupture.[4] This same Pope, Benedict XIV, had, "as a common father", wished in 1740 that all his neighbours would live in peace,[5a] but even had he genuinely wished to do so he was too weak a temporal Prince to deny passage through his State to the Neapolitan armies fighting on the French and Spanish side. Indeed he went further and abused his neutral privileges to the prejudice of the Austrians and British. It was probably difficult enough at the time and seems impossible today to estimate the exact effects on personal relationships in Rome of the three-cornered conflict between any Pope's duties as the spiritual leader of all the Catholic countries, his effective power as the ruler of a small Italian State and his own private and family predilections. Alessandro Albani, an immensely clever and likeable man and a gifted negotiator, quite evidently had his uses in many fields and it would be unwise to assume that his political associations necessarily alienated him from the Pope and his immediate circle. No situation in Rome could be seen in clear black and white, and Alessandro's great value to the British generally was the strength of his own personal position. He probably served them better than any official representative of their own nationality could have done.

Albani was acting jointly with the Austrian Minister in Rome, Count de Thun, Bishop of Gurk, but was himself corresponding directly with Mann by June 1743. His very first letters do not appear to have survived either in London or Vienna but one of his secretaries, Quarelli, wrote in that month to Mann apologising for Albani's not having replied and saying that he would write on his return from Soriano.[6a] Alessandro wrote to Mann himself in July 1743, returning him a book which the latter had sent him for Lord Hobart who had been in Rome.[6b] The rather elaborate style and fulsome compliments of the Albani–Mann letters would tend in any case to make them sound impersonal, but there appears to be no evidence that the correspondents ever actually met. There is no reminiscence of a meeting and Mann, if he had visited Rome in 1732 (p. 112), was too obscure a person to be mentioned in Stosch's despatches. It is virtually certain that although they quickly found each other highly congenial on paper they were not personally acquainted.

At the beginning of the war de Thun in Rome and Braitwitz in Florence, rather than Albani, seem to have been Mann's principal informants about the Pretender's affairs, but Alessandro must have started very soon after his new appointment to take under his wing people who might be of use to the British Government. In July 1743 Stosch reported the imprisonment, by the Inquisition, of an associate of Albani's, Dr Caffignoli, who was well known, he said, to English travellers and suspected of keeping up a correspondence prejudicial to the Pretender's interests (p. 98). In June 1742 Mann had written mysteriously to London, in a letter about postal arrangements: "My Friend tells me that the Knight's Letters come under the Cover of one Parker, a noted Antiquarian at Rome" [5b] and in August 1744 Albani himself wrote about this individual. Mr Mark Parker, he said, knowing the friendship with which Mann honoured him, had asked him to support with his good offices the request which he was making to him direct by the same post, to recommend him to the English noblemen who passed by on their way to Rome so that they should apply to him to be instructed in whatever there was of interest to be seen in the town. Albani assumed that Parker was well known to Mann, but added his testimony that he was a very honest man and very zealous for the welfare of people of his own nation. His profession, he said, was to act as antiquary and from this he derived all the income he had to maintain himself in Rome. Members of the Pretender's party, incensed against him, sought to discredit him so as to deprive him of the advantages he drew from his compatriots, but he hoped to see his enemies' efforts rendered unavailing if Mann would honour him with his protection.[7a] Parker was referred to by Horace Walpole in 1741, in connection with a statue for his mother's tomb and on several other occasions, and Mann spoke of him again in February 1743 as "that most sad fellow Parker", telling Horace Walpole he had been very negligent in answering letters.[3b] It becomes evident soon after this that he was involved in spying while catering for the artistic tastes of British travellers.

Albani also had much to do with naval affairs. Stosch spoke of him in August 1743 as making all possible efforts, with de Thun, to prevent Spanish vessels from unloading ammunition at Civita Vecchia for the Spanish army at Rimini,[1d] and in June 1744 Admiral Matthews was relying on him and de Thun to provision the British fleet.[7b] English officers came on shore to confer with the Austrian Ministers and Prince Lobkowitz, and Mann remarked to Horace Walpole that commanders of ships needed to know Italian and French because six captains had dined with Albani and de Thun, having only their mother tongue.[3c] Albani wrote to Mann at considerable length requesting the assistance of British ships to support hostilities against Naples and, without even waiting for consultation with Admiral Matthews, Mann gave the required instructions to a Captain Scott, so justifiably confident was he that he was thus interpreting the King's wishes.[8a] Albani possibly traded on these early favours, because in 1747 Villettes complained that he and the Austrian General asked for ships at short notice and without a plan, which was neither judicious nor fair.[6c]

In seeking the help of British ships Albani made use on at least one occasion of Richard Gaven, whom we have already noted as aspiring to the post of British Consul at Civita Vecchia on the Pope's or Pretender's nomination. He had been elsewhere since then and Villettes wrote from Turin in 1739 about a young Mr Newport who had been sent abroad without an escort and was giving much anxiety to his trustees. The young man, he wrote, was at Montpellier, deeply smitten with the wife of one Gaven, an Irish merchant there, who first seduced him.[9] Gaven, however, had now returned to Italy and in the summer of 1744 was sent by de Thun and Albani as Envoy Extraordinary to Thomas Matthews, Admiral and Commander-in-Chief of the British Fleet in the Mediterranean, to deliver a letter demanding prompt help from certain of the King of England's warships for his ally the Queen of Hungary.[10a] Gaven described this mission in an indignant letter to Albani dated from Rome in September 1744. He went, he said, to pay his respects to Count Lobkowitz and to ask him for a favourable recommendation to the Queen of Hungary. Lobkowitz, then commanding the Austrian armies, mistook Gaven for some other person employed by the British who, he thought, had been aboard Captain Long's ship a few days before in connection with provisioning the fleet, accused him of being a spy and said he would report him to the King of England. It seems possible that Lobkowitz had confused him with Chamberlayne, who might have been expected to act in just this way. Gaven denied any acquaintance with Captain Long or that he was employed by the British and reminded Lobkowitz of the arduous journey he had had round the islands of Hyères to find the fleet, risking his liberty and perhaps his life if his despatches were found by the French. Moreover, he said, for nearly all the voyage he had had no other bed than a chair at the bottom of the boat and such rough weather that the couriers from Genoa and Turin had not wished to put to sea when he had started from Lerici. The more Gaven explained the more furious did Lobkowitz become and Gaven, bursting, he said, with rage and shame at his humiliation before other officers who were present, fainted and nearly suffocated when, to do justice to His Highness, he had the humanity to hold to his nose a bottle of strong liquor.[10b] In 1745 Gaven was in Venice, employed by Maria Theresa as her agent to the British fleet, and Albani was seeing his wife and daughter in Rome and sending and receiving letters through them.[11a] In 1748 he was in London and presented a letter of introduction to Lord Chesterfield from Albani, which the former in due course acknowledged,[11b] and he evidently remained for he was there also in 1755. He then asked Albani to use his influence to get him back into the service of Maria Theresa as her agent to the British fleet at Nice. It was not so valuable as the agency on the ecclesiastical coasts which he had imprudently abandoned but the climate would suit his wife and daughter. In another letter of the same date he discussed deals in objets d'art, including a proposed sale of some of Albani's cameos to the Earl of Carlisle (formerly Lord Morpeth, Stosch's old acquaintance). We shall meet Gaven again during the Seven Years War.[12]

Alessandro wrote frequently to Mann during 1744 and seems to have been taking over more and more business from de Thun. He not only befriended the English in Rome when occasion arose but actually sought their acquaintance. In August 1744 he asked Mann to put him in touch with Lord Eglinton and allow him to render the latter some service.[7c] Mann had responded to his appeals on behalf of Parker and sent the latter various commissions including a small one for Villettes who wanted a "Fann upon a Leather drawn all in Indian Ink and with the pen without the assistance of any Colour. . . . . Price not exceeding Six or Seven *Zecchines*." [7d] Albani continued to deal with Stosch and addressed several packets of medals to Mann with the request that he should give them to the Baron.[7e] In November 1744 de Thun left Rome to assist at the election of a Bishop at Salzburg and never returned.[8b] Albani was thus left as Austrian Chargé d'Affaires in Rome and became Imperial Minister Plenipotentiary after the election of Maria Theresa's husband as Emperor Francis I in October 1745.

In January 1744 Mann had heard from de Thun that the Pretender's elder son had left Rome on the pretext of going to Cisterna to hunt and had passed through Florence on his way to take ship at Genoa.[3d] An incident of this party was the accidental shooting, by the Prince or one of his followers, of two oxen belonging to a nephew of the antiquary Ficoroni,[13a] who used to conduct tourists round Rome, and, impressed perhaps by these circumstantial details, Stosch himself believed that hunting had been the only object of the journey. After the Prince's departure Jacobite activities in Rome became more relevant than ever to the Austro-British cause, and in December Albani told Lord Holdernesse at Venice of the Abbé Grant's efforts to seduce the English in Rome and advised that the noblemen who came there should be warned not to be taken in by his insinuating manners.[14a] Grant seems to have made his first appearance in the official correspondence when in August 1744 Villettes sent a letter on for him from England, which with others, he said, had been so torn by the awkwardness of those who had endeavoured to open them on the road that he had had to add a cover.[7f] Mann told Newcastle in 1745 that several Englishmen corresponded with Grant as a man of learning, probably not knowing his attachment to the Pretender, and that the Abbé cultivated such acquaintance and correspondence in his interest.[15a] The war in Italy was not going too well and Albani, with a large party of the nobility who went to visit Lobkowitz's camp, had to retire in haste before the retreating Austrian army,[3e] but this did not entirely deter English travellers, who seem still to have been going to Rome in considerable numbers. Albani had already done so much for them and for the fleet that he probably felt he could now ask the British to do something for him, and he made the first of his somewhat embarrassing requests to the Government.

He wrote to Mann in November 1744 telling him that he had assigned an abbey of his in the Kingdom of Naples to Monseigneur Acquaviva, nephew of the cardinal of that name, in return for an annual payment of 5288 Roman crowns. To avoid any difficulty in getting this sum paid he had obtained from the Roman banker Jerome Belloni a *"cedola bancaria"* which put Belloni under the most solemn obligation to pay the money in any event whatsoever. The Court of Naples, however, regarding Albani as an enemy because of the services he had rendered to Prince Lobkowitz's army and the British fleet, had made a show of confiscating the revenues of the abbey and forbidden Belloni to pay. In order to avoid having to sue every few months, Albani proposed, he said, to send the *"cedola bancaria"* to every place where Belloni had agents, so as to get his assets sequestered, and as one of these places was London he enclosed a letter to Lord Carteret asking him to use his authority with the English merchants and bankers for this purpose and attaching the necessary documents for an English Court.[8c] Mann forwarded this request with a covering letter to Carteret in which he said that although he could not judge how far it might be possible to assist Cardinal Albani yet he humbly begged leave to represent to His Lordship the very particular services he had rendered to the Commanders of His Majesty's ships. He also noted his extremely obliging behaviour to all the King's subjects who applied to him and his repeated requests to himself to recommend to him all the young English people of rank so as to keep them out of the hands of ill-designing people at Rome who made it their business to draw them over to the Pretender's interest. These were the circumstances which Mann said had induced him to venture to assure the Cardinal that he was persuaded His Lordship would interest himself in his affairs and by his protection of them endeavour to procure him the justice which the laws of England would admit of.[8d] At the same time Mann protested to Albani his wish to help him but pointed out that the laws of England might present difficulties since if it were the case of the King himself it would be necessary to observe all the formalities and, further, that Belloni's assets would not be held in his own name and his agents would not disclose them.[14b] Count Richecourt, another Austrian Minister to whom Albani applied similarly in Florence, anticipated the same difficulty, saying too that Belloni's credit was so good that his letters of exchange were usually accepted by bankers without their holding funds for him.[16a] Albani probably knew well enough that he had no remedy in the English Courts but hoped to use English influence as a counterblast to the political prejudice which had been the cause of his injury. It was evidently with considerable relief that Mann heard of Belloni's spontaneous submission to the Roman Courts and he rejoiced that justice had been done in Rome without the inevitable embarrassment of calling in outside help.[16b] It must be admitted that Mann in his turn sometimes made embarrassing requests to Albani, who answered them with a courtesy equal to his own. He sought the Cardinal's help, for instance, for a certain Père Gérard who had complained of oppression by the ecclesiastical authorities in Florence and turned out to be a bad hat who had imposed on Mann.[11c]

Alessandro Albani had now become a most valued confidant of British Ministers by reason of his discretion and other personal qualities, it would seem, as well as by virtue of his office. Thus Lord Holdernesse wrote to him from Venice to ask his advice in strictest confidence as to whether he should yield precedence there to the Nuncio and received a careful statement of examples with Albani's advice that he should follow them and yield. "I tell you this", he wrote, "as a friend and honest man, without any regard to my status as a Cardinal and to the attachment I must have to the Ministers of the Holy See. I will keep it secret and no one will know that you have sought my advice on this subject and what I have replied." *[16c] It seems indeed that Albani assumed the mantle of the Greffier Fagel who retired at the end of 1744, having held office since 1690. He was spoken of with high esteem both by Mann and Albani and appears to have acted as a friend and confidential adviser to British Ministers throughout a period during which Britain and Holland had been closely allied. There was certainly a parallel in what Fagel and Albani, both, as it happened, notable collectors of coins and medals, did for the British in the matter of secret agents. Fagel had provided cover for Stosch, and Albani, who exchanged medals with the Baron and corresponded with Mann on matters of art as well as politics, now helped the British Resident to arrange his spy service in Rome. He wrote to him in January 1745 saying that he had given to the person who had asked him to write to Mann about it the cypher which the latter had sent him, to safeguard the correspondence this man hoped to have with him. Albani did not know, he said, whether he would be successful enough to use it but did know that Mr Parker, who was a confidant of the said person, would be making a journey to Tuscany in a few weeks' time and

* In French in the original.

would have an opportunity to arrange with Mann the plan for this correspondence.[16d] The "person" was afterwards referred to as "*l'Ami Hollandais*", and from subsequent events it appears that he was a Mr Born, sometime Dutch Consul in Rome.

All was apparently arranged satisfactorily because Albani wrote to Mann the following March saying that he had passed on promptly to the Dutch Friend the letter which he had sent him for him unaddressed. If the latter sent any reply to it he would enclose it and meanwhile was delighted that Mann was pleased with his correspondence and the trouble he, Albani, had taken to procure it for him.[16e] Parker, however, does not seem to have been quite so happy about it, and Mann wrote to Albani in May saying that he had not yet replied to a letter from Parker as its contents embarrassed him. He was complaining of his position and his fear of losing his pension and hoped that Mann would write to obtain one for him from his Court. He alleged that his attachment to his country and to the good of the service in general was the reason for the persecution he had suffered and still feared. Mann had pointed out to him, he told Albani, that he could not expect to have the patronage of two different parties and that if he had attached himself to that of the enemies of his country (of which he was incapable) he would not have enjoyed Albani's favour. At present he was being employed by all English travellers and would continue to be so far as it depended on Mann. Parker, however, had no reason to complain of not having been able to serve them all indiscriminately because those of the type of Holdsworth would only make use of people entirely devoted to the Pretender and they would never be protected, but on the contrary scorned by the Ministers of the King and all who were attached to him. Parker should also reflect that the troubles in Italy reduced the number of English travellers and it was in the exercise of his profession that he ought to expect advancement, because Mann very much feared that the Court would not be disposed to grant him a pension. Possibly, continued Mann, Parker had not told Albani all this, so he would leave it to his superior judgment to mention something of it to him if he thought fit.[16f] Albani wrote to Mann at the end of the month saying that he had passed on what he had said and was now impatiently looking forward to the visit of Messrs Chute and Whithed.[16g]

These distinguished visitors, the very special friends of Mann and Horace Walpole, arrived in Rome at a critical moment in Jacobite affairs and were taken into the close confidence of Mann and Albani. The former wrote to the Cardinal in May 1745 saying that as His Eminence had given him permission to recommend his compatriots to his protection he was profiting from this in favour of Messrs Chute and Whithed, two gentlemen who were very particular friends of his and with whom he had lived in Florence for several years in the most perfect goodwill. They were starting for Rome in two days' time by way of Bologna and Loretto and he would furnish them with a letter for Albani which they would have the honour of presenting to him on their arrival. Mann added that he would reply to Parker and the Dutchman by means of these gentlemen and begged His Eminence to tell his people to warn Parker about this.[16h] Chute sent various messages from Albani on matters which the latter did not think fit to raise directly with Mann and altogether made himself useful. Mann told Newcastle that he was indefatigable in procuring intelligence, for which he had good opportunities from frequenting the best assemblies. It is possible that, unknowingly, he was also used by the other side, for a young man whom Mann had hitherto thought a reliable informant managed to convince Chute that the Young Pretender was in Spain.[15b]

The visit of these two friends and their acquisition of a

A GROUP OF ENGLISHMEN IN ROME
Painting of the English School, c. 1749–52

BRANDENBURGH HOUSE

An engraving from Daniel Lysons, *Environs of London*, Vol. 2: *Middlesex* (1795)

particularly fine antique sculptured eagle for Horace Walpole was much discussed in the latter's correspondence with Mann, who told him that Albani had taken it upon himself to see that its export would not be forbidden by the Pope.[3f] It was not, however, a very agreeable time for loyal travellers to be in Rome. News of the Young Pretender's arrival in Scotland and initial successes there began to filter through as the year went on, and the Jacobites grew more and more arrogant, while it was taken for granted, Mann said, that every Englishman was in the Stuart interest.[15c] The lively Chute and the deaf and silent Whithed were thrown upon the goodwill and hospitality of Albani to a greater extent probably than any other English travellers who ever visited him, notwithstanding the fact that the Cardinal was in no very comfortable position himself.

The election of Francis I as Emperor gave rise to disorders between the Spaniards and men of the Imperial party, in which Albani had to mediate,[17] and he had ceased, temporarily at any rate, to trust Count Rivera, his colleague in Sardinian affairs, against whom he warned Chute.[3g] Having the care of English travellers he had to take up with Cardinal Acquaviva, Minister for Naples, the matter of their passports for that country, a delicate matter on which Mann made a report to the Duke of Newcastle. As an example, he wrote, of the arts and intrigues which were made use of to induce His Majesty's subjects to get to know the Pretender's people, Cardinal Albani had acquainted him that they were refused passports by Acquaviva unless they were recommended to him by Murray, who called himself Lord Dunbar. The object was to introduce to travellers certain people totally devoted to the Pretender and actually in his service, who would do their best to win over His Majesty's faithful subjects or at least to find out from them all they could. By means of the refusal of such passports, Mann continued, English travellers would be obliged to admit the emissaries of the Pretender unless they deprived themselves of the pleasure of seeing Naples. For the whole previous year all the English who had been there had been obliged to procure passports through Murray, who did not indeed insist positively on the English going to his house to ask for them but made use of a certain Abbé Grant, a Scotsman and agent of the Scotch missionaries. The latter, Mann said, was a very intriguing fellow, who put the blame on the Spaniard Acquaviva and offered out of friendship for the English to procure the passports they wanted by means of Murray. Cardinal Albani, Mann added, had on all occasions shown the utmost respect for His Majesty's person and service and the greatest zeal to prevent intrigues and cabals of this nature.[15d] He reminded Newcastle of the expenses Albani had incurred in despatching letters by special messenger,[15e] but neither on this or any other occasion does it appear that any direct payment went to him by means of Mann for his services to the British.

To his credit, Alessandro seems to have remained perfectly staunch to the Austro-British interests with which he was officially identified and not to have tried to improve his position with the other party in Rome in case the Jacobite rebellion succeeded. Mann wrote rather grudgingly of him to Horace Walpole, saying that he seemed sincere and that the Austrian and British interests were too nearly united to permit him to neglect giving him any notices,[3h] but in fact Albani must have done far more than could have been required of him by his Court, and even jeopardised his own reputation. There was a note of real apprehension in his letters when he thought, from a delay, that the Dutch Friend's despatches had been intercepted, and when Mann established that the negligence of his own secretary had been the sole cause Albani wrote his heartfelt thanks at the trouble taken to relieve his anxiety.[18a] The Cardinal gave a magnificent entertainment in January 1746 to celebrate the election of the Emperor and the favourable view taken in Rome of the Jacobite cause can be judged by the fact that Chute and Whithed were the only Englishmen he thought loyal enough to invite.[19a] When in the previous February he had given a similar party to celebrate one of the many successful accouchements of Maria Theresa, he had asked several Englishmen and was even affronted that Messrs Drake, Holdsworth and Dawkins, who had Jacobite sympathies, had absented themselves, and sent a false excuse.[16i]

Not least of the Jacobite crimes, in Mann's eyes, was the disparagement of his adored Chute and Whithed, and he asked Albani to forgive the heat with which he wrote on the subject. He had heard, he said, that Murray was putting it about that they were not gentlemen and that Chute was tutor to Whithed. He could, he said, assure His Eminence that this was the blackest of calumnies and that they were much better born than the calumniators themselves. Mr Chute was very much the gentleman as was also Mr Whithed, who had an income of more than four thousand pounds sterling per annum. Mr Chute travelled at his own expense, insisted Mann, and was related to Mr Whithed.[18b] In spite of all Albani's efforts, however, the two travellers found the atmosphere of Rome intolerable after a few months, and in the New Year of 1746 Mann welcomed them back to Florence, upon which many letters expressing mutual friendship and satisfaction were exchanged between them and Albani, and between Albani and Mann.

One particularly interesting letter written by Chute from Berlin on his way home shows how well informed he had become on diplomatic matters. When in Vienna he had, he assured Albani, explained the circumstances of that memorable summer in Rome and stressed his own gratitude to His Eminence. During the brief audience granted him by the Empress he had managed to slip in a word about Albani's gracious reception of British subjects, which must be interpreted as zeal for Her Majesty's faithful ally, since they did not personally merit such attentions. Some stupid people who did not know what they were talking about had criticised Albani's moderation, but he had insisted that this was nothing less than an "*affront sanglant*" both to their Imperial Majesties and to their Minister. Albani replied, apparently without undue concern, that there would always be people who judged of events without troubling to inform themselves fully, but that he was sure persons of good sense would appreciate what Chute had said to justify his conduct, and he was extremely obliged to him.[20a]

With his sophisticated continental outlook Mann had at once perceived, or at least he tried to persuade himself, that the Young Pretender's expedition was designed simply to prevent more English troops being sent to Flanders,[18c] and Stosch reported encouragingly in October 1745 that the Pope with his usual frankness had said that he thought certainly the elder son of the Pretender had set foot in Scotland but that he could well leave his head there too.[13b] Mann assured Albani that he had resolved not to be alarmed at the numerous rumours spread by France and the rebel partisans, who had announced repeatedly the capture of Edinburgh Castle. Marshal Wade, he said, was only waiting for the rebel army, which could not number more than 10,000 men, to advance farther so that he could cut them off without hope of retreat.[21] When in the spring of 1746 he received news of the rebels' minor successes in the Highlands he still tried to minimise the affair, but Albani was visibly anxious and fearful of the stimulating effect such reports would have on the Jacobite party and the French.[22a] At last, however, on 31st May 1746, Mann was able to send him the good news of Cumberland's victory at Culloden,[22b] and Albani described the effect in Rome. "There is today", he wrote,* "not one of the enemy partisans who counts on the

* In French in the original.

Scottish rebellion, each one being convinced that it is extinguished and will have no further result. In the Pretender's house all is dark, and the gloomy silence which they observe about everything relating to Scotland makes one realise that they expect nothing more from there. It is a fine reversal of the situation in which things stood last year." He had heard, from a cleric in the Pretender's confidence, that the latter had never thought well of his children's exploits and that it was only after being importuned for a long time by the Court of Paris that he had consented to deliver up his elder son to the French.[22c]

This grave anxiety out of the way, Albani sought some return for the considerable services he had recently rendered to the British. He had not only helped the fleet in his official capacity but had been endlessly good to British naval officers. Admiral Rowley was one who thanked him for the kindness shown to the officers of his squadron, of which the impression, he said, would never be effaced from his memory.[18d] It seems sometimes that private individuals showed insufficient gratitude to Albani, and it is pleasant to note that another sailor, Admiral Forbes, thoroughly appreciated his kindly offices at a rather later date. In answer to his request for an antique fragment carrying some maritime symbol, Albani found and sent him one *"avec l'empreinte du vaisseau de Neptune Dieu de la Mer"*,[23] and Forbes responded with a present and a charming letter.[24] He was, he wrote, giving him a trifle made of English porcelain, not because he thought it worthy of His Eminence's taste, but to enable him to boast that a work from his country had found a place in Albani's collection, and to remind the Cardinal of someone entirely devoted to him. Howe, the English merchant at Leghorn to whom it had been consigned, would at the same time deliver to him two fans which he humbly offered to the Countess (the latter was presumably the

Countess Cheroffini, Albani's mistress and always extremely hospitable to the English) (p. 227).

Other services by Albani were his attempt, albeit unsuccessful, to effect the arrest of a certain Thomas Shuttleworth who was in flight from England after defrauding the South Sea Company,[18e] and his obliging warning that the Neapolitans had got permission to use the Pope's colours on their supply ships and that the latter could be identified by their patents bearing the seal of his brother Annibale as Camerlengo.[15f] He had also transmitted information collected by the Dutch Friend about John Bouverie, the eastern traveller who, like his associate Dawkins, was a Jacobite sympathiser. Bouverie gave the authorities some anxiety when he left Rome in suspicious circumstances in March 1746 and was thought to have gone on some mission from the Pretender to the Court of Vienna.[19b] Although there were relatively few English visitors at this time Albani befriended a fair number. Mann had introduced to him in March 1746 Mr Walpole, son of Horatio, sometime Ambassador to France, with his companion Mr Turnbull; Mr Rice, who does not seem to have made the most of his opportunities and left without seeing a very magnificent ecclesiastical ceremony;[22d] in November four Scottish gentlemen, Lord March, Sir Thomas Sebright, Bt, Mr Treby, nephew of the Duchess of Leeds, allied to several of the principal families of England and very rich, with his companion Mr Fane. Mann indeed remarked that he was charmed that everyone of his nation regarded His Eminence as their Protector and that they paid their respects to him as such.[25]

The immediate reward which Albani hoped to obtain from the British Government was its intervention with the Court of Vienna on behalf, not of himself alone, but of his family. A marriage was arranged in 1747 between his nephew, Prince Soriano, and the second Princess of Massa, but the Duke of Modena was opposing it, Albani said, for his own ends. The eldest Princess and heiress of Massa was married to the Duke of Modena's only surviving son, who was thought incapable of begetting children. To ensure that the succession to his daughter-in-law's duchy did not pass out of his family on her death, the Duke, Albani feared, would try to get it diverted in his own favour as a term of the coming peace treaty, under which he might expect some compensation for damage to his territories. Should he attain his object the duchy might pass into a French family if the younger Princess of Modena married a Frenchman, or even into the Young Pretender's, since her engagement to him was at one time rumoured.[26a] This, as Mann corroborated, was contrary to British and Imperial interests, since Massa was virtually part of Tuscany.[26b] Albani's attempts to promote the succession to this isolated, minor duchy into a matter of international consequence were accompanied by ingratiating behaviour towards the Dowager Duchess Regent of Massa, mother of his intended niece-in-law. Her State was completely dependent on supplies coming through Leghorn and, so that the British Navy should not interfere with them, she had undertaken to observe strict neutrality towards the French troops in the neighbourhood. When some difficulties arose about this Albani sought Mann's help and asked him particularly to let the Duchess Regent know that he had intervened in her favour.[22b] His manœuvres were successful, the redoubtable Dowager Duchess and the Imperial Court consented to the marriage, the British Government gave its blessing, and in 1748 it took place, with every prospect that some day an Albani would be Duke of Massa.

Alessandro, however, was still anxious lest at the Peace Congress his family should be cheated of the fruits of what looked like a very brilliant negotiation on his part, and of a match which, as Mann said, would be esteemed by

any sovereign prince in Italy.[27] Albani pressed Mann to
ensure that the British peace delegates should have special
instructions in favour of his family and received something
like a snub from London. The Duke of Bedford, who had
succeeded Newcastle as Secretary of State for the Southern
Department, intimated that as this was a family affair it would
hardly be a matter for the general Congress and the decision
only concerned the Emperor, who could be relied on to
remember Albani's great services.[28a] The future of Massa
was not in fact affected by the Peace Treaty, but Alessandro
was still worried. In 1749 the Duke of Modena was going
himself to London and would, the Cardinal thought, try to
enlist British support for another attempt to secure Massa.[29a]
The fact that a son was born to the Princess Soriano in
September 1749 probably stimulated Albani to further effort,
and he again made representations to London, only to be
assured that there was no reason to suppose that the Duke
of Modena would mention Massa to the King or that the
latter would enter into the matter if he did.[30]

There one would have expected the matter to end, but
Albani now took up the lesser complaint that the Duke of
Modena, out of spite, was venting his animosity on an abbey
of his own situated almost entirely in the Duke's territories
and apparently being supported by the British. He was not
at all angry, he wrote with evident fury, that His Britannic
Majesty negotiated with the Emperor to the advantage of
the Duke, but he wished it need not be to the prejudice of
himself and his family. He had been of late, he pointed out,
the only friend whom the English had found at Rome in
spite of the trouble of appearing as such in the particular
circumstances of the late war, and he suggested that those
Englishmen who had been to Rome in his charge had not
cut a bad figure and that if any one of them had been annoyed there he had obtained for him the satisfaction due.[31]
Albani's testiness was evidently not directed against Mann,

who had most loyally supported his illustrious pen-friend's highly embarrassing requests and consistently urged upon British Ministers Albani's claims to their special consideration. The harmony between them was not disturbed and, as it happened, all Alessandro's efforts were wasted. The Princess of Modena, notwithstanding the oft-alleged incapacity of her husband, produced a daughter in 1750 who in due course inherited Massa and by her marriage with one of Maria Theresa's sons united it with the Hapsburg dominions. Moreover, the dowry of 30,000 crowns which the Duke of Modena should have paid to Prince Soriano was still outstanding in 1765[32] and probably never materialised.

This tremendous campaign of Albani's coincided with a change in his appointments. He wrote to Mann in April 1748 saying that Her Majesty the Empress-Queen had judged it fit to entrust her interests with the Holy See to Cardinal Mellini. His own Ministry, therefore, which he held *"pro interim"*, was now limited to managing the affairs of the Emperor as his Minister Plenipotentiary with the rank of Comprotector both of the Empire and of the Hereditary Estates of the Empress, with orders, however, to lend his aid in everything to Cardinal Mellini. To this favour, he said, the Empress-Queen had added another, which was a present of a Grand Cross to his Order of Malta, set with diamonds of which the value, though considerable, impressed him less than the gracious expressions with which the gift was accompanied.[28b] Albani was at this time joint Protector, with Cardinal Portocarero, of the Order of the Knights of St John.[29b] Mann does not seem to have commented on the change of appointments nor congratulated Albani, as the exquisite courtesy of their intercourse would appear to have demanded. He wrote, however, the following spiteful communication to Horace Walpole: "Pray tell the Chutes what, however, they won't be surprised to hear, that Cardinal Albani has been honourably dismissed from meddling with the Queen's affairs at Rome. She wrote to him to thank him for his past services, and accompanied it with a rich cross of Malta set with diamonds, and to soften the matter still more the Emperor has declared him compro-tector of the Empire and of the hereditary estates of the Queen. Cardinal Mellini has been appointed her minister plenipotentiary with, I believe, all the salary. The Cardinal is excessively mortified, though he does not own it in his letter to me." [3i] Making due allowance for the fact that Mann was sometimes less than generous to Albani when trying to reciprocate the sprightly malice of Horace Wal-pole's own letters, it must be conceded that he could hardly have been mistaken as to the light in which such a matter must be viewed, and Albani probably had enemies in Vienna (p.132). It is possible also that he had embarrassed the Imperial Court by his efforts to preserve the Massa inheritance for his own family and his tiresome disagreements with the Duke of Modena, who indeed had no reason to regard him with favour. If, however, there was a cloud it soon passed. Albani was to resume Mellini's post after the latter died in 1756 at the beginning of another war, and his relations with the Imperial House seem to have been harmonious for the rest of his own career.

Meanwhile the British Government still required intelli-gence about the Stuarts. Mann had hoped that the Young Pretender would return to Rome and live quietly there, but feared he was more likely to go to some seaport town in France and that the French would again use him against England, though they would abandon him when they had no more use for him.[11d] In fact Charles Edward used the one weapon available to him and was to keep British Minis-ters in an almost chronic state of suspense by moving about and concealing his whereabouts. He returned to Rome only after his father's death in 1766. The Old Pretender's younger son Henry, known as the Duke of York, became a cardinal in 1747, thus at the same time alienating his elder brother and doing something to reassure his enemies. He was henceforward known either as Cardinal Stuart or Cardinal York. The typically Roman compromise whereby his royal titles were recognised without unduly offending the British and their allies was described by Albani, who had been present at the relevant discussions and probably had something to do with their result. Henry was to be "*Altesse Royale Ementissime*", but the expression need not be used in addressing him orally and could be omitted by those who did not wish to write it. The only other special distinction granted to him was that the cardinals who paid him complimentary visits on his promotion were to do it in a red cassock instead of the customary black one.[6d] A year later Cardinal Stuart took full priest's orders, with the reluctant consent of the Pope, it was said, but with his father's approval. This surprised Mann, who thought he had taken minor ones for the sake merely of qualifying for ecclesiastical benefices and intended to retract later if the Jacobite cause required it.[29c] He noted, however, that there had been some instances of former Popes granting dispensations even from priests' orders, in particular cases to prevent the extinction of a family. In these surmises he almost certainly wronged the young Cardinal, who was to take his career seriously and distinguish himself in it. The prediction which Mann made to Albani, that Henry would prove to be the happiest member of his family,[33a] was both more generous and more accurate.

Regarding the Jacobites' plans generally, Albani told Mann that in the Pretender's house the greatest secrecy was maintained and that he thought only the Pretender himself really knew what was going on and told nobody. Alessandro seems to have had some contact with the household and even some degree of friendship, for among his correspondence in Vienna there is the following curiously conspiratorial letter.* [28c]

"From the Palace of the King of England, 24th July 1748.

Monseigneur,

In the fear of not finding Your Eminence, and also to be less importunate, Jacquim takes the liberty of leaving this note at Your Eminence's palace, and has the honour to tell you very humbly, Monseigneur, that the King of England his Master, has read with pleasure the note with which Your Eminence deigned to honour him yesterday. His Majesty and His Royal Highness the Cardinal Duke of York are very conscious of the generous and cordial attention of Your Eminence to their request in favour of Pascal Giacinti. They thank you warmly, Monseigneur, and command me at the same time to beg you to give them news of the health of the Cardinals of St Clement [Annibale Albani] and Francis Albani, in whom they are most genuinely interested, as well as in all which concerns your august House. This is what Jacquim has orders to tell you, to which he adds the declaration of his eternal and inviolable attachment, inseparable from his profound respect for Your Eminence."

This is one of the surprises of Alessandro's correspondence and suggests that his personal contact with the Pretender and his household was closer than might have been expected in the circumstances and that family reasons and the need for keeping up appearances in Rome modified any strictly political attitude.

No one by now relied very much on Stosch's information, and Villettes remarked that he had often observed that with all his penetration and refining in politics the Baron tended to overshoot the mark and that anyone who followed his way of thinking would often find himself misled. It did

* In French in the original.

not do, he said, to embrace the "airy and fantastical schemes" of such politicians as he, but a watchful eye should be kept on Murray, who no doubt had some diabolical scheme in the interests of the Pretender.[6e] Although Mann had apparently been receiving satisfactory intelligence by means of Albani, Parker and the Dutch Friend, supplemented by Stosch's information, for what it was worth, the Old Pretender's relations with the French Court remained of sufficient interest, in the opinion of Ministers in London, to warrant another regular correspondence. Mann had written to the Duke of Newcastle in May 1747 saying that he had received orders from Mr Walpole (presumably Horatio, the elder) to send His Grace any letters from Rome from a person with whom Walpole had a correspondence and to whom he was desired to forward letters. Mann remarked that he was not himself informed who the person was as he had been given a feigned name to write to him by and there was no direction on the letters meant for England, one of which he enclosed.[26c] The name of this correspondent never did appear, but from the evidence of the letters he was a Frenchman with a daughter in Gravelines under the care of a "Madame Hales" and a son who was also in France.[6f] His principal use seems to have been that he was a friend of "J. Towneley", who was in attendance on the Young Pretender in Paris and wrote long accounts of the latter's doings which were sent on to Mann and forwarded to England[29d] with the Roman address carefully removed. This man was presumably John Towneley (1697–1782) who had settled in Paris after helping Charles Edward in Scotland in 1745 and who later translated *Hudibras* into French. It is not clear whether he knew the purpose for which his letters were being used by his friend in Rome. He was also a friend of Dawkins, presumably James Dawkins who travelled to Palmyra and Baalbec, with whom he had, he said, drunk the health of the Roman correspondent.[29e] The Towneleys were a Jacobite family,

John's brother Francis having been executed for his part in the Forty-Five. In 1732 a Mr Towneley had visited Rome and Florence with Sir Marmaduke Constable, seen much of Charles Radcliffe and been eyed with great suspicion by Stosch, but it hardly seems likely that at thirty-five years of age he would have been described, as he then was, as having passed the age of travelling for pleasure.[34] More probably, therefore, this was not John but an older member of the same family. Albani does not seem to have taken any part in this particular correspondence, but he was still in close contact with Parker over various artistic commissions given him by Mann, and desirous of serving the latter however he could. He wrote that he envied Parker the happiness he had in being employed in the accomplishment of Mann's orders and begged the Resident, if he did not think him altogether unworthy, at least to divide the commissions between Parker and himself. Albani was writing on that occasion about an alabaster column which Parker had bought and kept, pending Mann's receipt of an answer from England, and which was exported from Rome through the good offices of the Cardinal.[35]

The introductions of Englishmen were by no means unilateral in the intercourse now firmly established between Albani and Mann. The latter only recommended personally to the Cardinal artists already of some standing, special protégés of his own or of a friend in England, and travellers who were well born, rich or famous. Albani, however, got to know many other Englishmen of all ranks who had come without Mann's introduction, or had reached Rome without passing through Florence and had probably sought his official protection. He had, for instance, got to know Richard Gaven independently, and had originally recommended Parker to Mann. At the end of 1748 the latter acknowledged Albani's introduction of a young sculptor, Prince Hoare, and promised to get him whatever permis-

sions he needed for making copies. He had also, he said,
an idea of employing him on works which would be advantageous for him at the present time as well as helping him to
establish a reputation in England before going there. Shortly
afterwards Mann introduced to Albani the artist and antiquary Richard Dalton,[33b] and with the coming of peace he
was followed by numerous other English travellers. Albani
and Mann were now to enter upon the busiest period of their
association in matters of art.

CHAPTER VI

Between the Wars

THE period between the ending of the War of the Austrian Succession by the Treaty of Aix-la-Chapelle in October 1748 and the beginning of the Seven Years War in 1756 saw the extinction of the Jacobite cause as an important element in international politics. For much of it no one in Rome knew exactly where the Young Pretender was, rumours that he had married always proved to be untrue and he was estranged from his brother because the latter had turned priest and thus weakened the line of succession. The Old Pretender was himself declining into the settled melancholy and ill-health which marked the last years of his life, and his wife, Clementina Sobieski, had died in 1735. There was, however, no reason why the Jacobites in Rome itself should not make the best lives they could for themselves, and indeed, with a prospect of lifelong exile for many of them, there was an added motive for doing so. Their numbers had been increased by participants in the Forty-Five Rebellion, including that admirable character, Andrew Lumsden or Lumisden, who became the Old Pretender's assistant secretary and studied the ruins of Rome in his spare time.[1]

The unofficial Jacobite leader seems to have been the egregious Abbé Grant, who himself had ambitions and evidently the capacity to act as cicerone and agent for the British. Trouble centred round him rather as it had round Charles Radcliffe when that impetuous character and his beautiful step-daughters had enticed English travellers in the 'thirties. The Jacobites had the official support of the Pope and, probably, the private sympathy of the majority of the influential Roman ecclesiastics; they were more permanent residents than most other Englishmen in Rome and comprehensibly enough they made their presence felt. Mann at any rate still took them seriously enough to write to the Secretary of State in 1751 saying that the least act or word in common conversation which the Jacobites could term a disrespect to the Pretender was a most unpardonable crime in Rome and usually produced a persecution in some shape or other from the Government, over which the Pretender had the greatest influence in things of this nature. As it had become the fashion, he continued, for English travellers to reside in greater numbers and longer at Rome than ever before, immense sums of money were being spent outside the country and some Englishmen won over to the Jacobites. He accordingly advised that some means should be found of preventing their going to Rome, or of imposing such limitations as would not be inconsistent with the liberty of the subject of which His Majesty was so tender.[2a]

Conspicuously little attention must have been paid to Mann's warning, judging from all the business connected with Englishmen which engaged Albani and Mann during the next few years. A particularly unsatisfactory though probably not intentionally disloyal visitor was a wild young Irishman, Mr St Leger, whom Mann recommended to Albani as Lord Doneraile's heir,[3a] and who was the unwitting cause of upsetting the intelligence service arranged with Parker. St Leger got into various scrapes, which seem to have started in March 1749 with a dispute over the wages of a servant whom both Albani and Mann thought he had treated ungenerously. Mann told him so,[3b] but he refused to take advice and the servant, who was French, started a lawsuit against him and enlisted the interest of the French Ambassador. The latter became so incensed by St Leger's conduct and his attitude towards himself that Albani thought by June that Rome was getting too hot for him[4a] and Mann advised him to leave. Meanwhile Parker, whom Mann and Albani usually referred to at this time as Mr Born's friend, had been ordered out of Rome by the Inquisition on evidence furnished by fellow-guests at St Leger's dinner table. British Ministers always suspected that the Inquisition used religion as a pretext for banishing from Rome persons who had become objectionable there for other offences which would be more difficult to prove or publish, particularly any against the Pretender. Albani himself told Mann that he had agreed with him at first that Parker's enemies had plotted against him in this way. On having looked into the matter he was, however, satisfied that there really was something in the accusation of impiety made against him. Although, he said, the fault was not perhaps so great as Parker's accusers wanted to make out, it was not intrigue alone which had caused his misfortune. Mann knew, he continued, what a delicate matter religion was in all countries and how easy it was to enter on the subject and exceed the bounds of prudence when merry at a meal, particularly in the company of people who thought themselves licensed to speak of everything and decide everything when they were thus heated. St Leger entertained at his dinner-parties many people whom he did not know well, and Born's friend, so as not to offend them, must have been the victim of their imprudence and bad faith. Fortunately, however, the Inquisition had confined itself to telling him quietly to leave without taking the more violent steps usual when the crime was established by accusers and witnesses such as those who had deposed in this case. Albani thought there was nothing to be done at present and that premature action might make the matter more serious. He doubted if it would end there and advised that St Leger should be warned not to stay in Rome too long after he returned from Naples. Mann knew, he added, how many Englishmen had enjoyed staying in Rome and, because they behaved correctly, had been treated with courtesy and never embarrassed, but St Leger unfortunately was different.[4b] Mann urged Albani to use his influence to divert from a poor family a thunderbolt which would other-wise crush them, as he put it, but Parker had to go. The accusations, Mann reflected, must indeed have been serious if Albani could do nothing for him.[3c]

The banishment of Mark Parker was not the end of the matter. While his servant's lawsuit was pending St Leger had gone off to Naples, leaving some of his belongings with Born, who obligingly consented to look after them. The result was that the sbirri descended on Born's house to seize St Leger's goods for his debt to the servant, and Born not unnaturally was terrified that his own liaison with Mann should be discovered. Born, wrote the latter, was so disturbed by what had happened to his friend that he con-fused everything and had convinced himself that this busi-ness was a result of the previous one, although really they had no connection. He refused to continue writing to Mann, who considered him as a sick man whose disordered ima-gination only time could cure,[3d] but his fears were not un-justified and Mann himself must have been either very dense, very unsympathetic or very frightened. Stosch, probably reporting current rumours, wrote that the Govern-ment had exiled from Rome an Englishman named Parker who had been established there for many years with a wife and children and acted as an antiquary to the travellers of his country, and that a Dutchman named Born, who lodged with him, had had the same fate.[5] This was probably in-correct, because in 1762 a Mr Born, described as "*Consul de la République de Hollande*" and obviously in Rome, was re-ferred to in correspondence between Albani and an official at The Hague,[6] and in 1759 Albani thanked Olivier Hope at Rotterdam for a cheese addressed to him through Born.[7]

A curious episode resulted from Parker's banishment.

A painter of the same name tried to step into his shoes, as Mann explained when Albani asked him to recommend an Italian, Costanzi, as a cicerone to English travellers in 1750. Many Englishmen, he said, who had come recently from Rome, had taken the trouble to recommend a painter named Parker who was attempting to fill the place of the other man of the same name who had been obliged to leave Rome. They supposed that this new Parker had all the necessary knowledge from long practice, and the reputation of being completely independent of the Jacobites. Mann however did not know him and indeed protested that he had never heard of him.[8a] This individual was presumably the history painter John Parker, who lived in Rome for several years prior to returning to England in 1762.

As though not content with the trouble he had caused already, St Leger in July had a quarrel with a Roman knight, but the latter was arrested as having been in the wrong and St Leger complimented Albani on the manner in which he had managed the affair for him.[4c] He stayed on in Rome until December 1749, when he left to attend to his own affairs in Great Britain, but by 1754 Albani and Mann were discussing him again. This time he had nearly killed a man in Ireland in circumstances which would not allow him to claim that it had been in a duel. Even though it was said not to have been his fault, Mann thought things might go badly with him if his adversary died, and Albani, knowing, he said, how severe the English laws were in cases of murder,[9a] earnestly hoped the victim would recover, which he fortunately did.

After the defection of Born and the apparent cessation of the correspondence with Towneley's friend, Mann had to make new arrangements for intelligence. In 1752 he wrote to Lord Holdernesse saying that he had settled an additional correspondence at Rome and for that purpose had been obliged to engage a person of some consequence whom he had thought fit to summon to Florence as it was impossible to make arrangements by letter with any degree of secrecy. By the last post, Mann said, he had received two letters from him, one written very late at night after his return from a company of people of rank in the Government of Rome who, not suspecting his views, had told him that the Pretender's eldest son was in Ireland.[2b] Possibly this was the unidentified "person of great rank at Rome" to whom Mann quite often referred and who was still writing to him about the Pretender in 1755.[10]

It is quite evident from the papers that Mann by no means told Albani everything about his intelligence service and always had agents in Rome additional to any he contacted through the Cardinal. When Sir Thomas Robinson became Secretary of State for the Southern Province in 1754 he was not aware that Walton and Stosch were the same person, and Mann, in putting him right on this point, said that since 1739 he had received instructions, expressly renewed in 1742, which had caused him to send people to Rome to establish them there, and that he had continued to do so ever since. He added that the news from Rome could not possibly be as important now as formerly, but the affair was still of so delicate a nature as to require constant attention and his correspondents at Rome were assiduous.[11] Albani, meanwhile, had continued to tell Mann whatever he could about the Stuarts, although in 1749 he was of opinion that nothing much was going on. The elder son, he said, had quarrelled with his father as well as with his brother, and the Old Pretender's finances would not allow him to make any sensational moves.[4d] In 1750 he had an interview with Cardinal Stuart, who asked him to find out through his friends and correspondents where Charles Edward was, and said that his father was in despair since the few letters he received from the Prince never carried any date or address.[2c] Albani told Mann he was sure the Cardinal spoke in good faith and in 1753 heard the same story from the Pope, who told him he knew nothing for certain but thought the young man was in France in some very out-of-the-way place. If, said Albani, they made a mystery of the son's whereabouts to the Pope, to whom the Pretender had so many obligations, it was easy to guess how much the others must know.[12a] It is evident that after the peace Mann had more time to spare for other more congenial concerns in Rome.

From his early days in Florence Mann had undertaken commissions from Englishmen for all kinds of things from Italy. Horace Walpole, for instance, wanted him to procure for Lord Islay some of Stosch's so-called Maltese cats which would figure prodigiously, he said, in His Lordship's cell as he was "of the mysterious, dingy nature of Stosch".[13a] Admiral Matthews, in his ship in Vado Bay, heard that the Austrians had captured a great many of the King of Sicily's horses and wanted a "fine Arab or Turk for Lord Godolphin" and a Spanish horse for himself, the qualities required being described in detail by this nautical lover of horseflesh.[14a] Another naval officer, James Paterson, wrote for an embroidered sky-blue waistcoat, for which he enclosed a pattern, begging him not to "skrimp" himself as he would trust Mann's taste and not begrudge whatever he spent.[14b] At a later date Lord Rochford, who was, he said, "excessively curious for plants", wanted a cutting of a rare kind of jessamine from the Grand Duke's garden, for which it was difficult to procure permission.[15] These are only a few examples of numerous miscellaneous requests. Mann had little or no private income and his expense accounts were often disgracefully in arrears from Whitehall, so it is probable enough that, as another writer has suggested, he supplemented his means by acting as a purchasing agent.[13b]

The most considerable of his commissions were for works

of art or furnishings, and once the War of the Austrian Succession was over he and Albani were able to make use of their official connection to promote on an increasing scale acquisitions for the great houses of England. So important indeed was this traffic to both of them that it may well have been one of the prime motives of their voluminous correspondence in peace time, and profitable financially as well as in terms of patronage and influence. In February 1749 Mann recommended Matthew Brettingham to Albani[3e] and in the following April the letter was presented, the Cardinal promising to render the young man all the services he could.[4e] Brettingham was the son of the architect who had carried out William Kent's designs at Holkham and was a protégé of Lord Leicester's, as recounted by Mann in a letter of September 1749.[16] His Lordship, he said, had contributed a great deal to the journey and maintenance of a young man called Brettingham at Rome, whom he had taken the liberty of recommending to Albani's protection some time before. This young man had bought at Rome for Lord Leicester five very badly damaged statues which he had had restored, but Cardinal Valenti had revoked his permission to export them. Mann thought perhaps this was for lack of some attention or other reason which he did not know, but as His Lordship had already prepared the niches for the statues in a very magnificent house which he had just built he was in despair at this setback. Lord Leicester, Mann said, had begged him to get the necessary consent and he implored Albani to intervene, being certain that when Valenti knew all the circumstances he would not wish to do Lord Leicester a bad turn. Albani wrote back by return of post to the effect that he had already tried to get these statues released as well as several modern ones which had been held up. The prohibition against exporting statues which had been published, he said, had been inspired by indiscreet zealots who, to ingratiate themselves with the Pope and the Cardinal Secretary of State, had suggested to them that everything fine in the way of sculpture was being taken away by foreigners. Until this opinion, which was absolutely false, had been entirely overcome there was no hope, but he would try to do everything he could to overcome it and did not despair of succeeding after a short time.[4f]

Brettingham wrote to Mann by the same post confirming that Albani had done all he could but had received a flat refusal. He had, he said, picked up these five statues in Rome, bought them conditionally and had them examined according to custom by the Pope's Antiquary, the Abbate Venuti. As the latter had declared they were ordinary figures and much restored, permission had been obtained in due form from the Cardinal Secretary, signed by his Auditor. Immediately afterwards, however, a rumour had got round and some spy or other had told Cardinal Valenti, the Pope's Secretary of State, that they were not as had been represented in the Memorial and were too good to go out of Rome. Upon this information Valenti had sent orders that they should not be removed until he had seen them. Brettingham was immediately told of this counter-order and called upon the Cardinal Secretary to ask that the statues might be examined quickly as he actually had a fine opportunity to send them away the same week in an English vessel taking in Gensano wines at Nettuno. The Cardinal, however, did not go. Brettingham had used all the influence he could, but the only result had been the deposition of Venuti in favour of a Flemish sculptor, von Strauffen, and the appointment of the celebrated seal-engraver, Costanzi, as a sort of Superintendent over all antiquities. The two antiquaries had examined the statues and agreed that all might pass except one small figure, but when they had left the sculptor's shop Costanzi had changed his tune and advised Brettingham to dissolve the bargain by pleading "unlawful commodities etc." as permission would never be given. Brettingham had then gone to see Valenti who, he believed, had told him, "not without some dissimulation", that the whole matter was now so public that he could not use his power secretly to help him.

Brettingham thought other means altogether must now be tried, but was apprehensive that Cardinal Albani would not be the most proper instrument to make use of on this occasion because he and the Cardinal Secretary hated each other mortally, and Albani was always suspected in these matters because he was so great a dealer himself and no one knew but that they might not be his own commodities which he was asking permission to send away. Brettingham suggested that instead Cardinal Mellini should be asked to intervene in the matter in the name of the Court of Vienna and he believed Lord Leicester had written to the Marchese Niccolini, who was a friend both of Valenti and of the Pope and might succeed in the matter if he came to Rome.[4g]

Notwithstanding Brettingham's doubts about Albani's qualifications for the task he seems to have made a successful application to Valenti and in October told Mann that Lord Leicester now only needed patience about his statues. They were not, he added, so ordinary as had been suggested, but had purposely been so described to facilitate their export.[17a] A week later he said they were now only held up until Valenti received a present, but afterwards qualified this by the rather subtle distinction that he thought Valenti did not actually need the spur of presents to induce him to be fair to Lord Leicester, but as he had heard there were some on the way for him from England he would wish to gain the good opinion of the person who sent them by releasing the statues.[17b] Brettingham, however, was not yet at the end of his troubles. A merchant, Lopez Rosa, to whom the letter of exchange was addressed, had gone bankrupt, so that the vendor of the statues had not been paid, and in January 1750 the resulting lawsuit was held up for the Court Vacations.[17c] Lord Leicester presumably got these statues in the end, but Brettingham was collecting for him over a considerable period and it may not be possible to date his acquisitions exactly. Several sculptures at Holkham were bought from Albani himself but they appear to have been later purchases and not those discussed here.[18]

One of the most useful services which Albani performed for English collectors such as Leicester was helping them to get home to England the works of art he had in the first place sold them or helped them to find. As early as 1701 the art-loving Clement XI had issued an edict restraining the export of antiques and works of art, and this was renewed by succeeding Popes in 1726 and 1733[19] as well as at the time so inconvenient to Lord Leicester. The general impecuniosity of the Romans makes it not unlikely that the payments exacted at all levels for the evasion of the regulations created a vested interest in their continuance. All the same, a combination of expertise, influence and sheer ingenuity was required as well as bribery, and although Albani was not the only practitioner he was certainly one of the most successful, and to him must be attributed many choice items in English collections. As Dodington said, such things either could not be found or were only to be sold at exorbitant prices, or could not be exported without the intervention of a great lord such as Albani.[20] His services were not entirely one-sided, for in Tuscany, where after 1754 there were similar prohibitions against exporting antiques, Mann was able to help the Cardinal in return. In 1756 the latter asked him to forward to England through the Consul at Leghorn a marble head which Stosch had bought for him, because the Baron's profession as antiquary would put the authorities immediately on their guard about anything he tried to send away,[21a] Albani said. A contemporary connoisseur, Count Caylus, himself rather an

BETWEEN THE WARS

unsatisfactory character, derided the taste of the English and the manner in which they could be fobbed off with spurious or inferior articles. He suggested that Albani himself was not above such practices,[22] but it seems more likely that any reputation he earned for trickery was rather in relation to his evasion of the export regulations. His restorations of arms, noses, etc., to antique statues were in the taste of the time and not intended to deceive, while the widespread fabrication of trivial fakes would seem beneath the notice of such a man as Albani.

There appears to be no evidence either in the London or Vienna archives that Albani and Bubb Dodington corresponded between the summer of 1733, when they had consulted together about Stosch, and October 1748, when Albani acknowledged receipt of a notice that Dodington was sending him a present.[23] In his next letter he thanked Dodington for his goodwill, shown not only by compliments but also by concrete proofs such as the case of porcelain which was going to be sent to Leghorn for him. He went on to discuss the inferiority of modern works of art as opposed to the antique but extolled the young sculptor, Hoare, as being very clever and anxious to succeed in his profession. He had, he said, made an admirable copy of his own beautiful bas-relief of *Antinous* for an English nobleman. He recommended Hoare to Dodington, saying that he would perfectly come up to his expectations and could contribute to the perfection of the beautiful gallery which His Excellency had resolved to build "*à l'Italienne*". Albani would, he continued, do everything he could for the young sculptor, Joseph Wilton, whom Dodington had recommended to him.[3f]

The house to which Dodington was now adding a gallery stood on the banks of the Thames at Hammersmith, was later known as Brandenburgh House and pulled down in 1822. It had been a notable seventeenth-century mansion,

155

with an interesting history, for General Fairfax had used it as his headquarters during the Civil War, and after the Restoration Prince Rupert had bought it for his mistress, Margaret Hughes. Dodington, who somewhat affectedly named it *"La Trappe"*, acquired it from a subsequent owner in 1748 and had it repaired and altered by the architect Roger Morris.[24] Servandoni, to whom the gallery was entrusted, was well known in Europe as a scene-painter and designer of pageants, and had organised a tremendous display of fireworks in St James's Park in 1749. He designed the porch of St Sulpice in Paris, but much of his work appears to have been of an ephemeral nature. His reputation *"au delà des Monts"* seems to have appealed to the cosmopolitan Dodington, who thought he had genius.[25a] He was also impressed by the German sculptor, Peter Verschaffelt, who, he told Albani, avoided the faults of the age by being *"ni Original monstrueux et estropié, ni Copiste fade et rampant"*.[26a]

The case of Dresden china was long delayed, and it was not until February 1750 that Albani received it together with some *"Bagatelles d'Acier"* and a snuff-box *"d'Email sur du Fer blanc, montée de faux Or, que nous apellons ici Métal de Pincebec"* which had been included for good measure and which Albani thought prettier than anything of the kind from elsewhere.[8b] In May 1750 Dodington wrote that he wanted four statues, not mutilated, for his gallery and would send a section-drawing of it. He knew things of the first rank could not now be found or paid for but he wanted works of real merit and asked Albani to look out for something and also for some busts and vases of fine workmanship.[25a] Albani took immense trouble over this commission and wrote back immediately to ask for measurements. It would not be easy to find what he wanted quickly and warned Dodington that it was also not possible to find complete antique statues and that he must content himself

with restored ones. He would, however, see that they were
the best obtainable, and wanted to know how much approx-
imately Dodington wished to spend on their purchase.[25b]
In August he wrote to tell him that he had found four
statues and was sending him drawings of two of them, the
others to follow when the artist had finished them. The cost
of all four, including packing, would not much exceed
1200 Roman crowns, but he was adding a drawing of a
fifth, a very beautiful statue, bigger than the others but very
fine, which would cost 500 crowns. Albani set out an estimate:[8c]

Baccante		500	crowns
Figure representing Paris		250	,,
,, ,,	Ptolemy	250	,,
,, ,,	Mercury	250	,,
Another Imperial Figure		250	,,
		1500	,,
Boxes and Carriage		200	crowns

The absurd and much derided Dodington always behaved to Albani in a most gentlemanly way, and he told him
that he could not judge of the statues from drawings but
would rely entirely on him. In a word, he said, if His
Eminence was pleased with them then so was he, perfectly.
Since he had already passed the limit of expenditure he had
proposed, he would take the additional figure if it were not
more than 500 crowns, but as his gallery was not yet ready
he would like them all kept for him in some safe place. He
added that if by chance Albani heard of anything really
worthy of the attention of a great Prince and available for
sale, in the way of columns, vases, busts, statues, paintings,
etc., he would be glad to know and thought the Cardinal
would understand what he meant. Dodington was, of course,

speaking of his patron and great friend, Frederick Prince of Wales. Albani however replied that marbles and paintings worthy of the attention of a great Prince were now very scarce and that people who possessed such things knew their rarity and how to get their price. Added to that there was so much rigour against the export of such things that they could only be got with extreme difficulty.[27a]

Horace Mann meanwhile was busy having a marble pavement of "*jaune de Siène, verd de Gênes et de blanc de Carrare*" made in Florence for Dodington's gallery.[28a] He told Albani that the design was not much approved of although the magnitude of the work was much admired,[8d] to which Albani replied that criticism was the fashion of the century and he expected as much himself, even with all the trouble he was taking to find four beautiful statues for the gallery.[27b] In December 1750 Dodington wrote to Mann expressing surprise at the beauty and cheapness of the statues, judging from the drawings, and gratitude to Albani for being such a good manager for him. He said, too, that 1700 crowns would be awaiting his orders at a banker's.[20] Dodington did not actually receive and unpack all his statues until the New Year of 1752 and, although he declared himself delighted with them,[26a] his pleasure was much clouded by the Prince of Wales' death in March 1751.

This event was a shattering blow to Dodington and he wrote to Albani from Eastbury in August 1751 saying that he had not had the heart to reply to his last letter after the loss he had just suffered of the most amiable friend and gracious master that ever was. He had lost the most enviable position and the most brilliant expectations that a man could lose. It was, however, only the sweetness of friendship and the pleasures of private life that he regretted. All the rest, he said, at his age and with no one to succeed him, only touched him very moderately. God, whom it had pleased to take from him the means of doing more good, would credit him with the sincerity of his intentions.[29a]

In June 1753 Albani told Dodington of an opportunity to get statues from the Villa d'Este at Tivoli, but the suggestion does not appear to have been taken up. The Cardinal reminded his friend of the beauty of the Villa and particularly of its statues, which the Duke of Modena was selling as he was dismantling the Villa. So that they should not all pass out of the State the Pope had bought the best, but the choice had not been made with such precision that there did not remain fifteen very good ones priced so modestly that it would pay a person to buy them to trade with. This, Albani said, was not the reason he suggested them to Dodington but he was just informing him that if he needed them for his gallery or for one of his friends there could not be a better opportunity for a profitable deal. They needed some restoration, but as that would be no great expense it would not detract from the bargain.[30a] Albani, in fact, had told Dodington on a previous occasion that all antique statues had arms, legs and noses broken by the ruins in which they were buried and the carelessness of those who got them out,[28b] and replacements were regarded as normal work by Roman sculptors and evidently taken for granted by purchasers. The Duke of Modena himself, continued Albani, would undertake to get permission for export out of the Ecclesiastical State and he begged Dodington to honour him with his commands. It may have been no coincidence that Alessandro, at about this time, was seeking a reconciliation with his old enemy the Duke of Modena, through the good offices of British Ministers.[31a]

In the same year Dodington introduced the young Lord Bolingbroke to Albani, thus assuring for him, he said in his usual flowery way, the protection of a Prelate who knew how to combine with the veneration attached to his position as a Prince of the Church, all the polish of a most accomplished aristocrat.[30b] Albani returned the compliment by the recommendation of Miss Catherine Read, an English artist, who had painted a portrait of himself from which Dodington could judge her skill. The other qualities with which she was gifted, he added, apparently without irony, His Excellency would soon perceive if he had the goodness to receive her.[32a] The recommendation says much for Albani's perception and kindness of heart. Fanny Burney, while praising Catherine Read's work and character, said she was "saturnine, cold, taciturn and absent to an extreme; awkward and full of mischances in every motion; ill accoutred even beyond negligence in her dress, and plain enough to produce, grotesquely, an effect that was almost picturesque".[33] What Dodington made of her does not appear.

The correspondence continued very amicably, Dodington taking some trouble to look into the case of a merchant in London whom Albani wanted to help,[32b] and sending the Cardinal the *Voyages of Pococke* which he had asked for, magnificently bound, and the *Ruins of Palmyra*, with preface in French, as an extra gift.[34] In 1754 the "Chevalier Stanhope", brother of Lord Chesterfield, presented a letter of introduction from Dodington, and Albani gave him the usual polite reception although he was concerned at Stanhope's getting into the hands of the Abbé Grant, who, he said, was not the man to give him good advice.[12b] In 1755 Dodington obligingly sent Alessandro the description of a long and complicated cure for the stone which he had wanted for a friend,[35a] and in 1756 wrote him general reflections on politics and of his distress at the disgrace of Admiral Byng. The Admiral's father had owed the first steps of his fortune to his own family and Dodington had been left in his charge during his minority, he said. It was therefore particularly painful for him to see the misfortune of a descendant of his guardian and special friend.[36] Albani replied to all these communications with warmth and exquisite politeness.

The proposal that Albani should find suitable purchases for the Prince of Wales had apparently come to nothing, but Mann had made a considerable purchase for him on Dodington's orders. It consisted of thirteen statues by Francavilla, of which four are now at Windsor, two (much restored) at Kew, one in America and the remainder probably lying in fragments near Windsor Castle.[37] Owing to their size, Mann told Albani, they would have to wait at Leghorn until a warship came in which was bigger than the ones usually calling there.[26b] They were eventually shipped to England in the spring of 1752 in a former naval frigate owned by a merchant, Fortunatus Wright.[37]

It was not unusual for the Navy to help in getting works of art home for collectors with sufficient influence. In 1720 the Consul John Fuller had written from Leghorn to the Secretary of State on the subject of marble for which Sir Thomas Hewet had contracted "for his Majesty's occasions", and had said that Sir George Byng would be sending a man-of-war for it.[38] Even in wartime this form of transport was not entirely abandoned although it had its drawbacks. Horace Mann, for instance, said he was afraid to send a choice sculptured eagle to Horace Walpole by means of a warship in 1746 as everything was cleared away even if action was only suspected, and so carelessly that things got broken and spoilt. Walpole agreed that Captain Townshend would hoist it overboard on the prospect of an engagement and think he could buy him another at Hyde Park Corner with the prize money. It was eventually sent to England in a store ship.[13c]

Soon after Albani had completed his commission for the adornment of Dodington's house he was asked to help with another major undertaking in England. In August 1752 Mann wrote saying that he hoped Brettingham would have communicated to him the plan of the gallery which he had sent him last week, but as great detail was required he supposed Brettingham had wished to take measurements to show Albani at the same time as he asked his advice. The necessity, he said, of conforming to exact measurements and many other difficulties, made him rather doubt the success of this commission.[39a] The Earl (subsequently the first Duke) of Northumberland, had been in Italy as Sir Hugh Smithson in 1732, according to Spence's list (p. 112), and he had now asked Mann to have copies made of paintings in the Farnese gallery to be used in his own house in the Strand, but without changing the scale of the originals. Brettingham in due course called on Albani, who made a list of artists who might be commissioned and of the paintings he thought most suitable as being the rarest in Rome. The proposed paintings were: Caracci's *Triumph of Ariadne* from the Palazzo Farnese, Giulio Romano's two *Feasts of the Gods* from the Palazzo at Mantua, for which Albani had sketches, Guido Reni's *Aurora* from the Villa Rospigliosi, and Raphael's *Assembly of the Gods* in the Farnesina. The artists suggested were Masucci, Placido Costanzi, Mengs, Battoni, Pozzi and Corrado,[39b] of whom the four first-named were employed. Albani, like Mann, anticipated difficulty over the scale and said that unless the gallery was the same size and height as that of the Farnese Palace there would be too great a disproportion between the figures and their setting. He advised Mann to consult his friend in England on this point[4h] and also about the cost, which would in any case be no small matter and would become exorbitant if he employed many people, each of whom would want his profit.[39c] It is not a very flattering commentary on Mann's character that in a letter to Bubb Dodington he gave Albani no credit for his advice and help. The idea was certainly Lord Northumberland's, he said, but the choice of the paintings and the execution of the design had been left to himself. Obviously he had some doubts as to the success of the undertaking for which he was so anxious to get the credit, but he rather naïvely suggested that the rapid decay of the originals would enhance the value of the copies and justify the great expenditure made upon them.[40]

The preliminary points were apparently settled to everyone's satisfaction and in December 1752 Albani told Mann that he was delighted Masucci was to be allowed 1100 crowns for his copy of Guido's *Aurora*, because, owing to his great reputation and the number of his commissions, he would never have done it for 1000. Albani was delicately going to insinuate some conditions in case death or illness should prevent his completing the copy. Battoni would do his two paintings for 1500 sequins, would leave the cost of the canvas and scaffolding to Mann and would expect to receive whatever he thought fit to give him as a present when the work was finished.[4i] Albani later told Battoni that he could not expect more than 1900 sequins in all,[12c] and consulted again with Brettingham as to the best way to please Mann and his friend in England,[31b] who does not seem to have been named at the beginning. Alessandro earnestly desired to see a drawing of the gallery in question, but Brettingham was reluctant to produce one, fearing, Albani thought, that he wanted the design so as to cut him out of the commission entirely.[12d] By February 1753 Alessandro thought he had got permission from the Minister of Naples and Sicily for Battoni to copy the Raphael paintings, but he had been hard to persuade as he feared lest the little nails necessary for attaching the canvases should damage them. In April the Minister said an express order would have to be obtained from Naples,[12e] apparently for the artist to attach a canvas to the original and transfer its outline on to this in chalk.

Meanwhile Mann had heard with some concern that

Pompeo Battoni and Raphael Mengs were at present engaged on painting portraits of travellers, and he was being pressed from England to send exact measurements so that the decorative work could be started.[30c] Albani reassured him by saying that Battoni, he knew, was only doing portraits of foreigners to fill in the time while he was waiting for permission to start work in the Farnesina. He had not seen Brettingham lately, but it was for him to supervise the artists and press them if he thought they were delaying. Albani had given the Court of Naples his personal guarantee that nothing should happen in the Farnesina as it had in the Vatican,[12f] and Mann hoped that the King of the Sicilies would reflect that there was a great deal of difference between a master like Pompeo Battoni and the young men of the French Academy who had worked at the Vatican. Evidently there had been some contemporary scandal about damage done there by students. Mann was also growing anxious about his contracts, thought he had made his initial payment too soon and that the artists would have been more punctilious about starting if he had delayed it a bit. The decorative work in the gallery would in consequence be held up for a year and he had also heard that Costanzi was very ill and did not know what condition had been made about his returning the money.[30d] In the end, the permission to fix canvases was not forthcoming from Naples, and Albani said he would get Battoni to make a free copy, which would be harder for him but also more to his credit. He was sorry he had not decided on this at the beginning as the work would have been well advanced by now.[12g] Mengs, however, had not wished to chalk the original of the *School of Athens*, thinking he could do more masterly work without it, and Mann thought Battoni might be put on his mettle by this.[30e]

Notwithstanding his illness, Costanzi finished first, and Albani told Mann in August 1754 that without disparagement to anyone else he thought his work would surpass that of the other painters, though he had had more fatigue than they in doing it. There had been both the difficulty of the task, because the figures being all nude required more application, and the lack of ease in manœuvring. He had had to draw everything from below upwards because he could not put up a canvas. He had even been put to more expense than the others, having used sixty crowns' worth of azure blue in his copy although he had worked for 500 crowns less than they.[12h] Albani urged Mann to give Costanzi something extra but Mann demurred, saying that he could not dispose of his friend's money as he liked and he thought Costanzi should stick to the bargain.[41a] Alessandro, however, continued to insist and Mann did eventually succeed in getting an extra 100 crowns from Northumberland for Costanzi, which Albani duly paid over to him. Masucci finished his *Aurora* in July 1755 in spite, Albani said, of the derangement of his health and his customary slowness.[42]

The fashionable portrait painter, Battoni, had meanwhile been hopelessly dilatory and Albani had remonstrated strongly with him in January 1755 about the Earl of Northumberland's commission which he had so neglected. He had made the painter understand, he said, that either he must do his duty with the most diligent haste or must give back the money he had taken, because there was no lack in Rome of painters as skilful as he and more honest, who would be honoured to serve with due exactness a person so distinguished by merit and birth as His Lordship.[35b] Mengs had promised his painting at the end of July 1755 and it is to be presumed that both he and Battoni fulfilled their contracts without much further delay as the subject dropped out of Albani's and Mann's correspondence.

The letters alone do not make it clear what paintings exactly were copied and by whom, but Dr Waagen in his

Treasures of Art of Great Britain, published in 1854, describes the gallery in Northumberland House in the Strand for which they were designed.[43] On the long wall opposite the windows, he says, was Raphael's *School of Athens* copied by Mengs and on either side of it the *Assembly of the Gods* and the *Marriage of Cupid and Psyche* from the Farnesina; at the two ends, Caracci's *Bacchus and Ariadne* from the Farnese Palace and Guido Reni's *Aurora* from the Villa Rospigliosi. Evidently the *School of Athens* in the Vatican and the *Marriage of Cupid and Psyche* in the Farnesina were substituted for Albani's original suggestion of Giulio Romano's paintings, probably for convenience, since the latter were at Mantua. Mengs did the *School of Athens*, Battoni the two Raphaels in the Farnesina, Costanzi the *Bacchus and Ariadne*, and Masucci the *Aurora*. The paintings must have arrived in England, or been thought to have done so, by October 1755, because Horace Walpole said then that he had never approved of the idea of the copies and was "adjourning his curiosity" until the gallery was thrown open at the first masquerade. It cannot, however, have been completed as soon as he expected, because it was not until May 1757 that he reported to Horace Mann that Lord Northumberland's great gallery was finished and opened.* "It is a sumptuous chamber," he wrote, "but might have been in better taste. He is wonderfully content with his pictures and gave me leave to repeat it to you. I rejoiced as you had been the negotiator—as you was not the painter, you will allow me not to be so profuse of my applause. Indeed I have yet only seen them by candle-light. Mengs's School of Athens pleased me: Pompeio's two are black and hard; Mazucci's Apollo, *fade* and without beauty; Costanza's piece is

---

* Northumberland sent Mann "a prodigious fine snuff-box, which must have cost a great deal" and "a drawing of the gallery extremely well done" in recognition of his services. Walpole V. p. 209; Mann to H. Walpole 3. vi. 58.

abominable." [44] Northumberland House was demolished in 1874[45] but one of the great twin fireplaces and overmantels from the gallery is preserved in the Victoria and Albert Museum in London and the other set up in the former Steward's Room at Syon. The Museum also has in store a large copy of the *School of Athens* by Mengs which was presented by the eighth Duke of Northumberland in 1926 (after having been on loan since 1917) and seems certain to be the one from the great gallery. The four remaining copies were sold more recently by the present Duke to Mr Charles de Bestigui and now hang in the Palazzo Labia in Venice.[46]

Lord Leicester's, Dodington's and the Duke of Northumberland's galleries seem to have been the largest single commissions from England in which Albani personally played a very considerable part with the co-operation of Horace Mann. Although the outbreak of the Seven Years War in 1756, or the building of his own Villa on the outskirts of Rome, or his advancing years, might well explain why he undertook no more, it may well be that the rise of other dealers, and particularly of Thomas Jenkins, had something to do with it. In July 1753 Mann wrote recommending to Albani Mr Jenkins, a young Englishman who was actually studying painting in Rome. The interest, he continued, which several of his friends in England took in whatever concerned this young man induced him to procure for him the honour of the advantage of being received by His Eminence, in the hope that he would show himself worthy of the benefits with which Albani saw fit to honour him.[32c]

In the following January Mann wrote to Albani saying that he had heard of some complaints about Jenkins and a bust which he had bought and sold at a profit.[9b] Albani replied that it was more the spirit of cabal than of reason which had made the gentleman concerned and his friends act as they had. His own opinion, in strict confidence, was that the matter was connected with a certain Abbé Grant, who accosted all the Englishmen of position who came to Rome and served them by showing them whatever there was to be seen that was remarkable. He was in alliance with another English painter, James Innes, and the two together did not like to see Jenkins approaching his compatriots and getting certain advantages from them, from which sprang misunderstandings. It was not proper for Albani to warn Englishmen to be on their guard against these two characters, but if Mann thought fit to warn those who passed through Tuscany on the way to Rome he was sure nothing like this would happen to them. Meanwhile he was delighted to hear that Mann had protested about the steps taken against Jenkins, as he highly disapproved of them himself. In a postscript Albani added that the English gentleman in question had complained to the Government of Rome before telling him, which proved it was an intrigue. He would do all he could but begged Mann to do the same, without letting anyone know that Albani had told him, because the Abbé Grant was one of the Pretender's firm supporters.[12i]

The accusation against Jenkins was that he had broken a contract by buying a bust for an English gentleman and then taking a profit on it himself. The dealer maintained that he had bought the bust on his own account and had the right to ask whatever price he liked afterwards, a position which Albani confirmed after seeing the papers.[12j] The Government of Rome threatened Jenkins with banishment, which was only narrowly averted. Lord Dartmouth and Lord North both wrote to Albani from Paris, saying that they had employed Jenkins on many occasions and found him most honest and they begged the Cardinal to save him.[9c] The matter was hotly contested in Florence between Mann and two English gentlemen, Smith and la Touche, who were interested in the dispute, told him all their views and refused to be persuaded in Jenkins' favour.[9d] However, through Albani's good offices or by other means, the threat of exile was withdrawn and, after this very shaky start, Jenkins was to flourish in Rome until Napoleon's wars induced him to return to England in 1798.

The young sculptor, Prince Hoare, whom Albani had recommended to Mann at the end of 1748, had remained in Florence ever since, and in August 1749 Albani, with many expressions of gratitude, sent Mann a letter in Italian which he had received from Hoare, describing all Mann's kindnesses to him. The sculptor thanked him for his own favours and particularly for the introduction to Mann, to whom he owed many obligations.[4j] In February 1752 Mann wrote to Albani about another notable English sculptor, Joseph Wilton,[26c] who must already have been some time in Rome, because Alessandro had promised Dodington in January 1749 that he would befriend him for his sake.[3f] He had won a prize in the Academy there, but had since moved to Florence, where he was now getting much work from England. Mann, having, he said, soon appreciated his merits, had allowed him to live in his own house. In 1752 Wilton was going to Rome for a few days just to wind up his affairs there and he was very anxious that Albani should get him permission to take a cast from the head of Julius Caesar in the Marquis Casali's house.[26c] The Cardinal told Mann he doubted whether he would succeed as the bust was kept locked in a great wooden case in a private part of the house. This jealous custodianship was caused, Albani said, by a very ill-founded conviction that it was the bust of Caesar, though it in no way resembled the Caesars to be seen on medals. He himself, knowing something of these matters, could declare that it was not only not the head of Caesar but a very badly made head of the fourth or fifth century. The bust was without dispute modern, the head was fixed on to it, people began to call it Caesar and, as there was no statue

of him as far as anyone knew, the House of Casali thought
they had the rarest thing in the world. Albani promised to
show Wilton all the portraits and medals of Caesar in every
metal and he could judge for himself, but meanwhile he
would try to get the permission. He wrote a week later
enclosing the answer from Casali who, by an exceptional
favour, would allow the bust to be copied without its being
removed from its box or touched, but not otherwise.[26d] On
receiving this absurd suggestion Mann said Wilton would
tell those who had commissioned it that there had been a
misapprehension.[26e]

Wilton was still with Mann in 1754 and the latter said his
reputation had been enhanced by the works he had done,
particularly his *Venus*, and that he also had a copy of the
Apollo to make. It would be very difficult for him to get a
model or even a plaster cast, but he had heard that the architect Paul Posi had made a cast for the Abbé Farsetti, and
Mann asked Albani on Wilton's behalf to get one for him
from Posi.[9e] There ensued a most complicated transaction,
since the moulds were now packed up to be sent away from
Rome, but Paul Posi thought Farsetti had an old cast he
would sell cheap and had written to him at Venice. Farsetti replied that he had given the cast to Posi, and the latter
told Albani that he could name his price, being obliged to
the Cardinal for helping him with Farsetti's commission to
make casts of the best statues in Rome. Not wishing to
penalise him, Albani had tried, he said, to find out what it
had cost Farsetti, and as Posi thought about thirty Roman
crowns he left Mann to fix the price on this basis and to
give orders for the despatch of the cast if required.[12k] Mann
wrote in February 1754 to say that Wilton was delighted
and had asked his friend Vierpyle to call on Albani, find out
the price and look after the cast until his own arrival in
Rome in two or three weeks' time.[9f]

Simon Vierpyle, who did much work for Lord Charlemont, had already been recommended to Albani, Mann having written in February 1753 saying that the kindness with which His Eminence honoured those recommended to him excited the ambition of the young students in Rome to enjoy the honour of his protection, and Mr Vierpyle, a clever young sculptor, had begged him to obtain him this favour.[47a] In October 1754 Mann wrote again, to ask Albani to get for Vierpyle the loan of the gesso of a statue in the French Academy which he wanted to copy for a commission. Albani was doubtful of success, though promising to do all he could,[41b] and the result of this request does not appear in the correspondence.

By no means all the artists Albani and Mann introduced continued to feature in the letters which passed between them. Thus we hear no more about a young painter, Astley, presumably John Astley, who afterwards flourished greatly in England. Mann, recommending him in February 1750, said he had been with him for two years, and in spite of having paid a previous visit to Rome wished to return there for a few months to study drawing. For this purpose he was going to attach himself to Pompeo Battoni, and connoisseurs thought he had learnt the art of colouring so well that he could now apply himself wholly to drawing. He had rare application for one of his age and was a deserving young man of irreproachable manners.[48] Richard Wilson was another painter of whom we hear too little. Mann wrote in March 1752 saying that he had taken the liberty of adding Mr Wilson, a painter of merit, to the number of those who desired to have the honour of paying their court to His Eminence as their Protector and at the same time of the Arts and Sciences.[26e] Albani merely acknowledged this with his usual courteous promises to do all he could,[26f] and the evidence that he subsequently had quite a lot to do with Wilson comes from another source.[49] He commissioned paintings from him but they have not been traced nor proved to have been carried out. He said more to Mann about the architect William Chambers, for whom Mann wrote an introduction in January 1753.[47b] Mr Chambers, he said, was a well-born young man with many talents, particularly in architecture, which he was studying mainly from inclination since he was very comfortably off. He had been in Rome some years before when he was quite young, but his taste was taking him there a second time so that he could perfect himself in his art, continued Mann, and his greatest ambition was to have the honour of being known to His Eminence, the Protector of the Arts and Sciences. Albani replied that Mann knew how much he welcomed those recommended by him and especially when they were distinguished by such talents as was Mr Chambers, who had brought his letter.[12l] Albani was also pleased with Clérisseau, whom Mann introduced in February 1755, saying that he had entrusted to him a set of engravings by Gordon which he hoped Albani would accept as a present from himself, for he was delighted when he was able to obtain from London some trifle worthy of the Cardinal's attention.[35c] Albani subsequently employed, or planned to employ, Clérisseau to paint landscape decorations in his Villa (p. 202).

The painter Thomas Patch was brought to Albani's notice in less favourable circumstances. In October 1751 Mann told him that Patch, who had been in Rome some time and was making landscape drawings at Tivoli for Lord Charlemont, had been warned by the Bishop of Tivoli to leave his diocese on the grounds that a man not a professing Catholic was prohibited from remaining more than eight days in one place. Mann expressed surprise that there should be such a law, or if there were that it should be enforced, and asked Albani to look into the matter. Alessandro made enquiries from the Bishop, who gave no other reason than the one already stated and, he thought, had not seen fit to put forward any others though there might well be some.

As Patch, in an effort to regain the Bishop's favour, had sought the help of Monseigneur Maresfoschi, Cardinal Stuart's Auditor, and Belloni, the banker, who provided all the necessaries for the Pretender's household, Albani thought that the painter himself did not attribute the order of expulsion solely to a religious cause.[28c] He had certain Jacobite connections, his father having been surgeon to the Old Pretender at St Germain, but the fact that he had gone to Rome on foot with Richard Dalton[50] suggests that he was not himself identified with the Stuart cause, for Dalton, afterwards Librarian to George III, seems always to have been a most correct person and unlikely to have risked being associated with the wrong side. Albani supported the Bishop of Tivoli's attitude and was grateful when Mann acceded to his own request and told Lord Charlemont that the painter's bad conduct was to blame. In November 1755 Albani again had occasion to write to Mann about Patch, this time to say that he had been banished from Rome by the Inquisition and was going to Tuscany. The Cardinal did not really know why this order had been given, but imagined it was for some outrageous talk on the subject of women. Whatever it might have been, however, he could testify that all the time Patch had stayed in Rome he had done nothing to tarnish his honour.[51] He later thanked Mann for the welcome he had given the painter and felt sure that in his hands he would find himself compensated for his regret at leaving Rome.[21b] As a commentary on Patch's temperament it may be noted that in a caricature group painted in Florence he portrayed his own head attached to the bodies of a lion and a bull. The figure on the right of this picture is Horace Mann (Pl. 9).

Albani's championing of individuals, especially artists, whom he thought in any way unjustly oppressed, is one of the most pleasing features of his "protectorship" of British interests in Rome. We have already seen how he insisted

that Mann should obtain a bonus for Costanzi from the
Earl of Northumberland, and in 1751 he similarly begged
him to intervene with Lord Malton, whom Mann had introduced to him with a certain Major Forrester in October
1749.[17d] His Lordship, on his departure from Rome, had
ordered an *Antinous* in Carrara marble from the sculptor
Bartolomeo Cavaceppi, who had undertaken the work and
not left it until he had brought it to perfection. Having
finished it he heard that Malton no longer wanted it, on the
grounds that it was badly done and the marble very defec-
tive. The sculptor had begged Albani to go and look at the
work, and having done this he could assure Mann that no
other sculptor in Rome, nor perhaps anywhere else, could
have made a more beautiful thing, and as to the marble there
was no fault other than a rather large black patch on a thigh
of the statue. Mann knew, Albani continued, that the quar-
ries of Carrara no longer provided marble of such perfection
as formerly and that no piece was extracted now which was
not marked by stains. Even so, whatever defects the piece
in question might have had, it was not the sculptor's fault,
because he defied anyone to guess the stains hidden within
the stone. This, however, was not the point. What vexed
the sculptor was the bad opinion of him which his enemies
had instilled into Lord Malton. Albani asked Mann to write
to His Lordship saying that Cavaceppi had made him such a
statue as no one else could have done so perfectly, that it
was for him to decide whether he took it or left it, but that
he ought not to believe what had been written to him against
the sculptor. It was only a slander, started by those who
were angry at not being able to surpass or even equal him
in his profession.[29b] Mann, pointing out in his punctilious
way that Malton had now become the Marquis of Rockingham, promised to put the sculptor's case to him.[28d]

While Albani and Mann had been happily corresponding
on matters of art and the private affairs of English travellers,

rumours in Rome about the Old Pretender and his elder
son, and about politics generally, had been assuming an
increasingly serious and international character. Finally,
in May 1756, the reason for this became apparent, for a
Treaty, of which Albani was not at first told and in which
for a time he did not believe, was signed between the erst-
while bitter rivals, Austria and France. This heralded a
revolution in diplomacy and in the system of alliances which
had more or less preserved the balance of power in Europe
for so many years, and its immediate result was the outbreak of the Seven Years War. The association between
Albani and Mann, which had first arisen from the community of interests of the States they represented, was not
interrupted but was inevitably affected.

CHAPTER VII

Albani's Concerns during the Seven Years War

WHEN the policies of Austria and England began to diverge, Mann still trusted to Albani's personal co-operation in regard to information about the Stuarts. He wrote to the Cardinal saying that, as the enemies of England would now become active and it must be expected that the French would give the Young Pretender a part to play, he wanted someone to watch over the Jacobite Court in Rome and tell him what was going on there. Albani's kindness, he wrote, encouraged him to open his heart to him and seek his advice as to whether for a fixed sum of money a person could be found who would carry out this assignment faithfully. Albani agreed with Mann as to the Young Pretender's probable emergence, but thought that people in Rome would be the last to get news as he and his brother the Cardinal hated each other and were not likely to communicate, while the father could now have no influence. Rome's part in any plan could only be a financial one and as the Apostolic Chamber was overburdened there were no funds to spare. Any money spent on getting information from Rome would in these circumstances be wasted and Mann could rely on him to tell him of the slightest movements. On hearing that some of the Young Pretender's servants had come from France and were going to rejoin him, Mann still wished that some person in low life should be hired as a spy, but Albani discounted any significance in the servants' errand and again insisted that Mann could safely rely on him.[1a]

Alessandro, on this as on other occasions, did not want

176

it to be known that he was passing information to Mann about the Pretender, and the former promised to use it only with the greatest discretion. Possibly his attitude was dictated mainly by personal and family reasons. His brother Annibale was dead, but his nephew Cardinal Gianfrancesco Albani had been for some time the close friend of Cardinal Stuart with whom Alessandro himself was evidently on excellent terms. When in 1752 the Old Pretender had differences with his younger son, Alessandro spoke of Cardinal Stuart's trials in a manner which showed both sympathy and an intimate knowledge of the household at the Muti Palace. He said that James was jealous of servants whom he himself placed about his son and dismissed when they became at all closely attached to him. Albani thought that the Cardinal had to live under too close a constraint for a man of his age and rank but had no choice except an open rupture with his father. According to Stosch a ground of disagreement at one time was the particular friendship which developed between Henry Stuart and Gianfrancesco Albani, whom the Pretender suspected of having a bad influence over his son and of giving him bad advice.[2] Probably, in the peculiar social and political conditions of Rome, Alessandro regarded himself as a mediator rather than a spy and saw no treachery in his relations with the Stuarts, but whatever his motives there was certainly some excuse for a certain reserve in his attitude to Mann at this time. He admitted that it was difficult to foresee all the results of the Franco-Austrian Treaty and anticipated a cooling-off between the Courts of London and Vienna.[1b]

The position during the war was to be that France and Austria would fight together against Prussia, and England would send troops to the continent to help Prussia against the French, with whom she would be at war on the sea and overseas. She would not, however, declare war on Austria nor clash with her directly. Albani and Mann were not therefore involved in hostilities on different sides and Mann had been brought up, he told the Cardinal, to believe that the interests of their two Courts were too interdependent to be separated, and counted on the continuation of his goodwill.[1c] With all their political acumen, neither Minister at first appreciated the full significance of the rise of Prussia and its effect on the old political system.

In spite of the confidence Mann had expressed in Albani's goodwill there came a period in 1758 when Mann feared that the affairs of the times might be preventing the Cardinal from sending him news either from Rome or the outside world and complained that he was limiting his replies to thanks for the reports which Mann had sent him.[3a] He told Dodington that his correspondence with their good friend the Cardinal was reduced "to such a point as shews that it only owes its existence to that sort of personal friendship which a long habitude has contracted, though the difference of our situations and much more that of our inclinations with regard to public affairs makes it very difficult to carry it on weekly, as we have done for many years".[4] He protested to Albani that the events of the town in which one lived were a suitable and non-controversial subject, and was sure that His Eminence knew that the soul of a correspondence was the exchange of information about everything except what a man's duty to his State might prevent his writing.[3a] It is likely enough that Mann, quite apart from official requirements, enjoyed the prestige and the literary aspect of his intercourse with Albani as well as valuing the material they provided for his own letters to Horace Walpole.

Albani hastened to assure Mann that if he sent no news it was because he had none to send,[5a] and that his friendship and esteem for him were based on his personal merit and could never change.[3b] The present disagreements could probably have been settled without bloodshed, but events must be taken as they came without letting friendship be affected and he really was getting no news that was not in the public gazettes. Certainly, as the war progressed, Albani's reserve with Mann disappeared and they soon returned to their old frank exchange of news and views. Alessandro rejoiced with Mann at British successes against the French, and Winckelmann even said that he liked the Austrians to be beaten and frequently said: "*Benedetto il Re di Prussia*".[6a] This is the more remarkable since Alessandro reverted to the post of principal Minister to Maria Theresa in Rome after Cardinal Mellini died at the beginning of the war. In 1757 the Empress awarded him 8000 florins a year in recognition of his services and of the losses inflicted on him by the Court of Naples in the previous war.[7a]

Although Albani's correspondence with Mann continued virtually unabated, communication with Bubb Dodington was necessarily interrupted. Having resigned his post in November 1756, he was reinstated as Treasurer of the Navy in April 1757, only to be dropped again for good in the following June. Mann wrote on this occasion that he was dying with impatience to see if Dodington was to be included in the new Ministry, and Albani, who never seems to have perceived in his old friend the absurdities, and worse, pilloried by other contemporaries, remarked that if Dodington were left out he was inclined to think it would be by his own choice, disposed as he knew he was to relish a little tranquillity.[8a] On the occasion of his earlier resignation he had said he was sure Albani would agree with him on the desirability of an interval between life and death "*pour pouvoir se lever de table décemment et avec Reconnoissance à l'Auteur du Festin*",[7b] and Albani, on paper at any rate, took him at his word.

Dodington was raised to the peerage as Baron Melcombe in 1761, and Alessandro wrote to Mann expressing his pleasure at the advancement of one of the best friends he had in England, for whom he had infinite esteem. Even if there were not so many other reasons for wishing for peace, he said, a sufficient one for him would be that he would have the pleasure, after the troubles, of resuming his correspondence with Melcombe.[9a] In May 1762, feeling peace to be imminent, he did in fact resume it. The silence, he wrote, which he had so long observed in spite of his desire to be always in communication with Dodington, had been due merely to a just concern not to distract him from the heavy and serious occupations with which he was surrounded. The joy, however, which he had felt on hearing of the new dignity with which His Excellency had been clothed, made him brush aside every other consideration. He hoped that he would not find amiss the sincere and affectionate congratulations he made him and his wishes for the preservation of his life in the enjoyment of a long series of honours which, however great they were, would never exceed his merits nor fulfil his own desires for his friend.[10] Only three months later Alessandro heard of Melcombe's death and wrote to Mann saying that he could not have received more distressing news. The merit of such a man would long be remembered in his own country, but for himself his memory would never be effaced. Dodington had honoured him with the most sincere friendship, which he reciprocated, and the loss of such friends, now suffered so frequently, was a warning of the necessity of following them soon. The short time Dodington had enjoyed the title with which he had been so recently endowed was a reminder that everything the world gave was but a dream.[11]

Although the activities of patrons of the calibre of Lord Leicester, the Duke of Northumberland and Bubb Dodington were curbed by the Seven Years War, Albani still had plenty of contacts with Englishmen because many were now residing in Rome and travellers were still going there in considerable numbers. In 1756, for instance, Mann intro-

duced to him the "Chevalier Davers", Lord Rosebery and
two brothers called Pennant with their tutor, Mr Hall. He
referred to Lord Brudenell and other English gentlemen
who were returning from Malta, asked Albani to help Lady
Orford, of whom he seems to have seen a great deal, and
also a Mr Woodfall who wanted to popularise inoculation
against smallpox. Albani thought there was great prejudice
against the latter procedure in Italy but was impressed by
Woodfall's lively conversation about his profession and his
experiences in the Lisbon earthquake.[12] In 1757 Mann asked
for passports through Germany for the architect Robert
Adam and the draughtsman, Clérisseau, and introduced a
Mr Bruce and his companion Mr Stuart, who were described
as gentlemen of good family and much merit.[13a] In 1758 he
introduced Lord Mandeville and Colonel Otway,[3c] the
"Chevalier Windham" and Mr Devismes;[14a] in 1760 the
engraver Robert Strange; in 1761 Mr Morrice, who wanted
to see the Holy Week ceremonies,[15a] and Mr Richardson,
"un gentilhomme si accompli";[9b] in 1762 the Duke of Roxburgh,
Mr Smythe and Mr Henry;[16a] and in February 1763 Mr
Stephenson.[17]

In addition to those specifically introduced, several English travellers or residents were mentioned by Albani and
Mann in various contexts, for instance a certain Richard
Noakes, a clockmaker who had absconded from Rome with
valuables entrusted to him;[8b] Mr Vane, who had obtained
a dispensation to marry a Sienese and was rescued from a
"dishonourable match" by the payment of a good sum of
money to the girl;[18a] Lord Fordwich, whose letters Mann
forwarded and Mr Mytton to whom Albani sent a *"joyeau
en fer blanc"*.[19a] It is evident that by now Albani knew a
great number of Englishmen and, as many must have
arrived by sea and not by way of Florence, his acquaintance
was by no means restricted to those introduced by Mann,
and indeed never had been. There appears, for instance, to

have been no discussion between Albani and Mann about the American-born artist Benjamin West who, according to his biographer, Galt, arrived in Rome in July 1760. He had letters of introduction to the Cardinal and, besides visiting him, met him at the house of Mr Crispyné, an English gentleman who had long resided in Rome, in the company of "Mr Robinson, afterwards Lord Grantham". This account, purporting to be based on West's own reminiscences, suggests that the artist's visit made a considerable impression on Albani, who thought that as he came from America he must be an Indian and would be black.[20] There are, however, reasons for doubting many of the details of this story. It is possible that Albani was seeing so badly at this time that he ran his hands over West's head to ascertain its shape, but incredible that he was so naïve as to think West might have been coloured or had the education of a savage. The following footnote in Raimbach's *Memoirs and Recollections* (1843) may provide the clue: "It must be admitted that West's talk did not contribute any aid to his talents as an artist, but rather the contrary. His everlasting subject, himself, paraded with all the garrulity of old age, and abundantly adorned with those figures of speech designated slip-slop twaddle and rigmarole, was equally out of keeping both with his works and with the shrewd and intelligent expression of his countenance."[21]

Although Mann had pressed Albani to write to him about local matters in Rome, there was always extremely little trivial gossip about individuals in his letters and a great part of them was taken up with comments on exterior affairs. Therefore, unless Albani performed some particular service for artists who were of interest to Mann we hear very little about them, and his letters throw little or no direct light on their day-to-day activities in Rome and the work they did there. He must have seen a great deal of Robert Adam, both before and after that architect went to

Dalmatia,[22] but all that appears to have survived about this in the Albani–Mann correspondence is a reference to his and Clérisseau's passports. On 27th September 1757 Mann wrote to Albani saying that he had just received a letter from "Mr Adams", whom His Eminence had honoured with his protection during his stay in Rome. He had since been in the Ancient Illyria, where he had made drawings of the Palace of the Emperor Diocletian and of many other antiquities, which he proposed to publish. He had begged Mann to tell His Eminence of the success of his journey and at the same time to inform him that he was obliged to beg him to give him a passport through Germany to England, without which he was afraid he would encounter difficulties. If Albani would do him this favour he begged that the name of Clérisseau should be added, with that of a servant.[13a] Albani replied on 1st October that he was the most mortified person imaginable, having such a great desire to oblige Mann and Messrs Adam and Clérisseau, for whom he had great esteem, and finding himself totally unable to do what was asked in regard to a passport. Mann would understand well that in the present critical situation an English architect would not be well received in Germany, and as his object was to see the country and make drawings of whatever he thought most beautiful in the country, the slightest pencil line he drew would expose him to tiresome contretemps. He wrote again a week later saying that he thought Mann understood that it would not do for Adam to risk going during the fermentation which false rumours of the British Fleet had provoked in Germany, because even if the Imperial Court had never believed in them it was not the same with the populace, which was always the first to take alarm and the last to forget it.[13b] Mann, however, seems to have taken the military situation less seriously than Albani, and, after his refusal, told William Pitt, the Secretary of State, that he had obtained two passports from the Regency

Government in Florence although they had been accompanied by a message that it could not be answerable for the event.[23]

Robert Adam's brother, James, was in Rome in 1762, acquiring works of art and antiquities of all kinds for resale in England. On behalf of George III he bought from Alessandro Albani for 14,000 crowns the Cassiano dal Pozzo and Carlo Maratta collections of drawings which had come to the Cardinal through his uncle, Pope Clement XI, and which he had frequently in the past refused to sell.[22] Richard Gaven (who had now ennobled himself as de Gaven) offered to approach George III in the matter, and it seems likely that he had become known to influential men in England not only through art dealing but also through some kind of cloak-and-dagger activity. In a letter written to Albani from London in January 1761 he said that he would not have missed sending his respects by letter for four years if he had not been very far away and in a place where it would have been very risky for such letters to fall into the hands of enemies. If His Eminence wished to sell from his collection gold medals, engraved gems and the collection of drawings of great masters assembled by Carlo Maratta there might be an opportunity in a short time so advantageous that it would be inexcusable for him not to warn him in advance. It concerned, he said, a person of the highest rank in England who had shown a liking for the drawings of great masters, drew himself, liked medals and intaglios and would soon be in a position to satisfy his curiosity. He had the means of introducing these collections and the drawings in such a way that His Eminence could, it seemed to him, get more advantage than from any Prince in Europe. So if the Cardinal wished him to undertake it he flattered himself that he could be useful to him in the deal.[15b]

Although Gaven had thus prepared the ground Albani

showed great reluctance to sell when James Adam made him an offer in 1762, but he was persuaded to do so by his mistress, the Contessa Cheroffini, whose elder daughter by Albani was needing a dowry, and the drawings are now in the Royal collection at Windsor. The Contessa herself received a present of 500 crowns for her mediation[22] and some connoisseurs with long memories might have reflected that she was not the first of Albani's mistresses to influence the art market. The Marchesa Grimaldi, whose name de Brosses linked with the Cardinal's when he visited Rome in 1739 and 1740,[24] was cited by Stosch in 1743 as putting up the price of engraved gems and antique medals which she had taken to buying,[25] being herself no mean connoisseur.

We have already noted that after the failure of the Forty-Five Rebellion a certain Andrew Lumsden arrived in Rome (p. 144) and became the Pretender's assistant-secretary. His sister was the wife of the celebrated Scottish engraver, Robert Strange, who had himself fought on the Jacobite side at Culloden, though perhaps his zeal was always rather less than that of the family into which he had married. Strange had to flee to the continent and although his Jacobite connections must have hampered him at least at the outset of his career, they were also the cause of his studying in Paris under Le Bas and acquiring an informed taste for European painting which was to put him in the top class of reproductive engravers and bring him international fame.

Strange was able to return to London in 1750, and according to his biographer, Dennistoun, he then "imported from Rome through Mr Lumisden, a number of engravings after celebrated masters, either as commissions for friends or, as seems more likely, for general sale with a view to extend in England a taste for works of a high class. . . ." By 1755 he was contemplating a visit to Italy, and Lumsden wrote that he expected to have little difficulty in getting him full access to all the principal collections in Rome. In October 1760 Strange arrived in Florence, where he was extremely well received by Horace Mann, to whom he presented a copy of his works.[26a] Horace Walpole had written to Mann in May 1758 saying that he was going to give a letter for him to Strange the engraver who was about to visit Italy. "He is a very superior artist and by far our best," he wrote. "Pray countenance him, though you will not approve of his politics." [27a]

Even with Horace Walpole's introduction Mann's thoroughly cordial reception of Strange is a little surprising. In October 1758 Lumsden had left Rome mysteriously for a journey north, which was reported by Albani as being connected with the Pretender's business, although probably not of great significance. Mann at that time had forgotten the secretary's name and Albani told him it was "Lombs",[5b] but it seems unlikely that by 1760 the British representative had not ascertained the name correctly nor found out the family connection between Lumsden and Strange. Perhaps he just ignored it as being harmless, for the former was very discreet and normally did not visit strangers unless they showed a desire to see him.[26b] The landscape painter, John Skelton, wrote in 1758 expressing surprise that his having called on Lumsden should have led to rumours that he himself was a Jacobite. Many of the students, who were very loyal to King George, visited Lumsden and other gentlemen attached to the Pretender without its being taken any notice of, he said, although they had done it for many years as publicly as he had.[28] Anyway, Mann gave Strange an introduction to Albani, apparently without mentioning his politics, and asked him to give his protection to one of the cleverest draughtsmen and engravers who existed at present in Europe. The reputation he had made for himself in England as well as France, Mann said, gave the finest hopes that he would not be unworthy of His Eminence's protection. He was travelling solely to educate himself further and to choose certain of the most famous pictures to draw so that he could engrave them when he got back to England.[15a] When Albani received the letter from Strange he told Mann that the description of this virtuoso which it contained made him conceive the highest esteem for him and he had made him the most ample and sincere offers of his services in everything that could befall him during his stay in Rome.[9c]

Strange remained there for some time and had the distinction, apparently rather unusual for his compatriots, of being closely acquainted with the famous German scholar, Winckelmann,[29a] who had been librarian in Albani's town house since 1758. In 1763 Strange wanted to make a drawing of Guercino's *Circumcision* in the church of Jesus and Mary at Bologna, and Mann asked Albani to give him a letter to the Cardinal Legate there, so that he might get permission to have the picture taken down, as it was in so dark a place that it could not be copied where it hung. Mann thought it would be an advantage for the public and the convent to have it engraved by one as famous as Strange. His merits, Mann said, had brought him, in Rome and elsewhere, extraordinary favours and facilities so that he could enrich the public by his works. Strange, he continued, expected soon to have finished the copy of Correggio's famous picture at Parma, where the Duke had loaded him with honours and benefits and made him a present of a magnificent gold snuff-box. Strange, however, received an answer rather like the one given to Wilton by the Marquis Casali (p. 170). He was told that the Bologna picture could not be moved, that he could not put up his scaffolding till after Mass at midday and must take it away every evening, conditions which in fact amounted to a refusal. Mann dared not judge whether it would be proper to approach the Pope himself in the matter[30] but Albani told him that the difficulties

probably came, not from Cardinal Malvezzi who had
intimated them but from the nuns who owned the picture,
and that if the Pope wrote to the Cardinal the result might
be the same as before. Mann knew, Alessandro said, what
women's heads were like and veiled ones were even more
opinionated than the others.[31a] Strange then got Cardinal
Stuart as well to press Malvezzi, who invited him to dinner
and eventually obtained the nuns' co-operation. Malvezzi's
friendliness went even farther and Strange wrote to Lumsden saying that he generally spent his evenings with the
Cardinal and his niece. He had some difficulties with
Richard Dalton and the engraver Bartolozzi who were, it
seems, competing in the reproduction of certain famous
paintings,[26c] and he also fell foul of Jenkins. He thought the
latter had defrauded Lord Fordwich over a picture, and
Lumsden's observations carry some echo of the old rivalry
of Jacobite and Hanoverian antiquaries. By consummate
impudence, he said, joined to the honourable office of a
spy, Jenkins got himself recommended to many of the
English travellers.[26d] The dealer seems to have turned the
tables well and truly on the faction which had once tried to
persecute him for his anti-Jacobite views (p. 168). Both John
Skelton, to whom we have already referred, and another
young painter, James Russel, complained at different times
that Jenkins damaged their prospects by impugning their
loyalty to King George.[28]

Although Albani was still so active in helping English
travellers and artists, he had many other preoccupations in
addition to his ecclesiastical and official duties. He had, for
instance, never ceased to communicate with Stosch. The
Baron had lived in Florence ever since he had had to leave
Rome, had fallen in and out of trouble with authorities in
Tuscany or the Inquisition, badgered various prominent
Englishmen to get the British Government to pay him his
arrears, provided many shocking stories for Mann to retail

to Horace Walpole, and compiled his weekly screeds about the Jacobites' doings. He had also continued to deal in objets d'art and to add to his collections, and although hardly any of his or Albani's letters to each other are to be found in the Vienna archives it is evident from various references that they corresponded regularly. Stosch recommended to Alessandro in 1755 the German scholar Johann Joachim Winckelmann, whose fame as an antiquary and historian of ancient art became so great that Albani is now better known outside Italy as Winckelmann's patron than in any other context. It must also have been through Stosch that Albani got to know in Rome the Baron's nephew, Wilhelm Muzell, who became his heir and the correspondent and close friend of Winckelmann as indeed of Albani himself.

Alessandro wrote to Muzell in Florence in June 1757 congratulating him on his safe return to his uncle's house,[32] and in August they were corresponding again about some clothes which Muzell thought had been stolen from him in Rome. Albani replied in affectionate terms, saying that he feared their exchange of letters would be ended when the matter of the clothes was settled. In fact it was only just beginning. Stosch was at this time in one of the mysterious predicaments which recurred frequently during his troubled life and was once more threatened with banishment from Florence. Muzell begged Albani to persuade his uncle to go to Rome if political affairs required it, and the desire, he wrote, of being able to pay his own court assiduously to His Eminence was his principal motive for wishing it. Albani replied that he would take every opportunity of pressing Stosch on the point and on his own account would certainly do his best for Muzell, desiring nothing more than the pleasure of seeing him again. Muzell wrote back saying that his uncle was the most contented man in the world, never foreseeing the slightest trouble and when any came taking it as lightly as he could. As Stosch was of this way of thinking it was not only useless but was even rather inhumane to talk to him of an uncertain future and to mention foresight would be to strike him down. He would begin to reflect when the order to leave arrived but not a quarter of an hour sooner. Albani observed characteristically enough that one submitted more philosophically to misfortunes if one did not add to them remorse at not having taken precautions. If they then came despite everything one could do it was possible, he thought, to pass one's time well with a few books, a few antiquities and a little conversation, and be happier than in governing States.[8c]

A few months later Stosch was dead. Mann told Albani on 1st November 1757 that he had been seized with an *"assoupissement"* which looked like having serious consequences, and Muzell also wrote the Cardinal an alarming account of his uncle's condition and of the remedies employed. On Monday, at supper, he said, he had noticed that he was very troubled and that memory failed him several times. He had asked him if he felt ill and he said no, but that he had been very sleepy all the evening. On Tuesday morning Muzell had sent for a surgeon who persuaded him, after some resistance, to consent to have himself bled. This almost certainly, Muzell thought, had prevented an apoplexy; his uncle had awoken as though from a deep sleep and had even been able to write a little letter to Albani, though with great difficulty. On Wednesday his memory had much deteriorated and he had talked with difficulty and without continuity. They had put four blisters on him, and on Thursday morning he had been much better, but by Friday evening he had grown a good deal worse, almost speechless and very drowsy. They had put a blister on the nape of his neck, which had comforted him greatly, but on Saturday evening he had been so bad that Muzell had sent for a doctor during the night, and as he was still worse on the Sunday morning the doctors had ordered an emetic. Muzell's account then seems to cover another week during which Stosch had lost his memory and, after the Friday, his speech, but did not appear to suffer and got up at his usual time. On the Saturday evening he had come to table but been so ill that his nephew thought he would die there. He did not wish to take anything nor do anything that the doctors ordered, and when they prescribed *sassaparilla* he closed his mouth with both hands and it was only after extreme effort that in the end they made him swallow a cup. Albani, Muzell said, could readily judge the anxiety he felt and he would not fail to send him news by the French courier.

Albani was greatly concerned at Stosch's illness, which had also been reported to him by Mann, and thanked Muzell for not concealing its seriousness from him. Interested as he was in the preservation of a man for whom he had so much friendship and esteem, he wrote to Muzell on 5th November, he suffered great anxiety on his account and would be most grateful for news. He expected it to be better following the bleeding, which had been done in time, and the other remedies, but above all he hoped for improvement from Muzell's attempts to make Stosch more obedient to the doctor's orders. He added that these sorts of ills were not treated with *sassaparilla* but with *Cornachina* powder and vesicants, and the doctor should be given a hint of this. Stosch, however, died on 6th November at 7.30 p.m., before Muzell received Albani's advice, and his end was described by his nephew. On the evening of 4th November, there had been every hope of improvement, but at midnight on the 5th the catarrh on the chest had increased considerably as well as the fever. Towards the morning of the 6th he had become completely unconscious, while the lower belly swelled a lot and by the matter he had vomited it was evident that he had a prodigious inflammation of the intestines. He had died without any return to consciousness and

without pain, Muzell thought. He had lost an uncle, or
rather a father and friend, whom he cherished greatly, and
if Stosch had lived longer he himself would no doubt have
profited by his knowledge and would have hoped to some
extent to replace him. Albani would be fully convinced that
he had neglected nothing to save him, but what could the
frivolous arts of men do against the hand of the Almighty?

Muzell then proceeded to tell Albani that Stosch had by
his Will left a fragment of red Egyptian marble to him as a
souvenir and he begged permission to send it to him. He
would also, he said, send him a copy of the Will under which
he was required to give up his own name and take his
uncle's with his arms and everything. Muzell hoped this
step would allow him to receive from Albani the kindness
which he had so generously promised, and His Eminence
could be assured that his own respectful attachment to him
had been increased by his uncle's death. He would have to
sell a great part of the collections, and begged to be recommended to the protection of His Imperial Majesty, a favour
which he would also seek from Marshal Botta. That morning he had sent the embalmed body of the deceased to
Leghorn, where he hoped to have an honourable epitaph
put up to him.[13c]

The harassed Muzell-Stosch, as we will now call him,
whose inheritance included no ready money,[33] found himself in great difficulties even though Mann exerted himself
strenuously on his behalf. By pleading Stosch's employment
by a foreign Court Mann hoped to get his estate exempted
from the tax of $7\frac{3}{4}$ per cent on the value demanded by the
Tuscan Government,[13d] but did not succeed. An edict had
been made in 1754 prohibiting the export of antiques from
Tuscany without the consent of the Regency, and Albani
thought this would be difficult to obtain, though he agreed
to approach Marshal Botta on the matter. In the meanwhile
he advised Muzell-Stosch to get his collections catalogued

CARICATURE GROUP, SHOWING HORACE MANN ON THE RIGHT
Painting by Thomas Patch, c. 1763

THE VILLA ALBANI

so that he might invite other offers in case the Emperor, who had been given the first refusal of everything, did not wish to purchase. He would himself, he said, suggest to the Pope that he might buy the great *Atlas* of Rome, but it was essential to have a proper list to show him. Albani was also interested in certain engraved gems, but Muzell-Stosch hoped to sell the collections as a whole, either to the Emperor or elsewhere, and was not in a position to accept individual offers. He also wished to keep any prospectus secret from those concerned in assessing the tax[13e] and through delay and indecision for which he can hardly be blamed he missed an excellent opportunity either of selling part of the *Atlas*, at least, outright to the Pope, or of getting from him a firm offer which could have been used to hasten the Imperial reply. The matter dragged on, and when in 1761 Albani was appointed Librarian of the Vatican he was unable to reopen the deal. No one, he said, wished more than he did to enrich the Vatican Library with the collection of maps, but there were not sufficient funds and the Apostolic Chamber was overburdened. The taste for beautiful and good things was languishing, and indeed Muzell's claims, he said, were too high.[34] The whole *Atlas* eventually did go to Vienna, where it is now divided between the Albertina and the geographical section of the National Library. It consisted of more than three hundred volumes, and among its treasures was a duplicate of a valuable set of drawings of Rome which had been commissioned by the King of Portugal and lost in the Lisbon earthquake. A short description of the *Atlas* was attached to Winckelmann's catalogue of Stosch's engraved gems, to which Muzell-Stosch contributed an interesting preface.

Winckelmann went to Florence in 1758 to prepare this catalogue, which was dedicated to Albani and published in 1760. In spite of such powerful advertisement the famous collection hung fire and some of it was sold piecemeal before

Frederick the Great of Prussia bought the bulk of it for a price which included a life annuity for Muzell-Stosch. Part at least of the collection of sulphur impressions, which once numbered 28,000, was acquired by the Scotsman James Tassie, who used them extensively for making the fine reproductions in which he,[35] and subsequently his nephew William Tassie, did a large trade. William left some 20,000 reproductions and sulphur impressions, presumably including many of Stosch's, to the Board of Manufactures, Edinburgh, and they are now in the National Portrait Gallery there. The extent to which engraved gems were copied was indeed the reason for this attractive and once aristocratic branch of collecting falling into disrepute. It became impossible to distinguish old copies, often very valuable as being the only versions of lost originals, from modern ones made either in good or bad faith, and what part Stosch took in making and trading fakes it is impossible to say. Equally mysterious is his possession of manuscripts, which Cardinal Passionei bought after his death for the Vatican and which were found in the following century to have come from there in the first place.[36] Other of Stosch's manuscripts were sold with his printed books at public auction in Florence, and in time the whole of his collections dispersed.[37]

While Winckelmann was in Florence Cardinal Archinto, who had been his patron and given him rooms in the Cancelleria, died suddenly and Albani stepped in with an offer to Winckelmann of quarters in his palace and a salary as curator of the great library which had come to him from Pope Clement XI.[29b] Albani, with his customary generosity, allowed Winckelmann to remain on in Florence after his expected time of return to Rome, to complete the work. Muzell-Stosch asked no favour, he said, in desiring him to leave the Abbé Winckelmann with him until he had finished the catalogue of his uncle's gems, which was so well advanced. He knew too well the importance of the work and the advantage it would be to the Republic of Letters, to deflect him from it.[14b] By October 1759, however, Winckelmann had finished and was installed in Albani's palace in Rome. His patron apologised for him to Muzell-Stosch for not answering letters. He was very well, he said, but too busy visiting ruins in the town to find a moment in which to write. He would, however, be a more punctual correspondent in future, when the season did not allow of such delicious outings as did October.[18b]

The young Muzell-Stosch, who seems to have had considerable charm and was greatly befriended by Mann, went to England in July 1760 with his introduction to Horace Walpole. The latter asked Mann whether he had come to sell his uncle's collection, and wanted to know on what footing he was to introduce him into society, when he returned from a three months' stay he was going to make with a clergyman in Yorkshire to learn English. In October 1760 he wrote that Muzell-Stosch was settled at Salisbury and wanted to be recommended as a travelling governor or companion, but, said Walpole, who travels now? He left England in August 1761,[27b] evidently having made good use of his opportunities to learn English and become acquainted with influential connoisseurs, for on 26th February 1761 he was proposed and on 16th April elected an Honorary Fellow of the Society of Antiquaries.[38a] Muzell-Stosch went to Constantinople with the Ambassador, Henry Grenville, as mentioned by Thomas Hollis at a meeting of the Society on 25th March 1762, presumably in some minor diplomatic post. Grenville, after complaining of boredom in Constantinople, wrote of him: "Our best, indeed our only possession here, which sweetens our days, is our amiable friend Stosch." Mann would know, he said, his engaging qualities, his personal merit and worth, and could therefore judge what a treasure he must prove in a country where, with all respect to the Corps Diplomatique, he scarce knew the man amongst them he could suspect of being gentleman, still less an agreeable companion. He could assure Mann without the least suggestion of flattery that Muzell-Stosch was an acquisition in all respects so valuable and estimable that to be deprived of him would be to render their situation there beyond all expression insupportable.[31b] Mann's great concern for Muzell-Stosch's welfare may not have been due solely to friendship. He hoped, fruitlessly as it turned out, to add the late Baron's emoluments to his own,[33] and probably a speedy settling up of his estate would be to his advantage.

Muzell-Stosch's election to the Society of Antiquaries was almost contemporaneous and evidently connected with that of Winckelmann on 9th April 1761. The latter was so proud of this distinction that he had the list of members framed and hung it in his room, and in June 1761 the Society discussed a letter from him to Muzell-Stosch in London. In it he proposed that he should send him for the Society "a short Sketch of his Eminence Cardinal Alexander Albani's Villa; a description of which, from several hints given in Mr Stosch's Letters, the Abbé found he was desirous of obtaining". The description was to be communicated in three parts, (1) The Villa, its Buildings and Ornaments; (2) Observations on works of Egyptian, Etruscan and Grecian Artists, their Statues and Relievos, in the Villa; (3) Works of other ancient artists in the Villa.[38b] The second part was to be communicated first, and duly arrived, but unfortunately the others never followed.

The admission of Alessandro Albani himself to the Society followed closely upon that of his protégés Winckelmann and Muzell-Stosch. His nomination was proposed on 21st May 1761 in the following terms: A Testimonial was presented and read, recommending His Eminence Cardinal Alexander Albani to be elected an honorary Fellow of this

Society, of which he is said to be desirous, and from his high Rank, distinguished Abilities, and Affection to the British Nation, which has remarkably appeared by his Civilities to British Travellers, and Artists at Rome, is certified as likely to prove a most useful and valuable Member. Signed by J. Parsons, H. Baker, E. M. da Costa, T. Tyndale, T. Hollis, M. Duane, W. Norris. He was duly elected on 19th November 1761, and even though, as Muzell-Stosch pointed out, the Secretary did not give him his correct title of *"Ementissimo Principe"*, the Cardinal was reported to be "extreamely proud of being a Member of the Academy".[38c] William Norris, Secretary of the Society, notified Albani in Latin of his election as a Fellow and the Cardinal replied similarly. The translation of his letter is recorded in the Society's Minutes: "Sir," he wrote, "What would have been extremely agreeable to me could I have presumed so far, the Courtesy of the Society of Antiquaries of London have effected, by electing me, as I understand from your Letter, as a Fellow of their Body. I set so high a Value upon this signal Favour, that I can scarce find Words to express the Gratitude I feel upon the Occasion. However that I might not be totally silent, where Words fall short of my Intention, I return you, Sir, infinite Thanks and beg you will pay the like Compliments for me to the Members of the Society, who have thought so honourably of me as to elect me into their Body, and assure them I shall omit no opportunity that shall offer, of making due Returns to the Favour they have done me. In the mean time I earnestly pray God to preserve you, and grant you a long and happy Life." [16b]

Albani had earned this gratifying recognition of his services while the war was still going on and the number of English visitors somewhat reduced. When peace came he was to have even greater opportunities of serving them, and he had been gradually creating a new background against which his hospitable activities should in future be visualised. In October 1753 he had told Mann that the Pope had done him the honour of visiting a vineyard which he had outside the town and had shown approval of the buildings he was erecting there.[39] He must have been speaking then of his new Villa at the Porta Salaria, and in 1755 he enquired from Mann the price of obtaining a large quantity of lead from England for his buildings. Mann was not encouraging in view of the length of time it would take to come and the risk of war, and after he had ascertained the price of lead from Leghorn, Albani decided it was cheapest after all to get it from Civita Vecchia.[40] After this episode it is rather curious that Albani apparently told Mann so little about the progress of his Villa, particularly as he was complaining in 1760 of a shortage of material for their correspondence and could only suggest that Mann should make more calls on his services as a means of providing some.[9d] He did, however, tell him of a fire in his town palace which had destroyed silver and porcelain vessels, all his table linen and tapestries and carpets which he had collected for the Villa Salaria. He consoled himself that no one had been killed and that the fire had been dealt with in time to prevent the whole palace perishing, of which at one time there had been evident danger.[5c]

To replace his china Albani asked Olivier Hope at Rotterdam to get him from the East a service of twenty covers. He could not touch Saxony china because it had become so dear, and while unwilling to forgo giving his friends a meal he did not want to incur great expense in serving them on porcelain.[41] The value and acceptability of the gifts Dodington and Forbes had sent him thus became apparent, for fine china was still scarce in Europe. Olivier Hope was a member of an influential family of oriental merchants who traded from Holland and whose fortunes, in the next generation, financed the great art collections of Thomas

Hope of Deepdene. Albani corresponded at times both with Olivier and Jean, and the former visited him in Rome in 1760. He struck a bad bargain in antique busts with the Baron Han, alias d'Hancarville, and Albani tried to extricate him, although he thought poorly of the prospects of getting satisfaction from such a man as the Baron.[19b] In 1766 Alessandro reopened the acquaintance by writing to Jean at Amsterdam for some "*calancas*" of the best kind to make dressing-gowns for his niece, the Countess of Potenza, and her daughter-in-law. One should have a white or gaily coloured ground for a very young lady, the other a darker one suitable for a modest taste. His confidence in Hope's judgment was not misplaced, for the stuffs he chose were, according to Albani, "*du dernier bon goût*". One had crimson flowers with green stalks on a dark ground, the other a large pattern of delicious little flowers on a ground of white with pale blue stripes, and Albani, who would go to endless trouble to please his friends, was evidently quite delighted.[42]

The architect of the Villa was Carlo Marchionne (1702–86), and the building seems to have been spread over a long period, although inscriptions both on the main block and the so-called "*Café*" give the date as 1757. It must have been virtually complete in 1761 when Albani replied to a letter from Richard Gaven, who had offered him some Dresden china and pointed out that it would become very rare now that war had closed the factory. He suggested that he might like to buy it or exchange some antiques for it, but the Cardinal refused. Having, he said, especially built a house outside the town, so as to put all his marbles there and everything he had in the way of antiques, he was simply not in a condition to sell the smallest item of his belongings and since Gaven saw his collection he had added to it some of the best things he had found. He would understand that he did not buy in order to sell, and that if he bought no more it was because his finances had been much diminished by the ruinous expenditure he had incurred, and would continue to incur yet for several years on his house. Perhaps some of Gaven's compatriots who had been to Rome had spoken to him of it because they all did him the honour of coming to see it.[15c]

The Villa stands in its own grounds just outside the Porta Salaria on the north-east side of Rome, but is unfortunately now backed by other buildings instead of a beautiful countryside. It faces south-east to a formal garden of clipped trees, hedges and statuary closed at the end by the semi-circular arcade of the "*Café*" and is set on a plinth from which twin ramps lead down into the garden. The main block is of two stories, the ground floor consisting only of a loggia of nine bays, arcaded and vaulted, running the whole length of the façade and occupying about half the depth of the villa from front to rear, the remaining space being accounted for by stairs on the left and a chapel on the right. The piano nobile is approached by a plain stone staircase with a wrought-iron ramp, the height of the fine downstairs loggia making the climb considerable. The oval entrance hall and a rectangular gallery occupy the centre of the block with smaller rooms opening out of them or of each other on either side. Some rooms were designed to display sculpture, of which much remains, and have reliefs such as the celebrated *Antinous* let into the walls. Others with the walls left plain must have been intended for the display of pictures and hangings. Many of the rooms have ceilings and walls painted with landscapes by Paolo Annesi, grisailles by Niccola Lapiccola and mythological scenes by Antonio Biccheriari.[43] The latter, at least, was in Albani's employment by 1756, for in April of that year Alessandro asked Mann to find a job in something like the Customs for a young man called Bicchierari, son of a painter who was working for him. He had to leave Rome because he had dangerously wounded a man in a quarrel.[1d]

The principal room was the great gallery, and for this Raphael Mengs painted a *Parnassus* which had considerable fame but is harsh in colouring and harmonises poorly with the magnificent work in walls, doorcases and window-frames. These are encrusted with antique reliefs and mosaics, variegated marbles and marble composition or scagliola in splendid gilt-bronze mounts. Although the whole effect is extremely rich there is a lightness and brightness about the room which probably reflects Albani's own exquisite taste. It is elsewhere apparent in the choice of antique fragments, which are combined with work of his own period to produce subtle effects of colour and texture. However deplorable from a purely antiquarian point of view such a use of Roman works of art may seem, the charm of the gallery is irresistible, and it is easy to appreciate why English visitors particularly were so impressed. In England, as in the Villa Albani, the tendency was to temper the ancient and modern styles of Rome with a certain neatness and gaiety.

It is impossible to say how much Albani influenced architectural fashion in England, for Robert Adam and some of his contemporaries were quite sufficiently original, and the taste of their patrons quite sufficiently formed by the contemplation of ancient sites, for it to have developed in the same way without Albani. Possibilities of influence can be pressed too far, and although Adam was in contact with the Cardinal when the Villa was being completed it need not be taken for granted that the transmission of ideas was unilateral. The Scotsman may well have contributed some. Perhaps it is enough to observe that in Britain, too, some of the very grandest patrons used genuine antiques to give the key for decorative schemes, the verde antico columns in the ante-room at Syon and the lion mosaic in the overmantel of the library at Holkham being striking examples.

The main block is flanked by loggias containing sculpture,

the one on the right joining the *"Bigliardi"* which has a
ceiling attributed to Bicchierari. This is a long narrow room,
the walls inlaid with veined, grey-and-white marble, varied
by niches containing statues on pedestals and, at the two
ends, verde antico columns with cornices above. The
"Café" at the end of the formal garden is a semi-circular
arcaded loggia containing antique statues. It has one rectangular room opening out of the centre with painted
decoration attributed to Annesi and Lapiccola, an antique
mosaic floor and two particularly fine antique mosaics let
into plinths. Clérisseau was to have filled the larger spaces
with views of Dalmatia and Baia,[6b] but nothing in the room
now answers to this description. The buildings are said to
have been in poor condition when the property was bought
by Prince Torlonia in 1866, and although the fabric of the
Villa and much of the decoration must be substantially as
Albani left it the restorations may have been fairly extensive.
A Latin inscription both on the main block and the *"Café"*
states that Albani built them in 1757 and that Torlonia restored them in 1871. The Villa was pillaged in the Napoleonic
Wars, and although many of the 294 statues removed to
Paris were subsequently replaced a certain number is known
to have been dispersed. Alessandro bequeathed the property
to his great-nephew, from whom, through marriage, it
eventually descended to the Castelbarcos. Prince Torlonia,
whose descendant owns it and keeps it in such excellent
condition, bought it from that family.[44]

It is something of a mystery how Albani ever managed to
stay in the Villa, as he is known to have done for forty-five
to fifty days every year, and still less how he put up distinguished guests.[31c] The *"Bigliardi"* may have been a dining-
room and the basement below it used for service, but the
whole place appears to have been designed primarily for the
display of statuary and other works of art and for receptions and brief outings from Rome. It is all surprisingly

small and neat, *"ein helles, heiteres, reiches Schlösschen"* as Justi called it, and an engraving of it by Piranesi distorts both its proportions and its character. Lady Miller, an Englishwoman who visited it in 1770 or 1771 and described it as a small palace rather than a Villa, evokes it more sympathetically. What charmed her much, she said, was the elegant order in which all was kept, joined to the most exquisite and universal cleanliness.[45]

CHAPTER VIII

Albani's Golden Age

IN February 1763 Maria Theresa signed a peace treaty
with the King of Prussia and the general pacification of
Europe followed. Albani said that posterity would be as-
tonished to see that, although millions of men had been killed
and millions of money spent, peace had been made without
any one of the parties gaining an inch of territory. Those
people who regarded war as one of the means Providence
made use of to punish the wickedness of men would not
however be surprised, he added.[1a] A few months later
Mann gave Albani the exciting news that the Duke of York,
brother of George III, was contemplating a tour of the
Mediterranean with the squadron commanded by Captain
Hervey. His Royal Highness, under the name of the Earl of
Ulster, would come from Leghorn to Florence, where he
expected to stay two months and then would go to Naples
for rather longer.[2a] This feeler had upon Albani exactly the
effect which no doubt Mann intended it should. The Cardinal replied by return of post that it seemed to him strange
that the Prince did not intend to see Rome if he was going
to Genoa, Leghorn and Naples. Had he so intended he
would himself have very much liked Mann to put him in a
position to show his respect.[1b]

Mann was probably already satisfied that on the Duke's
side no awkwardness would arise through the presence in
Rome of the Old Pretender and his son the Cardinal, who
also used the title of Duke of York. Major Richard Phelps,
Secretary at Turin, had written to Mann the previous
November reporting a conversation which he had had that
summer with the Duke, who had asked him what sort of a

man his namesake in Rome was, Phelps having seen much
of him. On Phelps telling him his true sentiments towards
both the brothers the Duke had replied: "Well, for the eldest
I heartily pity him and as for my Brother Duke England is
obliged to him, for he has done more to extinquish his
party by putting on the Cowle than could have been effected
by putting to death many thousands of their deluded
followers." [3] The fact that the Duke would travel incognito
would prevent any difficulties over procedure and precedence in Rome and the Old Pretender himself was so ill
that the Muti Palace had ceased to have any social importance. Mann had indeed written to England in May 1763
saying that the old man still held out, but that his death could
now interest the public in no other light than that of curiosity to see what effect it would produce on his elder son. [4a]
The awkward fact remained, however, that England had no
official diplomatic relations with the Holy See as had been
the case long before James Stuart's arrival in Rome and
still would be after his death. The approach therefore could
only be indirect and the ground was very carefully prepared
in a brisk exchange of letters.

Mann told Albani that he did not know what route the
Duke would take in Italy, but if it depended on him he
would persuade him to go by Rome, a town worthy of everybody's interest, and in any case he would not fail to make
known to His Royal Highness and elsewhere the benevo-
lent sentiments towards himself for which he would be very
grateful. [2b] Albani said that no one was in a better position
than he to offer the Duke a lodging by no means unworthy
of receiving him, a little distance from the walls of the town.
Having no doubt sounded Pope Clement XIII meanwhile,
he told Mann a week later that if the Duke wanted to stay
in Rome the Government and Court there would feel
bound to pay him all the honours due to his rank in spite
of the incognito he wanted to keep so strictly, and that

individuals would follow the example of the papal Court in showing that the difference of religion did not make them admire the less the rare qualities with which the Almighty had endowed him.[1c] The Pope's answer, it should be observed, stressed the old religious cleavage as a bar to normal official relations, rather than the more recent one of having a rival King of England in Rome, and its implications would not have been lost on Mann. Albani was also concerned about selecting an expert to show the Duke round Rome and said that no one was more likely to acquit himself so well of the task as Jenkins. He was a young Englishman who was perhaps known to Mann, had all the talents for serving the Duke well and the advantage over all the other competitors that he was born a subject of His Britannic Majesty.[1d]

Mann communicated to Lord Halifax, now Secretary of State, Albani's assurances and offers, with the additional news that the Nuncio at Florence had been instructed to wait upon His Royal Highness with similar courtesies as soon as he arrived there. He added the not irrelevant item that the Old Pretender was so ill that his physicians thought he could not hold out long.[5] In November 1763 Mann was able to convey King George's approval of Albani's suggestion for the Duke's visit and the Cardinal wished for nothing with more passion, he said, than the honour of showing the royal guest his respect.[1e]

The Duke arrived in Florence in March 1764 and Mann told Lord Halifax that the Nuncio had paid him especial attention, and by order from Rome had offered for his use there a house belonging to Duke Strozzi. The Grand Prior Corsini, who had been to England, and Prince Borghese had been informally appointed to attend him and it was going to be difficult, Mann thought, for him to preserve his strict incognito, as the Pope meant to give him a fine present and many of the nobility were preparing to entertain him.[6a] The Duke did, however, refuse Albani's and Strozzi's offer of quarters, and Mann arranged for him and his suite to lodge with a merchant, Barazzi, who had been to London and was well known to the English. Albani, meanwhile, had written again suggesting that the Duke might like someone to give a learned commentary on what Jenkins showed him and in that case the Abbé Winckelmann, who was well known to Mann as Antiquary to the Apostolic Chamber and to himself, was unquestionably the best qualified to satisfy the views and the curiosity of the Prince.[1f]

Albani wrote on 21st April to say that the Duke had arrived the previous Sunday and had delighted him by his gracious reception when he called. Although the ecclesiastical duties of Holy Week had prevented his seeing him often he would be receiving His Royal Highness at his Villa the next day and the following Tuesday.[6b] The latter visit, mentioned with such studied casualness by Albani, was to be for the purpose of attending a wonderful party which the Abbé Giordani, a correspondent of Mann's, described to him in glowing terms. "Yesterday," he wrote on 25th April,* "the Cardinal gave for him a magnificent ball at his country house outside the Salaria Gate. His Royal Highness was pleased with the music with which the party began, and the ball which ended it. He stayed until past midnight and everyone went on dancing until three hours after midnight. I assure you that it would be difficult to see in Rome a more brilliant party, both on account of the Great Prince who attended it and the order and magnificence of the house, than which there is no other richer nor in better taste in all Italy." [1g] Albani himself told Mann only that His Royal Highness had done him the honour of accepting a little entertainment at his house outside the Salaria Gate, and the next day had attended a very magnificent one at the

* In French in the original.

Corsinis'. The Duke of York, however, did not fail to do him justice for the party he had given for him at his Villa where, he said, His Eminence had assembled whatever Antiquity had produced that was most beautiful, joined to the most delicate taste and the greatest magnificence.[7]

The Pope had also honoured the Duke, sending him on arrival a present of eatables and drinkables as from Corsini and Borghese, having refreshments prepared for him when he visited the papal palace at Monte Cavallo, giving him a sturgeon and a number of citrons and, on departure, a picture in mosaic, another in tapestry, and a whole collection of prints (very finely bound) containing everything of that nature that was esteemed in Rome.[6c] Giordani told Mann that the Pope, in an interview with a cardinal, had said that he would be delighted to see so respected a Prince in Rome, that in his heart he recognised as King of England the one who reigned in London, though in appearance the one who lodged at the Santi Apostoli, and that when he had need of anything for the Catholics of his country he wrote to the King of Sardinia to ask the King of England for it, as he was obliged to render the honours due to the Pretender's birth.[1h]

The Duke of York's visit to Rome coincided with that of the charming Georgiana, Lady Spencer, whom Albani called the most accomplished lady in the world. She placed in the Duke's hands the present Albani made him of a gold snuff-box, in which was mounted a cameo of the greatest beauty, and because of its antiquity of an inestimable price. His Royal Highness said, as quite possibly Albani hoped he would, that it was so precious he would give it to the King of England, and Alessandro afterwards thanked Mann for sending it on with such recommendations as would ensure its acceptance.[1i]

Soon after she got back to England Lady Spencer got a letter from Albani saying that he was sending her a vase

THE LOGGIA, VILLA ALBANI

THE GREAT GALLERY, VILLA ALBANI

in transparent alabaster which he had had made for her, as she had expressed a wish to have one like those at his own country house. He begged her to tell him if there were anything else he could get for her and to remember him to the Duke of York when she saw him.[8a] Lady Spencer wrote a graceful letter of acknowledgement in French. What expressions could she use, she said, to make Albani understand the extent to which she felt herself honoured by the present she was going to receive from him? Every expression being inadequate she must leave it to His Eminence to appreciate that it would be impossible for anyone to be more struck than she by this mark of his regard. It was true that during her stay in Rome she had continuously enjoyed a series of attentions and very obliging courtesies on His Eminence's part, but she did not expect such a present. She was extremely impatient for it to arrive, and the vase, while giving her infinite pleasure by its beauty would at the same time enable her to have the honour of boasting of it as coming to her from the hands of His Eminence, and to show as a small example of the distinguished taste which so brilliantly marked the collections from antiquity with which his country house was filled. When she had the honour of seeing the Duke of York she would not omit to obey His Eminence's commands in regard to him. She did not know, she continued, if this country could produce anything which would please him, but if there were she hoped he would do her the honour of assuring himself that no one would be more charmed than she to execute whatever the commission might be with all the precision of which she was capable.[9a] Albani replied in equally courtly terms, belittling the value of his present and protesting his wish to give her pleasure.[8a] It is thirty inches high, of beautiful workmanship and is still in Earl Spencer's possession at Althorp.

In February 1765 Albani was hoping to see a very different kind of tourist. Mann announced that John Wilkes, who had been obliged to leave England as a result of Parliament's condemnation of the alleged libel he had published in the *North Briton* in 1763, was expected to pass through Rome on his way to Naples.[9b] Albani told Mann he was full of curiosity to see Wilkes, because although, he said, one could not from the build of the body judge much of the qualities of the soul it was always satisfactory to be closely acquainted with a person who had made such a stir, whether for good or ill. He did not know if the Court of Naples would long retain in its capital such a volatile person, who could still by his persistence in his view and by his headstrong way of never keeping his mouth shut about what he thought, embarrass it in relation to the Court in London.[10a] Mann wrote shortly afterwards to say that Wilkes had started for Rome furnished with a letter for Winckelmann, so that the latter could procure him the honour of being presented to His Eminence. He spoke from hearsay, he said, because his position did not allow him to meet Wilkes, but Albani would find him highly vivacious, very knowledgeable and, except on the subject of affairs in England, very amiable.[9c]

Albani looked forward to meeting Wilkes and reporting on him to Mann, but in the end his loyalty to the British representative triumphed and he added a postscript to his letter in which he said that in spite of all his desire to see him he would not receive him in his house as he was in disgrace with Mann's Court, for which he had so much veneration. He would, however, meet him at the house of a third party or perhaps at his own in the country. His plan failed, to his own great disappointment and ours. In spite, he wrote, of his wish to see Wilkes he had had to do without the pleasure because, having promised himself that he would meet him on neutral ground, namely his country house, Wilkes had gone there at a time when the rain fell in such abundance that Albani was not able to go. As he had now proceeded to Naples it was from there that there would next be news of him, unless past events induced him to keep quiet, as they should. According to what Winckelman had told him, Albani said, Wilkes had left in very beautiful company. Giordani amplified this a little, saying that Wilkes, unlike his compatriots who so loved antiquities, had stayed so briefly in Rome that he had not withdrawn his baggage from the Customs. He had gone to Naples with a beautiful dancer or singer and another woman who called herself her mother. All the English except Lord Bute's son had visited him, he added.

In June 1765 Albani told Mann that the woman whom Wilkes took round with him had not only left him but had escaped without his knowledge, taking all his money, effects and, what was more, his papers. No one doubted, said Albani, that the Court had done this and that material for distinguishing good from bad patriots would be found among them.[10b] Mann replied that Wilkes' companion had left him simply because their temperaments were incompatible and that the Government could have no interest in any documents he had with him,[11] drawing from Albani the rather disappointed rejoinder that it would always be a great advantage to discover them, either in order to know whom to trust in future, or to disperse a party.[10c]

Albani had told Mann in 1760 that all the symptoms from which the Old Pretender suffered from time to time were mortal,[12] and there had even been several rumours of his death. His household had of late provided little that was of interest, the more so since, in 1764, Cardinal Stuart had moved into the Cancelleria as his official appointments entitled him to do.[6d] For a long time he had only lived under his father's roof for the sake of appearances, while keeping his own establishment entirely separate. Mann had presumed rather prematurely in 1760 that when James died he need not send an express to England with the news,[4b] but his caution was justified. The Government would not have reimbursed him had the expense been regarded as unnecessary.

Mann had evidently underrated the determination of the Jacobite partisans to obtain for Charles Edward the formal privileges of royalty accorded to his father. In anticipation of James's death Cardinal Stuart, supported by the French Ambassador, made strong representations to Clement XIII, who replied, however, that he would not be responsible to Europe for an innovation mortifying to a sovereign who treated Catholics in his dominions so humanely.[10d] Begging Mann never to quote him as the source for the news, Alessandro Albani told him in 1765 that the Young Pretender (whose own death had at times been rumoured) was not only alive but inclined to return to Rome. In addition he had asked to be accorded the distinctions he had previously enjoyed there and to be recognised as a King when his father died. The Pope had ordered him to be told that he would see him again with pleasure, that he would treat him according to his distinguished rank, that he could count after his father's death on the emoluments already fixed for the Cardinal his brother, but that as regarded the marks of royalty he could not take it upon himself to give them, and would base his actions on those of some other sovereign.[13a] From another source Mann heard that the Pope's answer was to be conveyed to Charles Edward by Cardinal Gianfrancesco Albani, and thought it expedient to send early notice of it to England as the Courts of France and Spain would undoubtedly become involved.[14a]

Mann told the Secretary of State, Henry Seymour Conway, that the opportunity seemed very favourable totally to suppress for the future even at Rome the titles which the Pretender's son might attempt to assume on the death of his father. He had for a long time, he said, had the best grounds for a conviction that the papal Court thought this highly expedient and would gladly seize any opportunity that should offer to show its attention for England in return for the lenity with which His Majesty's Roman Catholic subjects were treated in every part of his dominions. This had been publicly the language of the late Pope, and was the sentiment of all sensible people at Rome, for they looked upon the residence there of the Pretender with the titles he assumed not only as a burden but as the greatest obstacle to that degree of harmony which, apart from religion, they wished to see established between the two States.[13b]

On 1st January 1766 the Old Pretender died and Albani sent Mann a special express with the news.[15a] Not waiting for specific instructions from England, Mann took the responsibility of putting to Albani as his own private views those which he knew the British Government would endorse. The Pope, in response to the importunities with which he was tormented, had weakened to the extent of saying that he would hear the advice of a Congregation of Cardinals on the matter, and Mann pointed out that he would not now be exposed to pressure from other Courts had he originally been more resolute in rejecting Cardinal Stuart's claims. The circumstances of Europe, he said, had changed so much since the late Pretender established himself in the Ecclesiastical State that such a refusal would have been justified, and although he had no orders from his Court he thought he knew its sentiments and those of the whole nation well enough to be convinced that neither the King nor his people would ever suffer such an affront. Thus he would rely on the wisdom and constancy of the Pope, to keep his first resolution, and on the prudence of the Cardinals he was going to consult, to prevent the very serious consequences that a false move in this matter could provoke.[14b]

Mann told the Secretary of State that he had chosen this indirect method of conveying his Government's views because everything at Rome was carried on by cabals and intrigues, and he was sure that Albani and other correspondents would use his letters well to make an impression both upon the Pope and the Cardinals he might consult, who were for the most part excessively ignorant of Courts and of the world. It is probably no accident that Mann's first very strong letter to Albani on the subject is missing from the Vienna files and known only from the draft in London. Mann had, he said, been very careful not to hazard His Majesty's dignity nor name, and added that he had accidentally met the papal Nuncio in Florence and talked to him so freely and forcibly that he felt sure his words would get back to Rome.[16a] He wrote again to Albani, hammering home the inadvisability of the Pope's complying with Cardinal Stuart's request, and pointing out that the interests of religion, which were the only excuse, by no means demanded it.[17a] Mann, however, surmised to Conway that as the Pope's health made it likely that a Conclave was near the cardinals might be fearful of incurring the displeasure of France and Spain. He also thought the French were loth to lose the nomination of a cardinal which the Old Pretender had claimed and had always exercised in their interest.[16b] This, of course, would be lost unless his son were recognised as a crowned head. The anticipation of a Conclave was, as it happened, premature, for Clement XIII lived until 1769.

Thanks to the firmness* and dexterity of Mann and Albani, the latter being "as staunch as a heretic" [18] in favour of England, the Congregation of Cardinals was faced with a clear issue, left with no illusions that Mann's Court was prepared to wink at continuance even of a perfectly empty form, and prudently decided against according the marks

* Mann was justifiably nettled because Horace Walpole belittled the importance of his coup. Walpole VI. p. 394. Walpole to Mann, Paris 9. ii. 66; p. 405, Mann to Walpole, 7. iii. 66.

of royalty. The result was soon publicly known, even though the "secret of the Inquisition" was imposed on all who assisted at the Congregation, reported Mann.[16c] In March 1766 the Arms of England, which together with those of the reigning Pope and the Senate of Rome, the late Pretender had always had over the door of his house, were taken down in the night time[16d] and as Lewis de Vismes, Secretary at Madrid, commented, "the Hunters after Antiquities will be no longer in danger of meeting with a Pageant King".[15b] Conway instructed Mann to convey the King's satisfaction, but as from certain circumstances, he said, there could be no immediate communication between the two Courts, His Majesty wished that Mann should avail himself of such opportunity as the proximity of his situation might afford him to convey the proper assurances to the Court of Rome that the King was extremely sensible of its correct and respectful conduct in not countenancing the idle claims of the Pretender. Mann, however, was not to be permitted to relax his vigilance. "I cannot but command Your Attention", continued Conway, "to what is doing at Rome, as that Court exhibits a Sort of common Stage where the several Popish Powers play their parts in such a manner as may frequently give intimation of the Dispositions they bear to one another and of the Characters they mean to assume elsewhere." [19]

The Pope's answer to Cardinal York on the subject of his brother's rights contained the face-saving formula "*per ora*", (for the present) and the younger Stuart at first refused to recognise the hopelessness of his cause. His close friend, Gianfrancesco Albani, evidently shared his family's addiction to intrigue, and long ago had been accused by Stosch of teaching Cardinal Stuart how to dissemble. When transmitting the Pope's message to Charles Edward he presented it in unjustifiably favourable terms, apparently at the instigation of Stuart, who afterwards left him to bear the brunt of the Pope's displeasure.* They no doubt believed, and with reason, that the Prince would not set out from Bouillon on hearing the true position, and staked everything on inducing him to show himself in Rome. They underestimated, however, the real strength, or perhaps desperation, behind the Pope's mildly worded resolution, and their trickery resulted in a deeply felt humiliation to the elder Prince and a total rupture between the younger and Gianfrancesco.[16e] When Charles Edward arrived, at the end of January, Alessandro, either referring to this incident or to his own advice against recognition given to the Pope, wrote that his own family, being suspect, was less than all others in a position to hear news of the Stuarts.[15c]

They did not at once give up hope. Cardinal Stuart went two stages out of Rome to meet his brother and, when the latter had recovered from the fatigues of the journey and the effects of being overturned in his coach on the way, drove him ostentatiously about the streets of Rome in his carriage and on his right hand, a distinction which according to convention no cardinal might show to anyone but a crowned head. This open defiance of the Pope's expressed wishes not unnaturally gave so much offence that all the Cardinals and Heads of Orders were instructed that the Court of Rome did not acknowledge the Prince Stuart as King and that it was expected that they should conform themselves in their behaviour agreeable to that declaration. There were, however, some signs that the Jacobite cause was still popular in certain quarters, and undoubtedly Mann's strong move to end the embarrassing pretence of royalty once and for all was both well judged and necessary. When the Young Pretender arrived in Rome it was reported that great crowds of people assembled at his house from curiosity to see him get out of his coach and a few of the nobility waited in his ante-chamber.[16f] More serious was

* Walpole VI. pp. 388–9; Mann to Walpole, 24. i. 66 and notes.

the fact that the Rectors and Students of the English, Scotch and Irish Colleges, as well as the Superiors of two Irish religious houses, received him in state in April, had a Te Deum sung for his return by the style of Charles III their Sovereign and members of the Colleges kissed his hand in homage. The Rectors and Superiors concerned were banished from Rome, although afterwards reinstated, and an order was also sent to the Abbé Grant "Agent for the Scotch Roman Catholicks", who had been very busy on this occasion, it was said. He was told not to dare to approach any of the Pope's palaces nor to frequent his Ministers, while his pension from the Roman Government was taken away from him.[16g] The Pope made his attitude even clearer by his manner of receiving the two Stuart Princes in audience in 1767. In accordance with his right as a cardinal the younger was immediately introduced into the Pope's room and seated on a stool, but his brother was left for some time in another apartment and then called for by the name of the "brother of Cardinal York". He remained standing up for the whole quarter of an hour that his audience lasted, although the Cardinal was seated the whole time. The Pope himself even thanked Mann through his Nuncio at Florence for having prevented him from taking a step in compliance with the strong solicitations that were made to him, that might have offended the King.[20a]

The Young Pretender himself, rotting in idleness and exile, completed the work of Clement XIII, Horace Mann and the cardinals friendly to England. Indeed it can be surmised that only the decorum and genuine piety of his father had enabled the latter to maintain his status and had prevented one of the several Popes who reigned in his time from finding a formula to exclude him from Rome or in some way to end the embarrassments created by his royal pretensions. Charles Edward quarrelled with his brother and with his own household, even that devoted Jacobite Andrew

Lumsden, leaving him within three years of James's death. In 1772 he married Princess Louisa of Stolberg, and rumours of his drunkenness and physical collapse were soon supplemented by ugly stories of his ill-treatment of his wife, who separated from him in 1780. He bought a house in Florence in 1776 but, after several sad and scandalous years there, returned to die in Rome in 1788, his illegitimate daughter by his old mistress Clementina Walkinshaw being with him at the end. Whether or not he still believed in them "this poor Vision of a Man", as his wife called him, clung to his ruined hopes and, according to her, always kept under his bed a strong-box with 12,000 sequins ready for the expenses of his journey to England whenever he should be called there.[21a] His doings soon ceased to be of any political importance and became little more than items of general interest in the letters of Albani, who now to his sorrow had to witness the persecution of the Jesuit Order organised by his old enemies the Bourbon powers with the acquiescence of the Court of Vienna, which he himself served.

Mann's informant about much that passed in Rome at the time of the Old Pretender's death and his elder son's subsequent return to Rome was a certain Abbé or Canon Paolo Bernardo Giordani. His identity is obscure, but Albani had known him since at least 1744 and had employed him as a secretary jointly with Quarelli, whom he afterwards preferred to him. He had written to him in Italian in various places, including Buda in 1752, but it is not clear whether he was originally a minor official in Austrian service, an agent for the British during the War of the Austrian Succession or simply a private dependant of Albani's. He shared, however, something of Albani's propensity for combining art-dealing with an intelligence service. He was writing to Mann in 1763, and in 1764 was complaining to him of having been passed over for some appointment although he had the great consolation that everyone who knew his life, his conduct and his actions wished him very well. Albani, he said, regarded him with similar consideration from a streak of gratitude and from his great heart, and perhaps would never forget that without the slightest interest and for no wage he had served him for eighteen or nineteen years.[1g] Despite these protestations it is evident that he harboured some grievance against Albani and was potentially dangerous to him. He seems to have been well acquainted with the British for when John Dick, Consul at Leghorn, arrived in Rome on a visit in 1764 Giordani offered to help him through the Customs and to present him to Albani who, he said, much wanted to see him although he was still tormented with his painful gout. He added that the Consul would on his return be able to tell Mann of his respect for him and how much he loved the English.[1j]

The letter containing these items was signed by Giordani, but several in the same handwriting and style and obviously from him are not, which suggests that at times he acted as something like a secret agent for Mann. Later, he described Albani's and Dick's mutual pleasure at meeting and said that he himself had told the Consul he could come every evening to see His Eminence, who never went out and preferred the conversation of Englishmen to that of all others.[1k] Mann wrote Albani his condolences on his gout,[8b] which must indeed have been severe, for the Cardinal hardly ever complained about his own ailments, and this attack must have been the reason that Giordani and not Alessandro took Mr and Mrs Dick to see the Villa for the first time. They would return there often, said the Abbé. It would be at their disposal and if the season permitted they would enjoy there a good situation and good conversation. The house was in the most charming part of the countryside, and for forty-five to fifty days of the year, when His Eminence went there to stay, there was great freedom and no etiquette for his friends.[1l] It may be observed that Albani even extended this pleasant informality to the Pope himself. On one occasion, when Clement XIII had been ill, Giordani reported that for his first outing he walked about the Villa of His Eminence, who waited on the Pope in country clothes in defiance of custom and etiquette. His Holiness had been pleased, saying that all dress was well outside the town, and Albani had gone on, Giordani said, to speak to him of many things with his customary candour and natural simplicity.[10e] At the time of the Dicks' visit Albani was looking for lead for the fountains of his Villa, and the Consul had apparently been asked to help, for Giordani wrote to Mann in May 1764 saying that the Cardinal was impatiently awaiting Dick's answer about it.[15d]

In June 1765 Giordani wrote to Mann about descriptions of pictures and mosaics evidently intended for sale to George III, to whom he sent compliments. He would, he said, be overcome with joy if he could boast of having procured for him the things which were the most considerable in the town. He actually enclosed a description of three bronze statues, mainly antique, a *"bustino"* and two antique bronze gueridons. These, he said, Albani did not wish to buy himself on account of the great expenditure he had already incurred on his Villa and also because he liked marbles and medals better than bronzes.[10f] Giordani wrote again in July 1765 saying that by now Mann would have received the envelope with the drawings of mosaics and description of pictures. He would only add, for the service of His Britannic Majesty, that if the good God willed that the affair should succeed and that his own taste for such things was approved, he would tell him how to make the finest collection of the best pictures in the world at a reasonable price. In that case he would come and visit Mann to tell him his ideas, but at present he asked no other favour than that of being trusted alone with this commission, if it materialised. When he remembered how much money had been lavished by one of Mann's friends, who had had big copies made by the best painters in Rome, and thought of the monopolies and plots that were made to cheat his compatriots, he was surprised that no one had spoken.[10g]

Shortly afterwards he wrote Mann a long letter commenting on Consul Smith's collection at Venice. He had not seen it, he said, but a friend, a good antiquary, had spoken of it to him in Milan and told him that it contained fine things, a very few rare ones and some mediocre. He remembered his saying that if Smith had been at Rome he would have been another Stosch for statues as Stosch had been for cameos, etc. Giordani went on to say that antique bronzes were extremely rare and that it would be very difficult to find any worthy of a Prince such as the King of England, but given time he would succeed. With regard to drawings he would like to know more details. The late Chevalier Ghezzi and Amerani, too, had had collections of which a part at least remained and were for sale. He went on to discuss Michelangelo's Sistine paintings (which perhaps it had been proposed to copy) and then spoke of antique mosaics which were available for sale to the King. He ended that he hoped his plans would be approved and that everyone would be pleased with him. He would like to know how the *Venus* bought in Rome by the Duke of York had been admired in England. The affair had been conducted in great secrecy and the statue was without question really beautiful. The man who sold it to the Duke had bought it for 400 to 500 crowns. The Duke had paid 5000 for it, according to what the Cardinal and the Abbé Winckelmann had told him many times. In another letter of the same date Giordani said that although the paper had come to an end he would never cease to write to Mann as to a friend, not to a Minister, to an Englishman who had the fine characteristics of his own nation and of Italy without being subject to the faults either of one or of the other.[10h] He remarked elsewhere that he was an Englishman as much as Mann and should be so all his life in regard to the interests of England.[15e]

Mann's drafts to the fulsome Giordani do not appear to have survived and it is not apparent from the correspondence whether these promising negotiations had any result. The death of the Old Pretender supervened and it becomes evident that Giordani, whether or not he had been doing so before, was also acting as Mann's secret agent in Rome. In January 1766 Mann told the Secretary of State that he was sending home a copy of the letter of his correspondent there, from which many lights might be gathered. He had acted with an uncommon zeal on this occasion and, being a Canon of the Church and a dependant of Cardinal Albani, had had free admittance to the other cardinals, with whom he had made the best use of his letters and of such other arguments as he knew were best adapted to those with whom he was speaking.[16c] Mann was certainly referring to Giordani, who also reported on the doings of the Young Pretender and his adherents after the Pope's decision on his status, as well as during the discussions which led up to it. When he spoke of the Abbé Grant's disgrace he said that, according to the proverb, he was neither Jew nor Samaritan, served the Pretender, assisted the English who came to Rome, and spied on both.[15f] It was from Giordani and not from Alessandro that Mann learned of the Young Pretender's having threatened to kill two or three of his gentlemen when in drink. The Canon thought Albani knew nothing of this, at least he had said nothing,[15g] but in general claimed to be in the Cardinal's closest confidence, telling Mann that when he saw him he would impart to him the whole story of the campaign of Velletri, known only to himself, Albani and Count Firmian[10i] (an Austrian Minister).

Pope Clement XIII, who had succeeded Benedict XIV in 1758, died in February 1769, and Giordani wrote to tell

Mann that the Jesuits had a strong party in the Conclave of which the young Cardinal Gianfrancesco openly and Alessandro secretly were the leaders.[22a] The Pope elected was however Cardinal Ganganelli, who as Clement XIV suppressed the Jesuit Order in 1773 and was thought to have died by poison in the following year. Shortly after the election Giordani told Mann that he was mortified to inform him that His Eminence cut the saddest figure in Rome and at Vienna. He had become melancholy to the last degree. The Pope and the Imperial Court had reproached him for his conduct and he was to be pitied in his old age. Giordani hoped he would get out of his difficulties, but equivocal or irregular actions, he said, such as were called "*alla romanesca*", sooner or later dishonoured anyone, whoever he might be.[22b]

Albani presumably cannot have been aware that Giordani, who evidently lived in his house, and whose correspondence with Mann went with his own mail, spied upon him in political matters and tried to undermine his reputation as an art dealer. The Cardinal must however have known that his protégé was closely associated with English travellers and indeed fostered the link. When the Duke of Gloucester, another brother of George III, visited Rome in 1772 Albani told Mann that Canon Giordani would attend him at papal functions because the Duke's incognito had made him refuse a companion of higher rank,[23a] and it is evident that Giordani was in Albani's confidence in artistic matters. For instance he shared his long-standing distrust of the adventurer d'Hancarville,[24] who after various shady transactions ingratiated himself with William Hamilton, Envoy at Naples, and edited a book on Etruscan, Greek and Roman antiquities from his collection. Giordani was still reporting on the Young Pretender's movements in 1772 and possibly continued to act as a secret agent after Albani's letters to Mann ceased.

Albani's uncharacteristic depression, upon which Giordani commented in 1769, may not have been due solely to political causes. He was ageing and in the previous year had suffered the loss of his friend, librarian and house companion, Winckelmann, in peculiarly distressing circumstances. The German scholar, accompanied by the sculptor Cavaceppi, set out in the spring of 1768 to make a tour of Europe, but was overcome by homesickness for Rome and turned back alone from Regensburg. While waiting at Trieste for a ship he was probably betrayed by his homosexual proclivities into striking up an acquaintanceship with a fellow-traveller, Arcangeli, who had already served a term of imprisonment for theft. Winckelmann showed him certain gold medals he had with him and Arcangeli murdered him by throwing a noose round his neck while he sat at his desk and stabbing him five times. Knowing himself fatally wounded, Winckelmann had a lawyer summoned and dictated a Will, which he was however unable to sign, bequeathing the residue of his estate to his patron Alessandro Albani. It might have been expected that the Cardinal would have commented to Mann on so shocking and presumably widely publicised an event, but it so happened that his admirable French-speaking secretary, Quarelli, was absent and Albani was only dictating short notes to Mann on official matters.

Quarelli went on a mission to Piedmont, was introduced by Albani to Mann in a letter of May 1768 and had returned to Rome by the following November, when Albani commented on his having seen Mann.[22c] Alessandro mentioned Winckelmann in March 1769 when he wrote that he was sending a portrait of him for forwarding to Muzell-Stosch and enclosing a copy of his Will to prove to Mann that a report of his having bequeathed medals to Wilkes was untrue.[22d] Albani wrote more fully to Muzell-Stosch at Berlin in January 1769. The tender feelings for the unfortunate

Winckelmann which he had expressed in his recent letter had, he said, only renewed the bitter memory of the sad loss which they had both suffered. There was, however, nothing more to be done for him except to pray God for his repose and to keep carefully, as Muzell-Stosch had resolved to do, the fragments of the work he would have given to the Republic of Letters had his misfortune not caused his premature death. Albani was very sorry, he said, not to be able to contribute at all in the matter of Winckelmann's productions. Everything remarkable among his papers was now at Vienna, where it was intended to publish an edition of his works. Whatever had been left among his effects, whether letters or rough drafts, he had been told was not worth the trouble of editing. He would send the portrait of the deceased to Mann as soon as he had returned from Pisa, having it rolled up by the painter who had painted it and packed so that it would reach him undamaged. He had not had this done before, he said, because Mann had been so long at Pisa and would not return to Florence until the Court did, so he had thought it best to leave the portrait open to get drier before being sent.[25]

Tragic for Albani as were the death of Winckelmann, the ganging-up of Austria with his old enemies France and Spain, the persecution of the Jesuits and the suppression of their Order, the last period of Albani's life was in many ways the most brilliant and the most personally rewarding. In spite of what the treacherous Giordani implied, Alessandro's relations with the House of Austria seem to have remained excellent, his health was still good and his Villa was one of the wonders of Europe. The most distinguished travellers of many nations, and particularly the English whom he so greatly loved, courted and honoured him, while his humbler neighbours looked up to him as their friend and champion. He had dug out antiquities in Rome while there were still priceless treasures to be found and could now, with his own collection completed as the inspiration and principal glory of his incomparable Villa, afford to leave digging and dealing to younger men such as Thomas Jenkins, Gavin Hamilton and James Byres. From his turbulent youth and the knife-edge politics of his middle age he had graduated to elder statesmanship and an unrivalled social position, with a good, long time in which to enjoy it. Maria Theresa herself showed him her warm approval when she wrote to him on the appointment of his great-nephew as Grand Master at the Court of Milan in 1772.

"Very Reverend Father in God," she wrote,* "Our good Friend and Cousin; in the sentiments which you have just shown me on the occasion of the little mark of esteem which I have given with pleasure to your worthy great-nephew Prince Charles Albani, I recognise still that old attachment and that way of thinking of which I have had so many proofs from you; I am sure that this young knight will follow in your footsteps in this; he has already earned general approbation at this Court and it will be very pleasing to me to make him feel at last, as occasion arises, the effects of that same benevolence and distinguished affection which with such good reason I have for you.

Your much attached
Maria Theresa.[26]

One of the humble people whom Albani helped was a certain Signora Guarnieri. He wrote to Mann in 1764 about her.[1m] For many years, he said, English gentlemen who came to Rome had lodged with the Chevalier Guarnieri, who seemed to have built his house especially for them, with a situation out of the way of the worst noise, the best air in the town, apartments divided so that several could stay there in comfort without disturbing each other and all the rooms fitted up with very suitable furniture. The

* In French in the original.

Chevalier Guarnieri having died, the innkeepers and caterers of the town had made every effort, and were still making them, to deflect foreigners from the house and attract them to themselves, and for this purpose they made use of antiquaries, servants and others to whom it was not fitting the widow should address herself. She had applied to him, Albani continued, and he in turn was applying to Mann, to beg him to intervene with his compatriots and persuade them not to allow themselves to be taken by surprise by those who had banded together to ruin this poor widow, who had no other means of subsisting with her family except what she made from the foreigners who lodged with her. By doing this he would perform a charity towards the widow, who by her goodness thoroughly deserved it, and would do him another favour which he would remember all his life. Mann promised to do his best but Albani did not let it go at that. He wrote again the following January reminding him about it and saying that while previously all the English had come to her house none came now because of the conspiracy against her.[10j] However, the widow evidently weathered the storm, because Mann recommended the Prince of Brunswick to go there in October 1766, although he was afraid he had been directed to another house in the Piazza di Spagna before he got to Florence. Incidentally, Mann had also on this occasion, at Albani's request, suggested to the Prince that Winckelmann should show him the antiquities of Rome,[27a] a favour evidently reserved only for the most august travellers.

Not all Albani's requests were so easy to comply with. In March 1766 he told Mann that Signora Vittoria Cheroffini, wife of Signor Lepri, was coming to Florence and that she was of a family in which he interested himself greatly and which had deserved well of the English by the offer of much hospitality. Any kindness which Mann did for her he would regard as done to himself.[15h] Mann replied that he would

offer the young lady all the attentions at his command so as
to render her stay in Florence agreeable, and later reported
her passing an evening with him and meeting many ladies.
She had also dined on another occasion to meet the Baron
St Odil.[17b] His guest was actually Albani's daughter Vittoria, supposed to have been depicted in Mengs' *Parnassus*
at his Villa. Her dowry had been provided by the sale of his
famous collection of drawings to George III, and in 1764
she had married the Marchese Giuseppe Lepri.[28] Encouraged probably by Albani, she wished to be presented at the
Court of Florence which, after the long, dull years of the
Regency Government of Emperor Francis I, was now pre-
sided over by his son the young Grand Duke Leopold and
his wife. Mann had to explain that this was impossible. The
Grand Duchess, he said, had made a rule that however
distinguished the birth of a lady none was to be received at
Court if she had married beneath her proper rank. This had
nothing to do with Madame Lepri's own birth, Mann added
with bold tact, and she would be received in all other
assemblies. Her friends had already tried to gain admission
for her, and he himself, without waiting to be approached,
had sounded those in authority, but the fact that many
others would then have similar claims was an invincible
obstacle.[17c] Albani, rather crestfallen, accepted the verdict
with his usual politeness but had hoped, he said, that the
rule might have been relaxed for a stranger just passing
through Florence.[15i]

At just about the same time Mann had to refuse another
awkward request. Albani wrote that his sister-in-law, the
Princess Albani, during her *villegiatura* at Porto d'Anzo, had
bought a fishing boat called the *Madonna della Speranza, e S.
Carlo Borromeo* built at Gaeta in 1764. She had put it in the
charge of a certain Pier de Campo who sailed his ships under
the Neapolitan flag, but to make hers safer from Barbary
vessels she wanted to fly the British flag, and Albani asked

Mann to get the necessary patent and permission from his Court.[15j] The British Representative was obliged to reply that the difficulties were insurmountable. The law of the sea as well as agreements made specifically with the rulers of Barbary expressly forbade such a thing, he said, and there had already been serious trouble when the Governor of Port Mahon contravened the regulations.[17d] Albani took this less well than he had his disappointment about his daughter's reception at Court. Though certain, he said, that Mann had done all he could, any more that might be said about the impossibility of obtaining the British flag for a ship not built in England only served to increase his mortification.[15k]

An attempt by Albani to get a protégé into the Royal Society of London was also unsuccessful. In April 1766 he asked Mann to get a place among the Academicians of the Royal Society of London for Canon Fantoni, Rector of a College at Bologna of which Albani was Protector, and a clever mathematician.[15l] He enclosed Fantoni's solution of a problem to be forwarded to the Society, and Mann asked Lord Hillsborough, who was a Fellow, to use his good offices.[17e] The Cardinal, having heard nothing more, wrote again in January 1767[29a] sending a book by Fantoni for forwarding, but the Canon never was elected and the matter appears to have been dropped.

Alessandro's attention was probably deflected by more important matters. In July 1767 Mann, who seems to have got the first news, told him that the Emperor was coming to Italy, strictly incognito, to accompany his sister Maria Josepha to Naples[30a] for her marriage with King Ferdinand of the Two Sicilies. Francis I had died in 1765 and the Emperor was now his eldest son Joseph who, immediately on his accession, had reappointed Albani as Protector of the Empire.[31] The proposed journey followed closely on the death of the young Empress from smallpox, which Maria

Theresa also caught but survived. In August 1767 Albani heard to his great delight that the Imperial visitors intended to stay the night at his Villa on their way through Rome, and he hoped that he could persuade them to remain at least another day. He was *"véritablement glorieux"*, he told Mann, that his house should have been chosen to receive such honourable guests.[30b] The Emperor, however, delayed until the late autumn, the roads threatened to become impassable and eventually the whole visit was abandoned because Maria Josepha died of smallpox. It has been suggested that she caught it from being taken by her mother to pray in the family vault of the Capuchin Church at Vienna, where lay the corpses of previous smallpox victims.[32]

After a short interval Ferdinand was betrothed instead, and this time married by proxy to his late fiancée's sister, Maria Carolina. Arrangements were made for her journey, but on this occasion the Emperor was not going to accompany her, and the Grand Duke and Duchess of Tuscany, her brother and sister-in-law, planned to take her to Naples. Unfortunately hostilities had broken out between the Ecclesiastical State and Naples, so for political reasons the royal party decided to go round the outskirts of Rome without seeing it. As Albani said, what ought to have been a subject of rejoicing for Rome became a mortification, since they were not to have the happiness of seeing the august persons. However, when the case was at its most desperate, Alessandro wrote three weeks later, Rome had the happiness of receiving within her walls and possessing for a few hours Her Majesty the Queen of Naples and their Royal Highnesses, who got out at the Church of St Peter, went in to say their prayers and then dined at the Villa Pinciana of the Borghese family, after which they returned to the town, crossed it and then pursued their way towards Marino. This honour was totally unexpected, he said, and as the Nuncio who sent word of it had said that the royal party would not get out of their carriages at St Peter's it was thought that the presence of the cardinals would constrain them. They therefore did not go and neither did the Pope, although he greatly wished to show the royal party his personal consideration. Thus, lamented Albani, the populace was more fortunate than the Pope and his cardinals, who had to stay at home, and Prince Borghese stole from him the pleasure, for which he had so long hoped, of receiving in his country house Sovereigns for whom no one could have more veneration than he had.[22e] Mann, who sometimes seemed to fail Albani in sympathy, could enter most fully into such a social mortification and hastened to assure him that it was only the situation of Prince Borghese's house which had secured that nobleman an unexpected honour.[33]

The Emperor did himself visit Rome the following year, 1769, but on this occasion the Conclave was in session[34] and Albani was confined in the Vatican quarters preserving his health as best he could in such a narrow and stuffy place, he said. Joseph, however, was taken to see the Conclave in session, so Albani saw him there and, it was reported, dissolved into tears. The Emperor and his brother Leopold, Grand Duke of Tuscany, stayed some days in the end and spent almost all their time seeing the beauties and antiquities of Rome. A rather appealing picture by Battoni in the Kunsthistorische Museum at Vienna shows the brothers hand in hand, posed against a background of Roman buildings, and this presumably was a souvenir of their visit. According to Albani, they showed great satisfaction at all the demonstrations of joy and at the public as well as private entertainments given for them, everyone having tried to show respect. He himself had had the honour of receiving these two amiable Sovereigns one evening in his country house,[22f] so at last he had his way.

Just before these events Albani had been expecting another royal visitor for the second time, namely the Duke of York, who was returning for a further visit to Rome. He never got there, for he was taken ill on the way and died at Monaco in October 1767. Albani who had the honour of being personally known to the late Duke and of being much distinguished by him, begged that his most respectful compliments of condolence should be mentioned to His Majesty through Mann.[20b]

Ever since the war ended Albani had continued to receive an increasing number of English visitors, who included the writer Laurence Sterne in December 1765 and the painter James Barry in January 1767. Of the former Albani said that the meeting did not last long because everyone was very busy these days, but for all that he appreciated Sterne's great wit. If he would not hurry so much to get on to Naples he would have the pleasure of seeing him on many more occasions and of enjoying his learning and his sallies.[10k] Mann asked Albani's protection for James Barry who, he said, had been in Rome for some time to perfect his studies in painting. The interest which Lord Shelburne, Secretary of State, took in everything that concerned Mr Barry had induced him to recommend him to himself, and consequently he was very anxious to procure him all the advantages he could command. That of the benevolence and protection of His Eminence, Mann continued, was the strongest proof he could give of his wish to help Barry.[29b]

A curious incident in 1766 was Albani's recommendation to Mann of the Abbé Grant, so recently in disgrace over the recognition of the Young Pretender and often previously in Albani's bad books. He was accompanying to Florence two brothers named Gastaldi, born in London, who were returning there to join their father, the Genoese Minister. Albani wrote that the Abbé Grant, a Scottish gentleman established for a long time with the best reputation in the world at Rome, was accompanying them as far as Aix.[27b] One cannot guess whether Albani had simply forgotten his previous remarks about Grant or with his habitual kindliness thought bygones had better be bygones, or had at times found him useful, as he was said to spy for both sides. Grant seems to have established himself in Rome more comfortably after his return there, because Mann's letter-book shows that he wrote to him several times in 1772,[35a] evidently in connection with the Duke of Gloucester's visit to Rome. Albani, however, advised that the Duke should be shown round by Jenkins and not listen to Grant's proposals.[23b]

Neither the London nor Vienna papers seem to contain letters or drafts by Albani and Mann later than 1772, but a rough list of letters despatched, made by Albani's secretary,[36] records almost weekly letters to Mann up till 29th January 1774. There is no note in London of letters to Albani after 8th December 1772, but this is not conclusive because from the beginning of 1773 Mann's letter-books seem to have been kept in a different way and cannot be satisfactorily compared with the earlier ones. It is to be supposed that Mann went on writing to Albani as long as the latter wrote to him, but it certainly seems that the correspondence ceased some years before his death. Mann, however, retained a useful correspondent in Rome, possibly Giordani, and hoped to obtain through him papers relating to the Gunpowder Plot, reputed on good authority to have been found in the Jesuit College of St Andrew after the dissolution of the Order.[35b] These hopes were however dashed by the death of the Pope and the suppression of the Congregation to which Mann's agent had access.[37a]

Albani died after a short illness on 11th December 1779, and Mann reported it in a strangely detached manner to the Secretary of State, Lord Hillsborough, who after all knew all about the Albani–Mann relationship because of the

Fantoni affair. "By the last post from Rome", he wrote, "I received an account of Cardinal Albani's death the 11th Instant. He has left his fine Villa under strictest entail to his Grand Nephew who is Grand Master to the Arch-duchess of Milan, Cardinal Hertzan is to succeed him, as the Emperor's Minister at Rome and the Com-Protectorship (as they call it there) of the Empire." [21b] If that was all Mann wrote on the subject it was a grudging tribute indeed and if they had been corresponding regularly till the end would seem positively peculiar.

In Albani's time and probably owing in great measure to him, the official attitude of the Ecclesiastical State to English visitors had been transformed. When in 1768 an inscription was set up to Baron Werpup, a young Hanoverian kinsman of George III's who was killed in a carriage accident, Mann said that for the first time since the Reformation the Pope had allowed the King of England's titles to be publicly displayed. [38] When the Duke of Cumberland visited Rome in 1774 the Pope not only gave him pictures in mosaic and tapestry, and volumes of prints such as the Duke of York had received ten years before, but he had the Cupola of St Peter's illuminated for him and, when he departed, lent him a frigate to Toulon, provisioned it and put the bargemen into new clothes for the occasion. [37b] The fact that the Duchess was not supposed to have royal honours paid her because the marriage had taken place without George III's approval [39] does not seem to have damped down the festivities. Other British travellers were also received by His Holiness with the greatest goodness and affability, and he made a present of a series of his gold and silver medals to the explorer James Bruce. [37c] So well indeed had Albani served the British that in the end his diplomatic intervention on their behalf appears to have become superfluous. It had been no light task looking after them, for, as William Hamilton wrote to Mann from Naples, the management of their own countrymen was not the least difficult part of their business.[23c]

Alessandro Albani's remains were placed in a plainly lettered stone sarcophagus in the catacomb beneath the Church of St Sebastian on the Appian Way. His only other memorial there is an inscription in the West Porch recording that as an Abbé he had restored in 1718 an ancient sarcophagus found nearby. He is, however, worthily commemorated elsewhere. The collections he sold to the Pope, the King of Poland and the King of England are still in Rome, Windsor and, it is hoped, in Dresden. His town house, the Palazzo delle Quattro Fontane, is now occupied with striking appropriateness by the British Council. His own cherished Villa remains in much of its original splendour as a testimony to his rare taste, his lifelong devotion to the arts and his most delicate and most magnificent hospitality. Above all, his intelligence and his kindness, his worldliness and his humour, his natural candour and his political tortuousness, in fact his whole character with the inconsistencies which are part of its attraction, stand revealed in the State Papers, which at the same time record so vividly the strange relationship created between Rome and England by the pitiable Stuart Court.

Notes

page

CHAPTER I

22   1   SP 98/58 f. 98 Walton 17.xii.51

22   2*a*   SP 85/13 f. 90-1 Ricci to Secretary of State, Rome 26.i.15

24   *b*   f. 178-9 Report of Board of Trade, Whitehall 4.ii.35

23, 26 3   SP 98/59 f. 368-9 Mann to Robinson 23.viii.55

23   4   British Museum Addit. MSS. 22. 515 f. 1-2 List of Ministers, Consuls and Governors in the Southern Province 6.iii.21

23   5   SP 98/34 Skinner to Newcastle, Leghorn 30.i.32

23   6   F. 161 de Gaven to Albani, London 7.ii.55

24   7   SP 98/33 Anon. to Colman, Rome 17.i.32, enclosed Colman to Newcastle, Florence, 9.ii.32

24   8   SP 92/33 (II) Allen to Newcastle, Turin 6.x.31

24   9   SP 92/37 Pailfield to Essex, Leghorn 21.viii.34, enclosed Essex to Newcastle, Turin 16.x.34

24   10   SP 98/37 f. 312 Walton 21.i.36

24   11*a*   SP 98/52 f. 304 Mann to Newcastle 27.xi.47

24   *b*   f. 302 Chamberlayne to Mann, Capranica 18.xi.47

24   12*a*   SP 105/283 f. 244-5 Albani to Mann 1.viii.44

24   *b*   f. 264 Long to Mann, Nonsuch off R. Tiber 30.vii.44

25   13   SP 98/63 f. 29 Mann to Fox 13.iii.56

25   14*a*   SP 98/50 f. 53-4 Mann to Newcastle 2.iii.45

26   *b*   f. 35-6 Albani to Mann 16.i.45

25   15   Dennistoun I p. 285

25   16   SP 98/51 f. 67 Mann to Newcastle 15.iii.46

25   17   Cust p. 260

26   18*a*   SP 98/57 f. 210-11 Mann to Bedford 28.v.51

31   *b*   f. 187 News Letter, Rome 3.iv.51

31   *c*   f. 301 Mann to Holdernesse 5.xi.51

26   19*a*   Stuart Papers I p. 166 James III to Clement XI, St Germain 7.xi.01

page

27	19*b*	Stuart Papers I	p. 243 James III to Gualterio, St Germain 22.ii.12
28	*c*	III	pp. 530–1 Clement XI to James III, Rome 20.ii.17
29	*d*	II	p. xxx
29	*e*	III	p. 148 Inese to Mar 29.x.16
29	*f*		p. 541 Narrative by John Paterson 1717
29	*g*	IV	p. 119 Inese to Mar 12.iii.17
29	*h*	VII	p. v
30	*i*	IV	p. xxvi
31	*j*	I	pp. 169–70 Queen Mary to Count Caprara 13.i.2
32	*k*	III	p. 536 Clement XI to James III, Rome 25.ii.17
		IV	p. 131 James III to Alessandro Albani, Pesaro 22.iii.17
32	*l*	IV	p. 288 James III to Mar, Rome 30.v.17
32	*m*	VII	p. 283 James III to Annibale Albani 15.ix.18
33	*n*		p. vi
33	*o*	V	p. 234 Mar to Wogan, Urbino 25.xi.17
34	*p*		p. 458 Nairne to James III, Rome 29.x.18
34	*q*		p. 402 James III to Carlo Albani, Bologna 18.x.18
34	*r*		pp. 123–5 James III to Gualterio, Urbino 8.viii.18, 10.viii.18
34	*s*		p. 323 Note: "Don Alexander's im[pertinent] letter to be taken notice of."
34	*t*	VII	pp. 417–18 James III to Nairne, Bologna 21.x.18
35	*u*		p. 543 James III to Dillon, Rome 15.xi.18
36	*v*		p. 265 Dispensation 10.ix.18
36	*w*		p. 662 Lease 15.i.19
28	20	SP 92/30	Molesworth to Stanyan, Augsbourg 27.x.20

page

28 21*a* Wiesener II p. 38
30   *b*   pp. 46–9
29 22 Tayler p. 98
31 23 Haile, *Mary of Modena* p. 348
31 24 SP 85/15 f. 312 Walton, Rome 10.iii.25
31 25 SP 98/35 Skinner to Newcastle, Leghorn 7.i.34
32 26 de Brosses II p. 293
32 27 Petrie p. 286
32 28 SP 85/16 f. 221 Walton, Rome 23.viii.27
33 29 SP 80/37 Stanhope to St Saphorin, Whitehall 17.x.18.
            Draft
33 30*a* SP 80/39 St Saphorin to Stanhope, Vienna 5.vii.19
35   *b*   „   „   „ 16.xi.19
35   *c*   „   „   „ 3.ix.19
33 31*a* SP 80/38   „   „   „ 4.i.19
36   *b*   „   „   „ 24.v.19
36 32 SP 98/24 Note enclosed Fuller to Secretary of State,
            Leghorn 19.v.19

CHAPTER II

38   1 The following biographical summary is based on these
        authorities: Stosch, *Antiq. Briefe*; Strocchi; Justi, *Preuss.
        Jahr.*; Winckelmann; Fleming; *Dizionario Biografico Degli
        Italiani* (G. Sofri's article on Alessandro Albani);
        Catholic Encyclopaedia and other standard works of
        reference
39   2 Strocchi
39   3 Winckelmann, *Briefe* III pp. 298, 299
40   4 *Il Settecento a Roma*, 1959 No. 236
40   5 SP 98/29 News Letter, Rome 14.viii.27 Enclosed
            Colman to Newcastle 23.viii.27
40   6 F. 134*a* Albani to Mann 21.x.47
41   7 Dennistoun II p. 80
41   8 Casanova, quoted Winckelmann, *Briefe* IV p. 223
41   9 SP 98/75 f. 160 Mann to Weymouth 22.ix.70
42 10*a* SP 80/39 St Saphorin to Stanhope, Vienna 16.xi.19
42   *b*   „   „   „ 22.xi.19
42   *c*   „   „   „ 23.xii.19
44   *d*   „   „   „ 26.vii.19

page

42   11*a*   SP 80/43 f. 76–7 St Saphorin to Townshend, Vienna 22.iii.21

45   *b*   f. 6–7 St Saphorin to Stanhope, Vienna 22.i.21

62   *c*   f. 135 St Saphorin to Townshend, Vienna 7.v.21; Sp 80/42 Townshend to St Saphorin 11.iv.21

43   12   de Brosses II p. 119

43   13   SP 84/276 f. 111 Dayrolle to Townshend, Hague 26.ix.21

44   14*a*   British Museum Addit. MSS.:

                22. 515 f. 142 Carteret to Sutton, Whitehall 1.vi.21

44   *b*   f. 44   „   Schaub   „   4.iv.21

44   *c*   22. 516 f. 40   „   „   „   25.ix.21

46   *d*   22. 515 f. 259–64 „   „   „   28.viii.21.

44   15*a*   SP 92/30 Molesworth to Townshend, Turin 29.iii.21

62   *b*   Memo endorsed 19.ii.21

62   *c*   Molesworth to Carteret, Turin 19.iv.21

44   16*a*   Wiesener I   p. 280

45   *b*   III p. 190

45   *c*   pp. 378–9

45   *d*   pp. 396–7

48   *e*   p. 388

44   17   SP 80/38 St Saphorin to Stanhope, Vienna 7.x.19. Copy

45   18*a*   SP 80/41 St Saphorin to Stanhope, Vienna 6.vi.20

46   *b*   Stanhope to Cadogan & St Saphorin, Pirmont 26.vii.20. Copy

46   *c*   Cadogan & St Saphorin to Stanhope, Vienna 10.viii.20. Copy

47   *d*   Cadogan & St Saphorin to Stanhope, Vienna 26.vi.20. Copy

48   *e*   Cadogan & St Saphorin to Stanhope, Vienna 18.ix.20. Copy

48   19   SP 98/59 pp. 30–1 Mann to Holdernesse 6.iv.53

49   20   The following biographical summary is based on these authorities: Stosch, *Antiq. Briefe, Gemmae Antiquae*; Justi, *Zeit*; Winckelmann, *Pierres Antiques*; Kinauer, R., *Der Atlas des Freiherrn Philipp von Stosch* . . . Vienna 1950 (Unpublished thesis Oesterreichische National-

bibliothek, Karten-S 797041-C). Standard works of reference. Justi wrote on Albani, Stosch and their circle from a variety of sources which are not always identified and which have not therefore been checked in the present work.

49	21	Bentley II p. 706 Stosch to Bentley, Rome 9.vii.29
49	22	Walpole III p. 477 Mann to Walpole 7.v.48
51	23	SP 98/45 f. 238 Mann to Newcastle 6.xi.42
52	24	Haile, *Mary of Modena* pp. 259–60
52	25	SP 85/14 f. 459 Walton, Rome 18.ix.23
52	26	Bentley I p. 432
52	27	Whiston, W., *Memoirs of the Life and Writings of*, London 1749 p. 302
53	28	Bentley, Dr, *Articles against*, London 1710 pp. 9, 12–13
53	29	Bentley, *Life of Horace*, London 1711 Preface p. 23
53	30	SP 92/31 (II) f. 166 Molesworth to Carteret, Pisa 30.xii.22
54	31	de Brosses I pp. 213–14
55	32	SP 105/326 f. 263 Stosch to Craon 4.v.39. Copy
56	33	SP 105/324 f. 18 Walton, Rome 2.iii.26. Draft
60	34a	SP 105/328 f. 170 Stosch to Duncannon 28.ii.49. Copy
60, 61	b	f. 180–1 Stosch to Carteret 22.iv.49 P.S. Copy
61	35a	SP 105/329 f. 31 Stosch to Duncannon 30.vii.51. Copy
61	b	f. 47 Stosch to Holdernesse 29.x.51. Copy
62	36	SP 80/42 Townshend to St Saphorin 11.iv.21. Draft

CHAPTER III

63, 64	1a	SP 85/14 f. 1–3 Walton, Rome 31.i.22
63	b	f. 287 „ „ 6.iii.23
64	c	f. 89 „ „ 15.viii.22
64, 86	d	f. 7–8 „ „ 14.ii.22
65	e	f. 9–12 „ „ 28.ii.22
68	f	f. 23 „ „ 14.iii.22
68	g	f. 238 „ „ 16.i.23
68	h	f. 45 „ „ 11.iv.22

page

68, 69	1*i*	SP 85/14 f. 81–3	Walton, Rome 20.vi.22
69	*j*	f. 104	,, ,, 5.ix.22
69	*k*	f. 213	,, ,, 3.i.23
69	*l*	f. 89	,, ,, 15.viii.22
70	*m*	f. 145	,, ,, 31.x.22
70	*n*	f. 188	,, ,, 5.xii.22
70	*o*	f. 205	,, ,, 26.xii.22
71	*p*	f. 181	,, ,, 1.xii.22
71	*q*	f. 451	,, ,, –.ix.23
72	*r*	f. 271	,, ,, –.ii.23
72	*s*	f. 229	,, ,, 12.i.23
72	*t*	f. 350	,, ,, 29.v.23
72	*u*	f. 219	,, ,, 5.i.23
73	*v*	f. 424–5	,, ,, 21.viii.23
73	*w*	f. 489	,, ,, 23.x.23
63	2*a*	SP 105/327 f. 92	Stosch to Carteret 29.x.43. Copy
63	*b*	f. 223–4	Undertakings by Philip and Henry de Stosch 4.vii.44
63	3*a*	SP 98/32 f. 317	Newcastle to Stosch, Whitehall 9.xii.31
85	*b*	f. 30	Walton, Rome 23.ii.30
85	*c*	f. 63	,, ,, 11.v.30
85	*d*	f. 245	,, Florence 25.viii.31
86	*e*	f. 44	,, Rome 23.iii.30
86	*f*	f. 225	,, ,, 11.vii.31
86	*g*	f. 304	,, Florence 23.xi.31
86	*h*	f. 181	,, ,, 17.iv.31
87	*i*	f. 146–9	,, Rome 25.i.31
87	*j*	f. 154	,, ,, 1.ii.31
88, 90	*k*	f. 159–61	,, Florence 24.ii.31
88	*l*	f. 165	,, ,, 3.iii.31
64	4*a*	SP 92/35 (I) f. 72	Essex to Newcastle, Turin 5.iv.33
78	*b*	f. 74	Stosch to Essex 28.iii.33
64	5	SP 105/324 f. 243–4	Walton, Rome 1.xi.27. Draft
64	6	Stosch, *Antiq. Briefe* p. 14	
66	7	*Dictionnaire de l'Académie Française:* "Maquereau: Terme dont il n'est pas honnête de se servir. Celui qui fait métier de débaucher et de prostituer des femmes. . . ."
68	8	Stosch, P. de, *Gemmae Antiquae Caelatae* or *Pierres*

Antiques Gravées, Amsterdam 1724 (Text in
Latin and French)

68	9	Quynn p. 336
69	10a	SP 98/26 Skinner to Newcastle, Leghorn 17.vi.30
81	b	„ „ „ 9.iii.26
84	c	„ „ „ 10.i.28
70	11	SP 92/31 (II) f. 161 Molesworth to Carteret, Pisa 23.xii.22
71	12a	SP 98/34 Skinner to Newcastle, Florence 19.xi.33
71	b	„ Delafaye „ 11.x.33
80	c	„ Newcastle „ 3.x.33
71	13	SP 98/33 Colman to Newcastle 28.xii.31
71	14	SP 98/35 Extract, Rome 13.xii.33, enclosed by Skinner 7.i.35
73	15a	SP 85/15 f. 28-9 Walton, Rome 1.ii.24
73	b	f. 38 „ „ 11.iii.24
74	c	f. 85 „ „ 25.iv.24
74	d	f. 34 „ „ 7.iii.24
74	e	f. 115 „ „ 16.v.24
74	f	f. 56 „ „ 4.iv.24
75	g	f. 127 „ „ 3.vi.24
75	h	f. 133-7 „ „ 10.vi.24
75	i	f. 149 „ „ 24.vi.24
75	j	f. 239 Newcastle to Stosch 4.v.24. Draft
75	k	f. 194-5 Walton, Rome 16.ix.24
76	l	f. 153-4 „ „ 8.vii.24
77	m	f. 197 „ „ 23.ix.24
77	n	f. 165 „ „ 29.vii.24
77	o	f. 145 „ „ 18.vi.24
77	p	f. 171 „ „ 5.viii.24
77, 78	q	f. 161-2 „ „ 22.vii.24
78	r	f. 350 „ „ 2.v.25
		f. 362 „ „ 9.v.25
78	s	f. 289 „ „ 24.ii.25
78	t	f. 274 „ „ 3.ii.25
79	u	f. 222 „ „ 2.xii.24
79	v	f. 468-9 Stosch to Walpole, Rome 17.xi.25
79	w	f. 237 Walton, Rome 30.xii.24
79	x	f. 251 „ „ 20.i.25
80	y	f. 490-1 „ „ 22.xi.25

NOTES

page

84 15 SP 85/15 f. 447 Walton, Rome 6.x.25
73 16a SP 105/323 f. 44 „ „ 24.iv.24
77 b f. 18 „ „ 12.ii.24. Draft
77 c f. 75 „ „ 15.vii.24. Draft
79 d f. 125 Bacon Morrice to Stosch, Rome 1724
75 17 SP 92/33 (I) Allen to Newcastle, Turin 20.xi.28, 27.xi.28
77 18 SP 98/29 Letter from Rome enclosed Colman to Newcastle 13.ix.27
80 19a SP 98/25 Bacon Morrice to Colman, Florence 10.ii.25
82 b Colman to Delafaye, Florence 6.xii.26
80 20 SP 98/28 Newcastle to Colman, Whitehall 22.ii.25
81 21a SP 85/13 f. 118 Edgar to M. le Ferme, Rome 28.xi.24
85 b f. 123 Secretary of State to Walton, Whitehall 1.iv.29. Draft
81 22a Bentley II pp. 632–6
82 b p. 650
82 23a SP 85/16 f. 188 Walton, Rome 14.xii.26
82 b f. 88 „ „ 1.vi.26
82 c f. 171–2 „ „ 16.xi.26
82 d f. 93 „ „ 13.vi.26
83 e f. 155 „ „ 3.x.26
83 f f. 272–3 „ „ 21.vi.27
83 g f. 176 „ „ 23.xi.26
84 h f. 249 „ „ 26.iv.27
85 i f. 572 „ „ 11.viii.29
85 j f. 589 „ „ 21.ix.29
85 k f. 586 „ „ 15.ix.29
83 24 Carutti, Domenico, *Storia della Diplomazia della Corte di Savoia*, 1879 p. 610
83 25 Archivi di Stato, Torino Sezione Prima (Piazza Castello), Lettere Ministri, Roma. The King to d'Orméa 13.viii.30. Note communicated by Mr R. Pommer.
86 26a Arnold, Ralph, *Northern Lights, the Story of Lord Derwentwater*, London 1959 p. 170
86 b *Northern Lights, the Story of Lord Derwentwater*, London 1959 pp. 192–3
86 27 SP 92/40 Essex to Newcastle, Turin 21.vii.36

244

page

86	28	SP 98/37 f. 35 Walton 6.ii.34
86	29	SP 98/41 f. 265 Walton 16.ii.39
88	30	Stosch, *Antiq. Briefe* p. 15
90	31	SP 98/31 Colman to Newcastle, Florence 24.ii.31
90	32*a*	Walpole I pp. 253–4 Note 30
90	*b*	II p. 225 Walpole to Mann 4.v.43

CHAPTER IV

91, 96,

98	1*a*	SP 98/32 f.179–81 Walton,		Florence	17.iv.31
92	*b*	f. 140–1	„	Rome	4.i.31
92	*c*	f. 187–8	„	Florence	5.v.31
93	*d*	f. 218	„	„	26.vi.31
94	*e*	f. 424	„	„	2.viii.32
		f. 436	„	„	13.ix.32
94	*f*	f. 496–9	„	„	7.iii.33
98	*g*	f. 197	„	„	12.v.31
99	*h*	f. 601	„	„	12.xii.33
103	*i*	f. 185	„	„	28.iv.31
92	2	SP 85/16 f. 172 Walton, Rome 16.x.26			
93	3*a*	SP 105/325 f. 85 Stosch to Colman, Florence 31.vii.31			
93	*b*	f. 110 Stosch to Churchill, Florence 20.x.31. Copy			
		f. 125 Stosch to Churchill, Florence 17.xi.31. Copy			
94	*c*	f. 318 Dodington to Albani, Eastbury 9.vii.33. Copy			
		Albani to Dodington, Rome 30.vii.33. Copy			
93	4	Michaelis p. 324 quoting Horace Walpole's *Aedes Walpoliana*			
94	5*a*	SP 98/38 f. 160 News Letter, Rome 8.x.35			
99	*b*	f. 127 Harrington to Fane, Hanover 30.ix.35. Copy			
94	6	F. 159 Dodington to Albani, London 9.v.54			
96	7*a*	SP 92/35 (I) f. 79 Essex to Newcastle, Turin 7.iv.33			

NOTES

page

101	7*b*	SP 92/35 (III) f. 256 Essex to Newcastle, Turin 13.x.33
113	*c*	f. 293 Essex to Newcastle, Turin 4.xi.33
96	8*a*	SP 92/34 (I) f. 2 Instructions
		f. 6 Pro Memoria of Interview, Essex with Newcastle
96	*b*	(II) f. 76 Essex to Newcastle, Turin 26.xi.32
98	*c*	(I) f. 44 „ „ „ 16.viii.32
96	9	SP 85/13 Newcastle to Waldegrave, Whitehall 5.vi.32
97	10*a*	SP 92/36 Newcastle to Essex, Whitehall 22.xi.33. Draft
105	*b*	Newcastle to Essex, Whitehall 20.vii.34. Draft
97	11*a*	SP 92/39 Essex to Newcastle, Turin 2.xi.35
98	*b*	Villettes to Newcastle, Turin 15.iv.35
97	12*a*	SP 92/37 Villettes to Newcastle, Turin 21.vii.34
97	*b*	Essex „ „ 17.iv.34
97	13	The Duke of Liria was the son of the Duke of Berwick, the Old Pretender's illegitimate half-brother, and himself an army commander of distinction
98	14	SP 98/85 f. 140-1 Walton 27.vii.43
98	15	SP 92/41 Villettes to Newcastle, Turin 11.v.37
98	16	de Brosses II p. 245
99	17*a*	SP 98/37 f. 160 Walton 11.ix.34
99	*b*	f. 164 „ 25.ix.34
99	*c*	f. 162 „ 18.ix.34
99	*d*	f. 260 „ 6.viii.35
		f. 261 „ 13.viii.35
110	*e*	f. 402-3 „ 15.ix.36
111	*f*	f. 254 „ 16.vii.35
99	18*a*	SP 98/41 f. 2 Walton 5.i.37
		f. 125 „ 6.i.38
		f. 288 „ 12.iv.39
99	*b*	f. 77 „ 12.viii.37
99	*c*	f. 38 „ 4.v.37
99	*d*	f. 146 „ 10.iii.38
		f. 228 „ 18.xi.38
		f. 356 „ 1.xi.39
114	*e*	f. 322 „ 19.vii.39

page

99	19*a*	SP 98/43 f. 4	Walton 10.i.40
115	*b*	f. 139	„ 18.ii.41
		f. 141	„ 25.ii.41
99	20*a*	SP 92/42 Villettes to Newcastle, Turin 16.ix.39	
100	*b*	„ „ „ 22.vii.39	
100	21*a*	SP 98/42 f. 97	News Letters, Naples 7.iv.39
		f. 133	„ „ Rome 9.v.39
113	*b*	f. 201	Mann to Newcastle 24.viii.39
113	*c*	f. 223	„ „ 29.ix.39
114	*d*	f. 207	„ „ 1.ix.39
100	22	Kettner, Hermann, *Die Bildwerke der Königlichen Antiken-sammlung zu Dresden*, 1856 pp. 5–6	
100	23*a*	SP 98/44 f. 34	Mann to Newcastle 14.ii.40
110	*b*	f. 439	Petition by Mann
112	*c*	f. 276	Newcastle to Mann, Whitehall 26.iv.40
114	*d*	f. 209	Mann to Harrington 27.ix.40
100	24	Walpole (Paget Toynbee) I p. 61 Walpole to H. Seymour Conway, Rome 23.iv.40	
		Supplement III pp. 107–8, Albani to Walpole from Conclave 3.vii.40	
101	25*a*	SP 98/26 Skinner to Newcastle, Leghorn 26.v.24	
101	*b*	Account enclosed Colman to Newcastle, Florence 10.ii.30	
		Newcastle to Skinner, Hampton Court, 14.x.31. Draft	
101	26	SP 92/31 (III) f. 345 Molesworth to Carteret, Turin 22.iv.24	
102	27	SP 98/25 Colman to Newcastle, Florence 5.x.26	
102	28*a*	SP 98/31 Colman to Stosch 30.i.31. Draft	
103	*b*	Colman to Newcastle 2.iii.31	
102	29	Walpole II p. 428 Mann to Walpole 7.iv.44	
103	30*a*	SP 98/33 Colman to Newcastle, Florence 23.i.32	
103	*b*	Newcastle to Colman 31.iii.32. Draft	
104	*c*	Colman to Newcastle, Florence 1.iv.32	
104	*d*	Colman to Delafaye, Florence 13.ix.32	
103	31*a*	SP 98/34 Skinner to Delafaye, Florence 21.xi.33	
104	*b*	„ „ „ 10.x.33	
		Petition 25.viii.33	
103	32*a*	SP 98/40 f. 179 Fane to Newcastle, Florence 26.viii.37	

111	32*b*	SP 98/40 f. 92	News Letter, Rome 18.v.37		
		f. 109	„	„	Florence 2.vii.37
111	*c*	f. 80	Fane to Newcastle, Pisa 21.v.37		
111	*d*	f. 94	„	„	Florence 18.vi.37
		f. 168	„	„	„ 13.viii.37
112	*e*	f. 121	„	„	„ 4. ii.37
112	*f*	f. 239	„	„	„ 3. ii.38
112	*g*	f. 259	Mann to Newcastle, Leghorn 21.iv.38		
112	*h*	f. 314	„	„	Florence 11.viii.38
113	*i*	f. 300	„	„	„ 30.vi.38
103	33*a*	SP 98/28	Newcastle to Skinner, Whitehall 2.iii.33. Draft		
105	*b*		Newcastle to Fane, Whitehall 20.vii.34. Draft		
110	*c*		Newcastle to Fane, Whitehall 16.vii.36. Draft		
111	*d*		Newcastle to Fane, Whitehall 11.vii.37. Draft		
104	34	SP 98/35	Notes enclosed Skinner to Newcastle, Florence 7.ix.34, 12.x.34		
105	35*a*	SP 98/36	Fane to Newcastle, Florence 27.xi.34		
106	*b*		„	„	5.ii.35, 1.iii.35
106	*c*		Rhodes to Courand	8.iii.35	
106	*d*		Fane to Newcastle,	„	30.iii.35
110	*e*		„	„	3.ix.36
110	*f*		„	„	21.xi.35
110	36	SP 98/48 f. 302	Mann's claims for arrears 13.x.44		
111	37	SP 105/281 f. 159	Newcastle to Fane 25.viii.37 P.S.		
112	38	B.M. Egerton MSS. 2235 f. 94 (referred to Walpole I p. xxx)			
112	39	F. 132	Mann to Albani 17.i.47		
115	40	SP 92/47	Villettes to Carteret 26.ix.43		

CHAPTER V

117	1*a*	SP 98/46 f. 161	Walton 9.ii.43		
117	*b*	f. 188–9	„	20.iv.43	
		f. 199	„	4.v.43	

NOTES

page

117	1*c*	SP 98/46 f. 215	Walton 15.vi.43
120	*d*	f. 235	„ 17.viii.43
117	2	Information communicated by Mr R. Pommer from researches in Turin archives
118	3*a*	Walpole II p. 56	Mann to Walpole 23.ix.42
120	*b*	p. 161	„ „ 18.ii.43
120	*c*	III p. 12	„ „ 9.iii.45
123	*d*	II p. 373	„ „ 21.i.44
124	*e*	p. 532	„ „ 24.xi.44
129	*f*	p. 149	„ „ 10.xi.45
129	*g*	III p. 142	„ „ 9.xi.45
130	*h*	p. 113	„ „ 5.x.45
138	*i*	p. 475	„ „ 9.iv.48
118	4	SP 98/45 f. 213 Mann to Newcastle 23.ix.42
118	5*a*	SP 98/44 f. 269 Mann to Newcastle 27.xii.40
119	*b*	f. 435–6 Mann to Courand 24.vi.42
119	6*a*	SP 105/308 f. 97 Quarelli to Mann, Rome 10.vi.43
119	*b*	f. 50 Albani to Mann, Rome 15.viii.43
121	*c*	f. 140 Villettes to Mann, Turin 10.v.47
139	*d*	f. 66 Albani to Mann 1.vii.47 (F. 133)
140	*e*	f. 101 Villettes to Mann, Turin 14.vi.47
141	*f*	f. 207, 216, 218
120	7*a*	SP 105/283 f. 247 Albani to Mann 1.viii.44
120	*b*	f. 374 Matthews to Mann, Namur in Vado Bay, 23.vi.44
123	*c*	f. 278 Albani to Mann 15.viii.44
123	*d*	f. 388 Villettes to Mann 8.vii.44
123	*e*	f. 362 Albani to Mann 11.vii.44
		f. 245 „ „ 1.viii.44
		f. 273 „ „ 8.viii.44
123	*f*	f. 250 Villettes to Mann, Turin 5.viii.44
121	8*a*	SP 98/48 f. 180 Mann to Albani 12.vi.44. Copy
123	*b*	f. 342 News Letter, Florence 24.xi.44
124	*c*	f. 345–6 Albani to Mann 21.xi.44
125	*d*	f. 343–4 Mann to Carteret (not dated) *c.* 21.xi.44
121	9	SP 92/42 Villettes to Stone, Turin 12.xi.39
121	10*a*	F. 133 Copy orders and instructions for Mr Richard Gaven 13.vi.44
122	*b*	Gaven to Albani, Rome 5.ix.44

page

122 11*a* F. 132 Albani to Gaven 15.iv.47, 23.iv.45
122   *b*   Chesterfield to Albani, London 30.xii.48
126   *c*   Mann to Albani 10.i.47
138   *d*   „   „   18.iv.47
122 12   F. 161 Gaven to Albani, London 7.ii.55
123 13*a* SP 98/49 f. 22 Walton 25.i.44
132   *b*   f. 219   „   5.x.45
123 14*a* F. 125 Albani to Holdernesse 5.xii.44
125   *b*   Mann to Albani 30.xi.44
124 15*a* SP 98/50 f. 232   Mann to Newcastle 31.viii.45
128   *b*   f. 286–9   „   „   2.xi.45
129   *c*   f. 202   „   „   10.viii.45
130   *d*   f. 33–4   „   „   26.i.45
130   *e*   f. 206   „   „   10.viii.45
134   *f*   f. 164   „   „   1745
125 16*a* F. 126 Richecourt to Albani, Florence 29.xii.44
125   *b*   Mann to Albani 23.i.45
126   *c*   Albani to Holdernesse 6.iii.45
127   *d*   Albani to Mann 30.i.45
127   *e*   „   „   6.iii.45
128   *f*   Mann to Albani 11.v.45
128   *g*   Albani to Mann 29.v.45
128   *h*   Mann to Albani 25.v.45
131   *i*   Albani to Mann 27.ii.45
129 17   SP 85/13 f. 249 *Copy of a letter from a Gentleman in Rome to his Correspondent in England,* 2.x.45
130 18*a* F. 127 Albani to Mann 31.vii.45, 7.viii.45
                    Mann to Albani 3.viii.45
131   *b*   „   „   20.x.45
132   *c*   „   „   -.iv.45
133   *d*   Rowley to Albani, à la rade d'Oristan la bord du Malbrough 15.x.45
134   *e*   Mann to Albani 20.vii.45
131 19*a* SP 98/51 f. 23 Mann to Newcastle 11.i.46
129   *b*   f. 75   „   „   22.iii.46
132 20*a* F. 130 Chute to Albani, Berlin 24.viii.46
135   *b* F. 130 Albani to Mann 30.vii.46
132 21   F. 128 Mann to Albani 28.xii.45
132 22*a* F. 129 Albani to Mann 23.iv.46

page

132 22*b* F. 129 Mann to Albani 31.v.46
133 *c* Albani to Mann 25.vi.46, 11.vi.46
134 *d* Mann to Albani 31.iii.46, 17.v.46
133 23 F. 162 Albani to Forbes 7.vi.55
133 24 F. 165 Forbes to Albani, London 3.viii.56
134 25 F. 131 Mann to Albani 1.xi.46, 22.xi.46
135 26*a* SP 98/52 f. 332-3 Albani to Mann 23.xii.47
            (F. 135)
135 *b* f. 327-8 Mann to Newcastle 26.xii.47
141 *c* f. 132 ,,   ,,   30.v.47
135 27 F. 135 Mann to Albani 26.xii.47
136 28*a* F. 137 Bedford to Albani, Whitehall 29.iv.48
137 *b* Albani to Mann 8.iv.48
139 *c* —— to Albani, *du Palais du Roi* 24.viii.48
136 29*a* SP 98/56 f. 336 Albani to Mann 28.vi.49
137 *b* f. 101 Mann to Newcastle 26.iii.48
139 *c* f. 189 Mann to Bedford 20.viii.48
        f. 199-200 ,,   ,,   13.ix.48
141 *d* f. 166 ,,   ,,   9.vii.48
141 *e* f. 56 Towneley to ——, Paris 9.i.48
        f. 57 ,,   ,,   ,, 24.xii.47
136 30 F. 140 Mann to Albani 1.vii.49
136 31 SP 105/309 f. 174-5 Albani to Mann 27.ix.49
            (F. 140)
137 32 SP 105/316 f. 177 Giordani to Mann 13.vii.65
139 33*a* F. 138 Mann to Albani 20.iv.48
143 *b* ,,   ,,   1.x.48, 5.xi.48
142 34 SP 98/32 f. 470 Walton 20.xii.32
142 35 F. 136 Albani to Mann 9.iii.48; Mann to Albani
            12.iii.48

CHAPTER VI

144 1 Lumsden ultimately obtained a full pardon and published a book: *Remarks on the Antiquities of Rome and its Environs*, London 1797
145 2*a* SP 98/57 f. 190 Mann to Newcastle 16.iv.51

page

149	2*b*	SP 98/57 f. 404	Mann to Holdernesse 14.viii.52
149	*c*	f. 107	Mann to Bedford 28.viii.50
145	3*a*	F. 139	Mann to Albani 21.i.49
145	*b*	„	„ 15.iv.49
147	*c*	„	„ 13.v.49, 20.v.49
147	*d*	„	„ 10.vi.49, 17.vi.49
151	*e*	„	„ 25.ii.49
155, 169	*f*		Albani to Dodington 4.i.49
145	4*a*	SP 105/309 f. 142	Albani to Mann 7.vi.49 (F. 139)
147	*b*	f. 111–12	„ „ 3.v.49 (F. 139)
148	*c*	f. 152	„ „ 12.vii.49 (F. 140)
149	*d*	f. 84	„ „ 29.iii.49 (F. 139)
151	*e*	f. 105	„ „ 19.iv.49 (F. 139)
152	*f*	f. 170	„ „ 13.ix.49 (F. 140)
153	*g*	f. 172–3	Brettingham to Mann, Rome 13.ix.49
162	*h*	f. 228	Albani to Mann 19.viii.52 (F. 152)
163	*i*	f. 234	„ „ 30.xii.52 (F. 140)
169	*j*	f. 163–5	„ „ 30.viii.49
		f. 165	Hoare to Albani 26.viii.49
147	5	SP 98/53 f. 247	Walton 30.v.49
147	6	F. 181	Baron de Reischach to Albani, The Hague 16.ii.62
147	7	F. 175	Albani to O. Hope 4.vii.59
148	8*a*	F. 144	Mann to Albani 8.ix.50
156	*b*		Dodington to Albani, Eastbury 25.vii.50
			Albani to Dodington 5.ix.50
157	*c*	„	„ 12.viii.50
158	*d*		Mann to Albani 1.ix.50
148	9*a*	F. 158	Mann to Albani 26.ii.54
			Albani to Mann 2.iii.54
167	*b*		Mann to Albani 22.i.54
168	*c*		Dartmouth to Albani and North to Albani, Paris 12.ii.54
169	*d*		Mann to Albani 5.ii.54
170	*e*	„	„ 15.i.54
170	*f*	„	„ 19.ii.54
149	10	SP 98/62 f. 41	Mann to Robinson 10.v.55
149	11	SP 105/291 f. 28	Mann to Amyand 7.vi.54
150	12*a*	SP 105/310 f. 135	Albani to Mann 22.ix.53 (F. 156)

page					
160	12b	SP 105/310 f. 253	Albani to Mann	2.iii.54 (F. 158)	
163	c		f. 7	„ „	6.i.53
163	d		f. 13	„ „	20.i.53
163,	e		f. 17	„ „	10.ii.53 (F. 154)
			f. 58–9	„ „	7.iv.53 (F. 155)
164	f		f. 63	„ „	14.iv.53 (F. 155)
			f. 64	„ „	21.iv.53 (F. 155)
164	g		f. 73	„ „	12.v.53 (F. 155)
165	h		f. 387	„ „	17.viii.54 (F. 160)
168	i		f. 228–9	„ „	26.i.54 (F. 158)
168	j		f. 233–4	„ „	2.ii.54 (F. 158)
170	k		f. 223–4	„ „	19.i.54 (F. 158)
			f. 243–4	„ „	16.ii.54 (F. 158)
172	l		f. 19	„ „	10.ii.53

150 13a Walpole I p. 164 Walpole to Mann 5.x.41; pp. 419–20 6.v.42

150 b pp. xxxi-xxxii

161 c III p. 246 Mann to Walpole 26.iv.46 p. 264 Walpole to Mann 6.vi.46; p. 420 26.vi.47

150 14a SP 105/283 f. 378 Matthews to Mann, Namur in Vado Bay 24.vi.44 This does not refer to Godolphin's acquisition of the famous 'Arabian', which was already in his stable

150 b f. 252–3 Paterson to Mann, Leghorn 6.viii.44

150 15 SP 105/285 f. 83 Rochford to Mann, St James's 2.vi.75 P.S.

151 16 F. 140 Mann to Albani, Pisa 8.ix.49
153 17a F. 141 Albani to Mann 11.x.49
153 b „ „ 18.x.49, 25.x.49
154 c „ „ 1.xi.49
174 d Mann to Albani 14.x.49
154 18 Michaelis pp. 71, 305, 306, 311, 312
154 19 SP 85/16 f. 167 Walton, Rome 2.xi.26 SP 98/32 f. 580–1
154,
158 20 F. 146 Dodington to Albani 17.xii.50

page

154	21*a*	F. 164 Albani to Mann 19.vi.56
173	*b*	„ „ 10.i.56
155	22	Caylus, [Comte de, *Correspondance Inédite*, Paris 1877I p. 2
		Caylus to Paciaudi, Paris 7.ii.57, p. 70 14.v.59
		II p. 33 27.viii.64
155	23	F. 138 Albani to Dodington 12.x.48
156	24	Woolfe and Gandon, *Vitruvius Britannicus*, 1767 IV pp. 26–9
		Lysons, Daniel, *Environs of London*, 1795 II pp. 402–4
		Colvin, H. M., *Dictionary of English Architects*, London 1954, entry for Roger Morris
156	25*a*	F. 142 Dodington to Albani, Richmond 3.v.50
157	*b*	Albani to Dodington 20.vi.50
156,		
158	26*a*	F. 150 Dodington to Albani, London 9.i.52
161	*b*	Mann to Albani 15.ii.52
169	*c*	„ „ 3.ii.52
170	*d*	Albani to Mann 19.ii.52, 26.ii.52
170,		
171	*e*	Mann to Albani 1.iii.52
171	*f*	Albani to Mann 11.iii.52
158	27*a*	F. 145 Dodington to Albani, London 11.x.50
		Albani to Dodington 14.xi.50
158	*b*	Albani to Mann 5.ix.50
158	28*a*	F. 149 Dodington to Albani, London 7.x.51
159	*b*	Albani to Dodington 13.xi.51
173	*c*	Mann to Albani 12.x.51
		Albani to Mann 23.x.51
174	*d*	Mann to Albani 21.ix.51; 28.ix.51
159	29*a*	F. 148 Dodington to Albani, Eastbury 12.viii.51
174	*b*	Albani to Mann 25.ix.51
159	30*a*	F. 155 Albani to Dodington 30.vi.53
160	*b*	Dodington to Albani, not dated but answered 17.iv.53
164	*c*	Mann to Albani 10.iv.53
164	*d*	„ „ 24.iv.53
164	*e*	„ „ 15.v.53
159	31*a*	SP 98/59 f. 83 Mann to Holdernesse 11.ix.53

page

163   31 *b* SP 98/59 f. 15–16 Albani to Mann 3.ii.53 (F. 155)
160   32*a*   F. 156 Albani to Dodington 15.viii.53
160   *b*   Dodington to Albani, London 21.vi.53
167   *c*   Mann to Albani 31.vii.53
160   33   Whitley, W. T., *Artists and their Friends in England 1700–99*, London 1928 I p. 238
160   34   F. 159 Dodington to Albani, London 9.v.54
160   35*a*   F. 161 Dodington to Albani, London 27.i.55
165   *b*   Albani to Mann 4.i.55
172   *c*   Mann to Albani 25.ii.55
             Albani to Mann 22.iii.55
160   36   F. 165 Dodington to Albani, London 2.vii.56
161   37   Scott-Elliot, A. H., *The Statues by Francavilla in the Royal Collection*, Burlington Magazine, March 1956 pp. 77–84
161   38   SP 98/24 Fuller to Craggs, Leghorn 12.iv.20, 19.iv.20, 17.v.20
162   39*a*   F. 152 Mann to Albani 1.viii.52
162   *b*   Albani to Mann 12.viii.52
162   *c*   ,,   ,,   26.viii.52
163   40   Mann to Dodington 28.vii.53 Unpublished letter in the possession and quoted by permission of Mr W. S. Lewis
165   41*a*   F. 160 Mann to Albani 20.viii.54
171   *b*   ,,   ,,   1.x.54
             Albani to Mann 12.x.54
165   42   F. 162 Albani to Mann 5.vii.55, 17.v.55
166   43   Waagen I p. 394
167   44   Walpole (Paget Toynbee) III p. 360 Walpole to Mann, Strawberry Hill 27.x.55; pp. 52–3, Arlington St 5.v.57
167   45   London County Council, *Survey of London* Vol. XVIII, *The Strand*, 1937
167   46   Information from the Duke of Northumberland and Mr C. de Bestigui
171   47*a*   F. 154 Mann to Albani 13.ii.53
172   *b*   ,,   ,,   21.i.53
171   48   F. 142 Mann to Albani 12.ii.50
171   49   Constable p. 30

173 50 Watson, F. J. B., *Thomas Patch (1725–1728)*, Walpole
Society, Vol. XXVIII 1939–40

173 51 F. 163 Albani to Mann 27.xii.55

CHAPTER VII

176 1*a* F. 164 Mann to Albani 13.i.56, 20.i.56
              Albani to Mann 17.i.56, 24.i.56

177   *b*   ,,   ,,   26.vi.56, 29.vi.56

178   *c*   Mann to Albani 22.vi.56

200   *d*   Albani to Mann 10.iv.56

177 2 F. 150 Albani to Mann 19.ii.52, 26.ii.52, SP 98/61 f. 167
              Walton 9.viii.54, f.191–2 1.xi.54

178 3*a* F. 170 Mann to Albani 4.iv.58, 11.iv.58

178   *b*   Albani to Mann 8.iv.58

181   *c*   ,,   ,,   24.i.58

178 4 Mann to Dodington 8.v.58 Unpublished letter in the
possession and published by permission of Mr W. S.
Lewis

178 5*a* SP 105/312 f. 9 Albani to Mann 15.iv.58 (F.170),
                          8.iv.58 (F. 170)

186   *b*   f. 67 Albani to Mann 14.x.58 (F. 172)
               f. 68   ,,   ,,   21.x.58 (F. 172)

198   *c*   f. 98   ,,   ,,   6.i.59 (F. 173)

179 6*a* Winckelmann, *Briefe* II p. 36 Winckelmann to
                                Muzell-Stosch, Rome 2.x.59

202   *b*   III p. 57 Winckelmann to H.
                                  Füssli, Rome 22.ix.64; to
                                  Muzell-Stosch 7.xii.64

179 7*a* F. 166 Albani to Mann 5.iii.57

179   *b*   Dodington to Albani, London 12.xi.56

179 8*a* F. 168 Mann to Albani 12.vii.57
              Albani to Mann 16.vii.57

181   *b*   ,,   ,,   23.vii.57

190   *c*   Muzell to Albani 9.viii.57, 16.viii.57
              Albani to Muzell 13.viii.57, 27.viii.57

180 9*a* SP 105/313 f. 462 Albani to Mann 18.iv.61 (F. 178)

181   *b*   f. 470   ,,   ,,   25.iv.61 (F. 178)

187   *c*   f. 300   ,,   ,,   3.xii.60

page

198   9*d*   SP 105/313 f. 29 Albani to Mann 23.ii.60 (F. 178)

180   10   F. 182 Albani to Dodington 1.v.62

180   11   SP 105/314 f. 281 Albani to Mann 28.viii.62 (F. 183)

181   12   Mann to Albani 28.ix.56, 16.xi.56, 23.x.56, 9.xi.56, 18.x.56
             Albani to Mann 13.i.56

181,

183   13*a*   F. 169 Mann to Albani 27.ix.57, 9.ix.57

183   *b*   Albani to Mann 1.x.57, 8.x.57

192   *c*   Mann to Albani 1.xi.57
            Muzell to Albani –.xi.57, –.xi.57
            Albani to Muzell 5.xi.57

192   *d*   Mann to Albani 14.xi.57

193   *e*   Albani to Muzell-Stosch 12.xi.57, 19.xi.57
            Muzell-Stosch to Albani 18.xi.57

181   14*a*   F. 172 Mann to Albani 15.x.58

195   *b*   Albani to Muzell-Stosch 18.xi.58 (Published
            Winckelmann, *Briefe* IV p. 125)

181,

187   15*a*   F. 178 Mann to Albani 13.xii.60, 17.iii.61

184   *b*   de Gaven to Albani, London 13.i.61

200   *c*   Albani to de Gaven 4.ii.61

181   16*a*   F. 181 Mann to Albani 2.iii.62, 8.xi.62

197   *b*   Norris to Albani 18.xii.61 (Latin)
            Albani to Norris 17.ii.62 (Latin), transl.
            Minutes, Society of Antiquaries VIII p. 419

181   17   F. 185 Mann to Albani 17.ii.63

181   18*a*   F. 176 Mann to Albani 20.xi.59, 27.xi.59, 4.xii.59

195   *b*   Albani to Muzell-Stosch 27.x.59 (Published
            Winckelmann, *Briefe* IV p. 126 dated, appar-
            ently in error, 23.x.59)

181   19*a*   F. 177c Mann to Albani 2.ix.60, 14.x.60

199   *b*   Albani to O. Hope 9.viii.60

182   20   Galt, J., *Life . . . of Benjamin West*, London 1820
            pp. 101–4

182   21   Raimbach, A., *Memoirs and Recollections*, London 1843
            p. 50 Footnote 67

183, 184,

185   22   Fleming

184   23   SP 98/64 f. 139 Mann to Pitt 8.x.57

185   24   de Brosses II p. 164

page

185   25   SP 105/327 f. 50 Stosch to Carlisle 2.vi.43. Draft
186   26a   Dennistoun I pp. 244, 260, 286
186   b   p. 279
188   c   II pp. 3, 10, 11, 22
188   d   I pp. 287–9
186   27a   Walpole (Paget Toynbee) IV p. 388 Walpole to Mann, Strawberry Hill 7.v.60
195   b   IV p. 411 Walpole to Mann, Arlington St 1.viii.60
186, 188   28   Skelton, John, *Letters of*, Ed. Brinsley Ford, Walpole Society Vol. XXXVI 1956–8
187   29a   Justi, *Winckelmann* II p. 425
194   b   p. 335
187   30   F. 186 Mann to Albani 10.v.63, 7.vi.63
188   31a   SP 105/315 f. 137 Albani to Mann 11.vi.63 (F. 186)
196   b   f. 208 Grenville to Mann, Constantinople 1.viii.63
202   c   f. 796 Giordani to Mann 1.xii.64
189   32   F. 167 Albani to Muzell –.vi.57
192, 196   33   Doran I pp. 424–5 Mann to Walpole 12.xi.57
193   34   F. 180 Albani to Muzell-Stosch 12.xii.61
194   35   Schlichtegroll, F., *Dactyliotheca Stoschiana* . . . 2 Vols. Nuremberg 1805
          Raspe, R. E., *Descriptive Catalogue* . . . *of Collection* . . . *of* . . . *Engraved Gems cast by James Tassie*, London 1791
194   36   Quynn pp. 342–4
194   37   Justi, *Zeit.* p. 338
195   38a   Antiquaries, Society of, *Minutes* Vol. VIII pp. 302, 328
196   b   Antiquaries, Society of, *Minutes* Vol. VIII pp. 322, 343, 412
197   c   Antiquaries, Society of, *Minutes* Vol. VIII pp. 336, 358, 411
198   39   SP 105/310 f. 153 Albani to Mann 6.x.53 (F. 157)
198   40   F. 162   Albani to Mann 7.vi.55
198   41   F. 175   Albani to O. Hope 4.vii.59
199   42   F. 195/6 Albani to J. Hope 28.vi.66
          Hope to Albani ——. 18.xi.66

page

199	42	F. 197 Albani to Hope 18.iii.67
200	43	Thieme-Becker
202	44	Winckelmann, *Briefe*; Justi, *Preuss. Jahr.*; Noack, F., *Das Deutsche Rom*, Rome 1912; Veysset, J. (especially for excellent illustrations); *Country Life* XVII (1905) pp. 738–48, 774–82 (Villa Albani)
203	45	Miller, A., *Letters from Italy*, London 1776 III pp. 130–3

CHAPTER VIII

204	1a	SP 105/315 f. 71	Albani to Mann	26.iii.63	(F. 185)
204	b	f. 230	,,	,, 10.ix.63	(F. 187)
206	c	f. 246	,,	,, 17.ix.63	(F. 187)
		f. 258	,,	,, 24.ix.63	(F. 187)
206	d	f. 300	,,	,, 22.x.63	(F. 187)
206	e	f. 316	,,	,, 19.xi.63	(F. 187)
207	f	f. 539	Giordani to Mann 15.iv.64		
		f. 521	Albani to Mann 31.iii.64		(F. 188)
207,					
219	g	f. 547	,,	,, 21.iv.64	(F. 188)
		f. 551	Giordani to Mann 25.iv.64, 16.vi.64		
208	h	f. 256–7	Giordani to Mann 21.ix.63		
208	i	f. 314	Albani to Mann 12.xi.63		(F. 187)
		f. 575	,,	,, 12.v.64	(F. 189)
		f. 555	Giordani to Mann 28.iv.64		
219	j	f. 780	,,	,, 14.xi.64	
219	k	f. 784	,,	,, 17.xi.64	
219	l	f. 796	,,	,, 1.xii.64	
226	m	f. 748	Albani to Mann 13.x.64		(F. 190)
204	2a	F. 187 Mann to Albani 6.ix.63			
205	b	,,	,, 13.ix.63		
205	3	SP 105/314 f. 380 Phelps to Mann, Turin 24.xi.62			
205	4a	SP 105/293 f. 233 Mann to Neville 21.v.63. Draft			
211	b	f. 18 Mann to Pitt 5.iv.60			
206	5	SP 98/68 f. 249 Mann to Halifax 1.x.63			
207	6a	SP 98/69 f. 67–8 ,, ,, 31.iii.64			
207	b	f. 86 Albani to Mann 28.iv.64 (F. 188)			
208	c	f. 82 Mann to Halifax 24.iv.64			
		f. 90–1 ,, ,, 5.v.64			

page

211 6d SP 98/69 f. 96–7 Mann to Halifax 12.v.64

208 7 F. 189 Mann to Albani 8.v.64

209 8a F. 190 Albani to (Georgiana) Lady Spencer 29.xii.64, 16.iii.65. Noted Hist. MSS. Commission 2nd Report, Spencer MSS. p. 13

219 b Mann to Albani 20.xi.64

209 9a F. 191 Lady Spencer to Albani, London 4.ii.65

210 b Mann to Albani 5.ii.65

210 c „ „ 12.ii.65

210 10a SP 105/316 f. 32 Albani to Mann 9.ii.65 (F. 191)

211 b f. 40 „ „ 16.ii.65 (F. 191)

f. 44 „ „ 23.ii.65 (F. 191)

f. 135 „ „ 8.vi.65 (F. 192)

f. 46 Giordani to Mann 23.ii.65

211 c f. 145 Albani to Mann 15.vi.65 (F. 192)

212 d f. 3–4 „ „ 4.i.66 (F. 194)

220 e f. 188 Giordani to Mann 31.vii.65

220 f f. 161 „ „ 29.vi.65

221 g f. 174 „ „ 3.vii.65

221 h f. 175–6 „ „ 13.vii.65

f. 178 „ „ 13.vii.65

222 i f. 167 „ „ 6.vii.65

227 j f. 14 Albani to Mann 12.i.65 (F. 191)

232 k f. 352 „ „ 28.xii.65 (F. 193)

211 11 F. 192 Mann to Albani 11.vi.65

211 12 SP 105/313 f. 87 Albani to Mann 26.iv.60 (F. 177b)

212 13a SP 98/70 f. 188 Albani to Mann 6.xi.65 (F. 193)

213 b f. 193 Mann to Conway 16.xi.65

212 14a SP 105/294 f. 184 Mann to Rochford 15.xi.65. Copy

213 b f. 206–7 Mann to Albani 7.i.66

213 15a SP 105/317 f. 1 Albani to Mann 1.i.66

215 b f. 65 de Vismes to Mann, Madrid 8.ii.66

216 c f. 44 Albani to Mann 25.i.66 (F. 194)

f. 46 „ „ 25.i.66 P.S.

220 d f. 138 Giordani to Mann 10.v.66

222 e f. 48 „ „ 25.i.66

222 f f. 126 „ „ 26.iv.66

222 g f. 298–9 „ „ 15.xi.66

227 h f. 92 „ „ 8.iii.66 P.S.

page

| 228 | 15*i* | SP 105/317 f. 116 | Albani to Mann 12.iv.66 (F. 194) |

222,

229	*j*	f. 122	„	„	19.iv.66
229	*k*	f. 136	„	„	3.v.66
229	*l*	f. 128–9	„	„	26.iv.66 (F. 194)
214	16*a*	SP 98/71 f. 17–19	Mann to Conway 10.i.66
214	*b*	f. 23–5	„	„	17.i.66
215	*c*	f. 30	„	„	21.i.66
215	*d*	f. 118	„	„	22.iii.66
216	*e*	f. 63	„	„	28.i.66
216		f. 70	„	„	1.ii.66
		f. 101–2	„	„	11.ii.66
217	*g*	f. 124–6	„	„	15.iv.66

Mann to Shelburne 8.xi.66

214	17*a*	F. 194 Mann to Albani 14.i.66
228	*b*	„	„	11.iii.66, 15.iii.66, 18.iii.66
228	*c*	„	„	8.iv.66
229	*d*	„	„	22.iv.66
229	*e*	„	„	6.v.66
214	18	Doran II p. 158 Mann to Walpole 3.i.66
215	19	SP 105/284 f. 51 Conway to Mann, St James's 1.iv.66
217	20*a*	SP 98/72 f. 88–9 Mann to Shelburne 19.v.67
232	*b*	f. 181	„	„	14.xi.67
218	21*a*	SP 98/82 f. 430 Mann to Weymouth 30.xi.79
234	*b*	f. 434 Mann to Hillsborough 21.xii.79
223	22*a*	SP 105/319 f. 384	Giordani to Mann 25.ii.69
223	*b*	f. 532	„	„	6.vi.69
224	*c*	f. 112	Albani to Mann 14.v.68 (F. 200)
		f. 117	„	„	21.v.68
		f. 272	„	„	19.xi.68
224	*d*	f. 420	„	„	22.iii.69
231	*e*	f. 103	„	„	23.iv.68 (F. 200)
		f. 111–12	„	„	14.v.68 (F. 200)
231	*f*	f. 370	Mann to Albani 18.ii.69
			Albani to Mann 2.iv.69
223	23*a*	SP 105/321 f. 160	„	„	14.xii.71
233	*b*	f. 158	„	„	30.xi.71
235	*c*	f. 35	Hamilton to Mann, Naples 19.ii.71

page

223 24 SP 105/320 f. 32 Giordani to Mann 17.ii.70
225 25 F. 201b   Albani to Muzell-Stosch 28.i.69 Published
                   Winckelmann, *Briefe* IV pp. 21–2
226 26 F. 205   Maria Theresa to Albani, Vienna 23.xi.72
227 27a F. 195/6 Mann to Albani 7.x.66, 14.x.66
233   b   Albani to Mann 23.xi.66
228 28 Fleming
229 29a F. 197 Albani to Mann 3.i.66
232   b   Mann to Albani 24.i.67
229 30a F. 198   ,,   ,,   8.vii.67
230   b   Albani to Mann 29.viii.67, 12.ix.67
229 31 F. 193 Mann to Albani 5.xi.65
230 32 Acton, Harold, *The Bourbons of Naples*, London 1956
                   p. 125
231 33 F. 200 Mann to Albani 17.v.68
231 34 SP 98/74 f. 59 Mann to Weymouth 25.iii.69
233 35a SP 105/296 f. 7, 9, 12, 14, 18
233   b   f. 75 Mann to Rochford 24.iv.73. Copy
                 f. 99   ,,   ,,   12.x.73. Copy
                 f. 100 ,,   ,,   23.x.73. Copy
233 36 F. 258
233 37a SP 98/79 f. 139 Mann to Rochford 26.vii.74
234   b   f. 57   ,,   ,,   16.iv.74
                 f. 61   ,,   ,,   23.iv.74
234   c   f. 5   ,,   ,,   1.i.74
234 38 SP 98/73 f. 9 Mann to Shelburne 16.i.68
234 39 SP 105/285 f. 39 Rochford to Mann, St James's
                   3.xii.73

Principal Sources

Public Record Office, Chancery Lane, London W.C.2
State Papers Foreign

Reference	Chapter	Reference	Chapter
SP 80/37	1.	98/35	1. 3. 4.
38	1. 2.	36	4.
39	1. 2.	37	1. 3. 4.
41	2.	38	4.
42	2.	40	4.
43	2.	41	3. 4.
84/276	2.	42	4.
85/13	1. 3. 4. 5.	43	4.
14	2. 3.	44	4. 5.
15	1. 3.	45	2. 5.
16	1. 3. 4. 6.	46	5.
92/30	1. 2.	48	4. 5.
31	2. 3. 4.	49	5.
33	1. 3.	50	1. 5.
34	4.	51	1. 5.
35	3. 4.	52	1. 5.
36	4.	53	6.
37	1. 4.	56	5.
39	4.	57	1. 6.
40	3.	58	1.
41	4.	59	1. 2. 6.
42	4. 5.	61	7.
47	4.	62	6.
98/24	1. 6.	63	1.
25	3. 4.	64	7.
26	3. 4.	68	8.
28	3. 4.	69	8.
29	2. 3.	70	8.
31	3. 4.	71	8.
32	3. 4. 5. 6.	72	8.
33	1. 3. 4.	73	8.
34	1. 3. 4.	74	8.

Reference	Chapter	Reference	Chapter
98/75	2.	105/313	7. 8.
79	8.	314	7. 8.
82	8.	315	7. 8.
85	4.	316	5. 8.
105/281	4.	317	8.
283	1. 5. 6.	319	8.
284	8.	320	8.
285	6. 8.	321	8.
291	6.	323	3.
293	8.	324	2. 3.
294	8.	325	4.
296	8.	326	2.
308	5.	327	3. 7.
309	5. 6.	328	2.
310	6. 7.	329	2.
312	7.		

Österreichisches Staatsarchiv
Abt. Haus-, Hof- und Staatsarchiv, Wien 1, Minoritenplatz 1
Gesandtschaftsarchiv Rom/Vatikan

Reference	Chapter	Reference	Chapter
Fasz. 125	5.	Fasz. 141	6.
126	5.	142	6.
127	5.	144	6.
128	5.	145	6.
129	5.	146	6.
130	5.	148	6.
131	5.	149	6.
132	4. 5.	150	6. 7.
133	5.	152	6.
134a	2.	154	6.
135	5.	155	6.
136	5.	156	6.
137	5.	157	6. 7.
138	5. 6.	158	6.
139	6.	159	4. 6.
140	5. 6.	160	6.

PRINCIPAL SOURCES

Reference	Chapter	Reference	Chapter
Fasz. 161	1. 5. 6.	Fasz. 182	7.
162	5. 6. 7.	183	7.
163	6.	185	7. 8.
164	6. 7.	186	7.
165	5. 6.	187	8.
166	7.	188	8.
167	7.	189	8.
168	7.	190	8.
169	7.	191	8.
170	7.	192	8.
172	7.	193	8.
173	7.	194	8.
175	6. 7.	195/6	7. 8.
176	7.	197	7. 8.
177b	8.	198	8.
177c	7.	200	8.
178	7.	201b	8.
180	7.	205	8.
181	6. 7.	258	8.

Bibliography

BENTLEY, Richard, *Correspondence of*, 2 Vols. London 1842.

BROSSES, Charles de, *Lettres d'Italie*, 2 Vols. Dijon 1927.

CAMBRIDGE New Modern History, VII, *The Old Régime 1713-63*.

CONSTABLE, William George, *Richard Wilson*. London 1953.

CUST, Lionel, *History of the Society of Dilettanti*. London 1898.

DENNISTOUN, James, *Memoirs of Sir Robert Strange, Kt., and Andrew Lumisden*, 2 Vols. London 1855.

DORAN, John, *Mann and Manners at the Court of Florence 1740-86*, 2 Vols. London 1876.

FLEMING, John, *Cardinal Albani's Drawings at Windsor*, The Connoisseur, November 1958, pp. 164-9.

HAILE, Martin, *Queen Mary of Modena*. London 1905.
James Francis Edward, the Old Chevalier. London 1907.

HAUSMANN, Friedrich, *Repertorium der Diplomatischen Vertreter aller Länder*, II, *1716-63*. Zürich 1950.

HORN, David Bayne, *British Diplomatic Representatives 1689-1789*, Royal Historical Society, Camden 3rd Series, XLVI. London 1932.

JUSTI, Karl, *Philip von Stosch und seine Zeit*, Zeitschrift für Bildende Kunst, VII, 1871, pp. 293-308; 332-46.
Der Kardinal Alexander Albani, Preussische Jahrbücher, Vol. 28, September 1871, pp. 248-63; 338-53.
Winckelmann und seine Zeitgenossen, 3 Vols. Leipzig 1923.

MICHAELIS, Adolf, *Ancient Marbles in Great Britain*, transl. C. A. M. Fennell. Cambridge 1882.

NOACK, Friedrich, *Des Kardinals Albani Beziehungen zu Kunstlern*, Der Cicerone, XVI, 1924, pp. 402-13; 451-9.

PETRIE, Charles, *The Jacobite Movement*. London 1959.

QUYNN, Dorothy Mackay, *Philip von Stosch . . .*, Catholic Historical Review, XXVII, No. 3, October 1941, pp. 332-44.

STOSCH, Baron Philip von, *Antiquarische Briefe*, edited by Karl Justi. Marburg 1871 (University Publication).

STOSCH, Philip de, *Gemmae Antiquae Caelatae . . .* Amsterdam 1724.

STRANGE, Norah K., *Jacobean Tapestry*. London 1947.

STROCCHI, Dionigi, *De Vita Alexandri Albani, Cardinalis*. Rome 1790.

STUART Papers, I–VII, Historical Manuscripts Commission.

TAYLER, Alistair and Henrietta, *The Old Chevalier*. London 1934.

VEYSSET, Jacques, *Les Merveilles cachées de la Villa Albani*, Connaissance des Arts, March 1960, pp. 37–42.

WAAGEN, Gustav Friedrich, *Treasures of Art in Great Britain*, 3 Vols. London 1854.

WALPOLE, Horace, *Correspondence with Sir Horace Mann, I–III, 1740–8*, Yale Edition, London 1955; *IV–VI, 1748–68*, London 1960.

 Letters, 16 Vols., edited by Paget Toynbee, Oxford 1903–5; with Supplement, 3 Vols., Oxford 1918–25.

WIESENER, Louis, *Le Régent, L'Abbé Dubois et les Anglais*, 3 Vols. Paris 1891–9.

WINCKELMANN, Johann Joachim, *Briefe*, 4 Vols. Berlin 1952–7.

 Description des Pierres Gravées du feu Baron de Stosch. Florence 1760.

 History of Ancient Art, 2 Vols. Transl. G. H. Lodge. Boston 1880.

Various standard works of reference, including the following:
  Dictionary of National Biography.
  The Catholic Encyclopaedia.
  Dictionnaire de Biographie Universelle.
  Enciclopedia Italiana.
  Thieme-Becker Künstler Lexikon.
  Moroni's Dizionario di Erudizione Storico-Ecclesiastica.
  Cardella's Memorie Storiche de Cardinali.
  Dizionario Biografico degli Italiani, Vol. 1, 1960. (The entry on Alessandro Albani by G. Sofri, with supplementary note by the author, includes a comprehensive list of sources.)

Index

Acquaviva, Cardinal, 32–3, 100, 129, 130
Acquaviva, Monseigneur, 124
Adam, James, 184, 185
Adam, Robert, 181, 182–3, 201
Albani, Alessandro, Cardinal: apparent interest in Old Pretender, 98, 99, 100, 139–40; artists patronised by, 169–74, 182, 183, 187–9; attached to interests of Great Britain, 11, 83, 92–3, 98, 116, 117, 118, 124 *et seq.*; attack on coachman of, 92; Austrian Chargé d'Affaires and Imperial Minister Plenipotentiary in Rome, 11, 12, 14, 123, 137, 179; on Benjamin West, cited, 182; biographical details, 11, 38–42; busts and vases given as presents by, 93, 209; cameos sold by, 122; Canon Fantoni nominated for Royal Society by, 229, 234; collection of drawings, 39, 184, 228; collector and patron of the arts, 38–9, 55, 92, 93, 99–100, 126, 184–5, 235; Comprotector of the Empire, 137, 138; correspondence with Bubb Dodington, 94–5, 155–161, 179; correspondence with Horace Mann, 11–18, 115, 116, 118 *et seq.*; correspondence with Wilhelm Muzell-Stosch, 189 *et seq.*; Countess Cheroffini mistress of, 133–4, 185; death of, 233–4, and burial, 235; decline of Jacobite sympathies, 82–4, 100, 116; elected Hon. Fellow of Society of Antiquaries, 196–197; at election of Pope Benedict XIII, 73, 74, 75, and of Clement XIV, 223; friendship with Cardinal Stuart, 177; friendship with Philip von Stosch, 64–5, 82–4, 92, 188–92; and John Wilkes, 210–11; Joint Protector of Knights of St John, 137; letter from James Stuart to, 140; letter to, from Maria Theresa, 226; Librarian of the Vatican, 193; made a cardinal, 45–6, 47, 48; marriage to Princess of Massa of nephew of, 134–6; medals sent to Philip von Stosch by, 123, 126; meeting with Horace Walpole, 16, 100; nomination to Sacred College, 34–5, 42; Nuncio at Congress of Cambrai, 45, 46–8, 56; Palazzo delle Quattro Fontane belonging to, 235; papal envoy at Vienna, 24, 42, 44, 47, 48, 62; patron of Abbé Winckelmann, 11, 189, 194–5, 207, 224–5; porcelain and snuff-box given to, 155, 156; portrait of, 160; Protector of King of Sardinia, 83, 98, 117; Protector for Maria Theresa, 24, 116, 117 *et seq.*; reports to Marquis d'Orméa, 98; Signora Guarnieri befriended by, 226–7; snuff-box given to Duke of York by, 208; Villa of, at Porta Salaria, 16, 196, 197–203, 207–8, 219–20, 225, 226, 230, 234, 235; and visit of Duke of York to Rome, 204–8; Vittorio Cheroffini daughter of, 227–8; works of

art, etc., procured for English-men, 151 *et seq.*; *et passim*, 32, 34, 77, 82, 112

Albani, Annibale, Cardinal: antiquarian tastes, 38; death of, 177; Jacobite sympathies, 31, 34, 36, 82, 99; at Papal elections, 62, 73, 75; portrait of, 40; Protector of Saxony, 99; seal of, as Camerlengo, 134; *et passim*, 26, 31-2, 38, 45, 48, 77, 140

Albani, Carlo, Prince, 32, 34, 38

Albani, Charles, Prince: Grand Master at Court of Milan, 226; Villa Albani left to, 202, 234

Albani, Francis, Cardinal, 140

Albani, Gianfrancesco, *see* Clement XI, Pope

Albani, Gianfrancesco, Cardinal: 27, 212; appointed Protector of Poland, 22; at election of Clement XIV, 223; friendship with Henry Stuart, 177, 215, and quarrel with, 216

Albani, Orazio, 32, 38

Albani, Princess, attempt to sail fishing-boat under British flag, 228-9

Albani, Teresa, 36

Alberoni, Cardinal, Minister in Madrid, 52, 64, 66, 76-7, 79, 82, 94

Allen, Edward, Chargé d'Affaires, Turin, 75

Althan, d', Cardinal, 62

Amerani, collection of works of art, 221

America, statue by Francavilla in, 161

Anne, granddaughter of Charles I, wife of King of Sicily, 28

Annesi, Paolo, painter, 200, 202

Antinous: bas-relief of, 155, 200; statue of, 174

Antiquaries, Society of, 16, 195-7

Antiques and works of art, restriction on export from Rome, 151-2, 154

Antium, Roman fort, 84

Arcangeli, Abbé Winckelmann murdered by, 224

Arundel, Lord, 52

Astley, John, painter, 171

Atella, vase found in ruins of, 93

Augustus II, Elector of Saxony and King of Poland, 56, 60

Augustus III of Poland and Saxony, statues sold to, 100

Baccante, statue of, 157

Bagnall, George, 29

Baker, H., 197

Barazzi, Rome merchant, 207

Barry, James, 232

Bartolozzi, Francis, engraver, 188

Battoni, Pompeo: paintings copied by, 162, 163, 164, 165, 166, 171; picture of Emperor Joseph and Grand Duke Leopold by, 231

Beaufort, Henry, 3rd Duke of: antiquarian tastes, 82; audience with the Pretender, 82

Bedford, John, 4th Duke of, Secretary of State for Southern Department, 136

Belloni, Jerome, Roman banker: 98, 173; attempt to sequester assets of, 124-5

Benedict XIII, Pope: election of, 74-5; policy of, 76, 83

Benedict XIV, Pope: 31; election of, 100, 116; relations with Austria, 118

Bentivoglio, Abbé, 91, 107, 110

Bentley, Dr Richard, Master of Trinity College, Cambridge: 49, 53; friendship with Philip von Stosch, 52-3, 81

Bentley, Thomas, 81, 82
Beranger, banker, 67
Bestigui, Charles de, 167
Bicchierari, Antonio, painter, 200, 202
Blaeu, John, atlas published by, 60
Blanchet, Louis-Gabriel, portraits of Old Pretender's sons by, 111
Bolingbroke, Frederick, 2nd Viscount, 159
Bologna (Italy): Guercino's *Circumcision* at, 187; Old Pretender at, 83, 84
Borghese, Prince, 206, 208, 231
Born, "Mr", *see* "Dutch Friend"
Botta, Marshal, 192
Bottari, John Gaetano, 68
Bouverie, John: 25; Jacobite sympathiser, 134
Bradford, Samuel, Bishop of Rochester, 73
Braitwitz, . . . , 111, 113, 119
Brandenburgh House, Hammersmith, 155–6
Brettingham, Matthew: 161–2, 163; statues bought by, 151–4
Britain, diplomatic relations with Papal Court, 21–7
British Council, 235
Brosses, Charles de, 54, 61, 185
Bruce, James, 234
Bruce, "Mr", 181
Brudenell, George, Lord (later Earl of Cardigan, etc.), 181
Brunswick, Prince of, 227
Bubb, George, *see* Dodington
Buckingham, Catherine, Duchess of, 89, 90
Burney, Fanny, 160
Button's coffee-house, Covent Garden, 52
Byng, Sir George, 161
Byng, John, Admiral, 160
Byres, James, 226

Cadogan, William, 1st Earl of, 46, 47
Caffignoli, Dr: 98; imprisonment of, 119
Caligula, bust of, 93
Cambrai, Congress of, 45, 46–8, 56
Caprara, Cardinal, Protector of Jacobite interests at Papal Court, 22, 26
Caracci, Annibale: *Triumph of Ariadne* by, 162; *Bacchus and Ariadne* by, 166
Carlisle, Howard, 3rd Earl (Lord Morpeth), 52, 122
Carteret, George, 1st Lord, collector of coins and medals, 53
Carteret, John, 2nd Lord: 53, 124; antiquarian tastes, 63, 67, 68; friendship with Philip von Stosch, 53, 59; Secretary of State for Southern Department, 23, 53, 62; von Stosch employed by, 62, 63 *et seq.*
Casali, Marquis, 169, 170, 187
Casanova, James, 41
Cassilis, John, 8th Earl of, 26
Castelbarco family, 202
Castel Gandolfo, palace at, 32–3, 99
Cavaceppi, Bartolomeo, sculptor, 174, 224
Cavallo, Monte, Papal palace at, 208
Caylus, Count, 154–5
Chamberlayne, Thomas: attempt to kill British spy, 24; Consul at Civita Vecchia, 22, 23, 121; Consul at Messina, 24; plot against Duke of Cumberland reported to Mann by, 24; relations with British Government, 24, 26; with British naval officers, 24
Chambers, Sir William, architect, 172

Charlemont, James, 1st Earl of, 26, 170–1, 172

Charles Edward, Prince (Young Pretender); audience with Clement XIII, 217; birth of, 36; character of, 110, 114, 115; deterioration of, 217, 218, 222; increasing importance of, 176–177; landing in Scotland, 129, 132; leaves Rome in 1744, 123; marriage to Louisa of Stolberg, 218; proposed landing in England, 115; proposed visit to Turin, 98, 99; rebellion of 1745, 132, and subsequent movements, 138, 149, 150; refusal, as a child, to kiss the Pope's feet, 75; return to Rome, 212, 216–217; rumoured engagement to a Princess of Modena, 135; suggested visit to Spain, 100, 128; titles claimed on death of his father, 212–17; and visit of Duke of York to Rome, 205; visit to Florence, 111–12.

Charles VI, Emperor, 29, 33, 35, 44, 55; death of, 114

Charles VII, Prince of Bavaria, claim to Holy Roman Empire, 114; elected Emperor, 115

Charles XII, King of Sweden, 29, 30

Charles Emanuel III, Duke of Savoy, King of Turin, 28, 92, 96, 116

Cheroffini, Countess: fans presented to, 133–4; mistress of Alessandro Albani, 185

Cheroffini, Vittoria, see Lepri

Chesterfield, Philip, Earl of, 122

Christina, Queen of Sweden, 38; sale of statues, etc., formerly belonging to, 75

Churchill, Brigadier Charles, 93

Chute,.... : 137; in Vienna, 131–2; visit to Rome, 128, 129, 131

Cienfuegos, Cardinal, Imperial Minister in Rome: 64, 69, 70, 91, 105, 106, 108–9; conversations with Charles Fane, 106–7; Old Pretender spied on by, 106

Civita Vecchia (Italy), British Consul at, 22, 23; port of, 120

Clavering, Captain, 26

Clement XI, Pope: 26, 27, 154; career of Alessandro Albani furthered by, 38, 39, 41–2, 46; collection of drawings, 39, 184; death of, 48, 57, 62; decline of temporal power under, 43; pension and other benefactions given to Philip von Stosch by, 54–5, 57; relations with James Stuart, 11, 27, 30–3, 34–7, 43, 47; represented by Alessandro Albani at Congress of Cambrai, 45, 46–8

Clement XII, Pope: election of, 85; support for Jacobites, 85

Clement XIII, Pope: 205, 208; at Villa Albani, 220; audience given to Young Pretender and Cardinal Stuart, 217; death of, 222; relations with George III and the Young Pretender, 205–206, 212–16

Clement XIV, Pope, election of, 223

Clementina (Sobieska), wife of James Stuart, 33–7, 66, and estrangement with, 80–1; arrest at Innsbruck, 33–4, and escape from, 35; death of, 111, 144; use of the Pope's litter, 81

Clérisseau, Charles Louis, draughtsman and painter, 172, 181, 183, 202

Clocer, Ladislas, 101

Colman, Francis, British Resident in Rome, and in Florence: 40, 71, 79, 80, 82, 93, 101, 102, 103;

death of, 104; protection of Philip von Stosch in Florence by, 87, 89

Colonna, Constable, widow of, 65

Commodus, bust of, 93

Constable, Sir Marmaduke, 141

Conti, Cardinal, see Innocent XIII, Pope

Conway, Henry Seymour, Secretary of State, 212, 213, 214, 215

Corrado, Giaquinto, painter, 162

Corsini, Cardinal, Governor of Rome, 87, 104–5; conversations with Charles Fane, 107–9

Corsini, Cardinal Lorenzo, see Clement XII, Pope

Corsini, Chevalier Gisiori, 105

Corsini, Grand Prior, 206, 208

Corsini family, 104, 105, 109, 111

Cortona (Tuscany), memorial inscription to Philip von Stosch prepared by Academy of, 55

Coscia, Prelate, 77

Costa, E. M. da, 197

Costanzi, Placido, 148, 174; painting copied by, 162, 164–5, 166, 167

Costanzi, Superintendent of antiquities, 152

Craon, Prince, Imperial Minister in Florence, 55

Crispyné, "Mr", 182

Culloden Moor, Battle of, 11, 132, 185

Dalton, Richard, 143, 173, 188

Dartmouth, William, 2nd Earl, 168

Davenant, Henry, Envoy Extraordinary to Tuscany, 68–9

"Davers, Chevalier", 181

Davia, Cardinal, 27, 62

Dawkins, James, Jacobite sympathiser, 131, 134, 141

Dennistoun, James, 11, 185

Dereham, Sir Thomas, Jacobite, 23, 55, 86, 109

Devismes, Lewis de, 181, 215

Devonshire, William, 2nd Duke of, 52

Dick, John, Consul at Leghorn, 219–20

Dodington, Bubb (George Bubb, later Lord Melcombe): correspondence with Alessandro Albani, 94–5, 154, 155–61, 179, 180; death of, 180; friendship with Philip von Stosch, 94–5, 104; gallery added to Brandenburgh House, 155, pavement for, 158, works of art for, 156–159, 167; porcelain and snuffbox sent to Cardinal Albani by, 155, 156, 198; visit to Rome, 94–5, 113; et passim, 178, 179, 180

Drake, . . ., 131

Duane, M., 197

Dubois, Abbé, 27, 44; Cardinal, 44–6, 51

Duckett, Dugood or Ducat, William, jeweller, imprisoned by Inquisition, 70–1

Dunbar, Lord, see Murray

"Dutch Friend" or "Dutchman" (Mr Born), Dutch Consul in Rome: 134; correspondence with Horace Mann, 126–7, 128, 130, 141; defection of, 147, 148; friend of Mark Parker, 146, 147, and of St. Leger, 147

Edgar, James, Pretender's secretary, 80

Edinburgh (Scotland), impressions of engraved gems in, 194

Edward Augustus, Duke of York: death of, 232; snuff-box given to, by Alessandro Albani, 208;

Venus bought by, 221; visit to Italy, 204–8, 209, 234

Egizzio, Matteo, 93

Eglinton, Alexander, 10th Earl, 122

Essex, Lady, visit to Rome, 105–6

Essex, William, 3rd Earl of, Ambassador to Turin: 63, 101; information concerning Old Pretender supplied by, 95–8

Eugene, Prince, 30, 52, 55 . . .

Fagel, Franz, Greffier of Assembly of States General: collector of coins, 51, 126; friendship with Philip von Stosch, 51, 59, 60–1, 64, 126; retirement, 126

Fahrenheit thermometer, 88

Fairfax, General, 156

Fane, Charles, British Minister at Florence: 99, 104, 111–12; conversations with Cardinals Cienfuegos and Corsini, 106–9; financial difficulties of, 110; visit to Rome, 105–6, and return to England, 112

Fane, "Mr", 134

Fantoni, Canon, 229, 234

Farnese, Elizabeth, wife of Philip V of Spain, 114

Farnese, Palazzo, copies of paintings in, for Northumberland House, 162–7

Farnesina, copy of painting in, for Northumberland House, 162–7

Farsetti, Abbé, 170

Ferdinand, King of the Two Sicilies: betrothal to Maria Josepha, 229; and her death, 230; betrothal and marriage to Maria Carolina, 230–1

Ficcoroni, Francis, antiquary, 123

Firmian, Count, 222

Flemming, Count, Prime Minister of Augustus II, 56, 57, 58–9

Florence (Tuscany), senior British diplomat accredited to, 22

Fontanini, Justus, Papal Chamberlain, 54

Forbes, Admiral, gifts exchanged with Alessandro Albani, 133, 198

Fordwich, Lord, 181, 188

Forrester, Major, 174

Fotheringham, . . ., 103

Fountaine, Sir Andrew, 52

Francavilla, statues by, 161

Francis I, Emperor: 112, 114, 123, 129, 131, 228; death of, 229

Franco-Austrian Treaty, 177

Frederick the Great, King of Prussia, 115, 194, 204

Frederick, Prince of Wales: works of art procured for, 157–8, 161; death of, 158

Freemasons, Society of, 111

Fuller, John, Consul at Leghorn, 161

Galt, John, 182

Ganganelli, Cardinal, *see* Clement XIV, Pope

Gastaldi brothers, 232–3

Gaven Richard: 22, 142; accused of spying by Prince Lobkowitz, 121–2; art dealer, 14, 23, 122, 184, 199, 200; Maria Theresa's agent to British fleet, 23, 121, 122

George I, King: 33, 44; death of, 36, 84

George II, King, 90

George III, King: 173; drawings bought for, 184, 228; works of art bought for, 220–1

Gérard, Père, 125–6

Gersdorf, Baron von, 56, 57

Ghezzi, Chevalier Pier Leoni, 40, 67, 68, 221

Gilly, Xavier, 25

Giordani, Abbé Paolo Bernardo, secretary to Alessandro Albani, 18, 40, 207, 208, 211, 218, 225; art-dealing, 218–23; correspondence with Horace Mann, 218–23, 233

Giudice, Cardinal, Imperial Protector: 94; death of, 117

Glenshiel (Ross-shire), Jacobite rising quelled at, 30, 36

Godolphin, Francis, Lord, horse purchased for, 150

Gordon, . . ., Jacobite agent, 65, 172

Grant, Abbé, Jacobite supporter, 123–4, 130, 144, 160, 168, 217, 222, 232–3

Grantham, Thomas, Lord, 182

Grenville, Henry, 195–6

Grimaldi, Marchesa, 185

Gualterio (or Gualtieri), Cardinal, Protector of British Jacobite interests at Papal Court, 26–7, 68, 72

Guarnieri, Signora, widow of Chevalier Guarnieri, befriended by Alessandro Albani, 226–7

Guercino, Circumcision by, 187

Gunpowder Plot, papers relating to, 233

Halifax, George Montagu, Earl of, Secretary of State, 206

Hamilton, Gavin, 226

Hamilton, Sir William, Envoy at Naples, 223, 234

Han (d'Hancarville), Baron, 199, 223

Hay, John, Earl of Inverness, 70, 71, 73, 89, 103

Hay, . . ., Countess of Inverness, 80, 81

Henry, "Mr", 181

Henry Frederick, Duke of Cumberland, visit to Rome, 234

Henry Stuart, Cardinal (Cardinal Stuart or York), 173, 188; appointed Arch-Priest and Prefect of St Peter's, 31; audience with Clement XIII, 217; birth of, 31; differences with Old Pretender, 176, 177; friendship with Alessandro Albani, 177; friendship with Gianfrancesco Albani, 11, 177, 215, and quarrel with, 216; made a cardinal, 138–9; move to Cancellaria, 211; title of Duke of York used by, 204; Young Pretender's claims supported by, 212–17

Hervey, Captain, 204

Hewet, Sir Thomas, 161

Hillsborough, Lord (Wills Hill, 1st Marquis of Downshire), Secretary of State, 229, 233

Hoare, Prince, sculptor, 142, 155, 169

Hobart, John, Lord (1st Earl of Buckingham), 119

Holdernesse, Robert, Earl of, 61, 123, 126, 127, 148

Holdsworth, . . ., 131

Holkham (Norfolk), 151, 154, 201

Hollis, Thomas, 195, 197

Hope, Jean, 199

Hope, Olivier, 147, 198, 199

Hope, Thomas, 198–9

Howe, . . ., merchant at Leghorn, 133

Imperial Figure, statue of, 157

Imperiali, Cardinal, 27, 64, 77

Innes, James, 168

Innocent XII, Pope, 84

Innocent XIII, Pope: death of, 73; election of, 62

Inquisition, The: Dr Caffignoli imprisoned by, 119; Mark Parker banished from Rome by,

146–7; Thomas Patch banished by, 173; William Duckett imprisoned by, 70–1

Islay, Archibald, Earl and Viscount of (later Duke of Argyll), request for cats for, 150

Jacobite Court, diplomatic relations, 25, 26, 27

James II: 22, 26, 90; death of, 31 tender): audience with Benedict XIII, 75; at Bologna, 83, 84; cardinals nominated by, 34–35, 42, 45, 214; death of, 213, 222; decline of, 144, 205, 206, 211–12; diplomatic appointments made by, 26–7; lack of support from Duke of Savoy, 28–9; marriage to Clementina Sobieski, 33–7, and estrangement from, 80–1, 83; medals struck by, 114; Philip von Stosch employed to spy on, 61 et seq.; relations with Alessandro Albani, 82–4, 98, 99;

James Edward, Prince (Old Pretender): removal to Rome, 11, 27, 29, 30–3, 35, 36; support from Clement XI and Albani family, 30–3; suspicions of Capt. Morrice, 79–80; withdrawal to Avignon, 27; et passim, 94, 97, 98, 99, 106, 175, 204

Jansen, Sir Theodore, 63

Jenkins, Thomas, art dealer, 167–169, 188, 206, 207, 226, 233

Joseph, Emperor: death of the Empress from smallpox, 229; visit to Rome, 229, 231

Julius Caesar, bust wrongly stated to be of, 169–70

Justi, Karl, 16, 56, 203

Kew (Surrey), statues by Francavilla at, 161

Knights of St John, 137

Küster, Ludolf, 49, 52, 53

Lagnasco, Count, 99, 109

Lambertini, Cardinal, see Benedict XIV, Pope

Lampo, Abbé, 97

Langlois, "Mr", Leghorn merchant, 50–1, 63

Lanti, Cardinal, 27

Lapiccola, Niccola, painter, 200, 202

Leghorn (Italy), British Consul at, 22, 23

Leicester, Thomas, Earl of: 167, 180; difficulties of obtaining statues bought for Holkham, 151–4

Leopold, Grand-Duke of Tuscany, 228, 231

Lepri, Vittoria (Cheroffini): daughter of Alessandro Albani, 228; visit to Florence, 227–8

Ligorio, Pirro, architect, 75

Liria, Duke of, 97, 103

Lobkowitz, Prince, 111, 120, 121–122, 124

"London, City of, with a Rising Sun", on Jacobite medals, 114

Long, Captain, R.N., 24, 121

Louis XIV: 43; death of, 27

Louis XV, 27

Lumsden, Andrew, Pretender's secretary, 11, 25, 41, 144, 185, 186, 188, 217–18

Malton, Charles, Lord (Marquess of Rockingham), 174

Malvezzi, Cardinal, 188

Mandeville, George, Lord (later Duke of Manchester), 181

Mann, Horace: 23, 40, 41, 48, 102; appointed Resident to Grand Duke of Tuscany, 112, 115; biographical details, 112; commissions for works of art, etc., undertaken for Englishmen, 150 *et seq.*, for Lord Leicester, 151-3, for the Duke of Northumberland, 161-7; complaints of Xavier Gilly by, 25; correspondence with Alessandro Albani, 11-18, 116, 118 *et seq.*; correspondence with "Dutch Friend", 126-7, 128, 141; correspondence with Henry Conway, 212, 213, 214, 215; correspondence with Horace Walpole, 15, 50, 54, 120, 130, 137-8, 178, 186, 188-9; financial difficulties of, 110, 150; Giordani employed by, 222-3, 233; relations with Philip von Stosch, 49, 50-1, 113; relations with Thomas Chamberlayne, 24

Manteuffel, Count, Royal Polish Antiquarian, 59

Mantua (Italy), Palazzo at, copies of paintings in, 162, 166

Maratta, Carlo, collection of drawings, 184

March, William, 3rd Earl of (later Duke of Queensberry), 134

Marchionne, Carlo, architect, 199

Maresfoschi, Monseigneur, Cardinal Stuart's auditor, 173

Maria Carolina, Princess, betrothal and marriage to Ferdinand, King of Sicily, 230-1

Maria Josepha, Princess: betrothal to Ferdinand, King of Sicily, 229; death from smallpox, 230

Maria Theresa, Empress: 204; Alessandro Albani Protector for, 24, 116; letter to Alessandro Albani, 226; Richard Gaven agent to British fleet for, 23; smallpox contracted by, 229-230; succession to throne of

Charles VI, 35, 114-15, and coronation, 117

Mary of Modena, Queen of James II, 31

Massa: Dowager Duchess Regent of, 135; marriages of Princesses of, 134-6

Masucci, Agostino, painting copied by, 162, 163, 165, 166

Matthews, Admiral Thomas: 115, 120, 121; request for horse, 150

Mazzanti, Lodovico, 40

Medici, Grand Duke Cosimo III, 55, 88

Medici, Grand Duke Gian Gastone: interview with young Pretender, 111; death of, 112

Melcombe, Lord, *see* Dodington, Bubb

Mellini, Cardinal, 137, 138, 153, 179

Mengs, Raphael: painting copied by, 162, 164, 165, 166, 167; "Parnassus" painted by, 201, 228

Mercury, statue of, 157

Miller, Lady, 203

Millo, Cardinal, 117

Modena, Duke of, 134-7, 138, 159

Modena, Princess of, 135, 137. *See also* Mary of

Molesworth, John, Envoy Extraordinary to Turin, 28, 44, 53, 62, 70

Montefiasconi (Rome), James Stuart married at, 36

Montemileto, Prince of, 77

Montfaucon, Bernard de, 54

Morpeth, Lord, *see* Carlisle, Lord

Morrice, Capt. Bacon: attempt on life of, 79; banishment from Rome, 80; drawings ordered by, 79; mail of, intercepted by Jacobites, 79

Morrice, "Mr", 181

Morris, Roger, 156

Murray (Lord Dunbar), Old Pretender's Secretary, 25, 99, 100, 129, 130, 140

Muti Palace, Rome: 177, 205; leased to James III, 36; royal and other arms removed from, 215

Muzell-Stosch, Wilhelm, nephew and heir of Philip von Stosch, 50, 189–94; correspondence with Alessandro Albani, 189 et seq.; elected Hon. Fellow of Society of Antiquaries, 195–6; visit to England, 195; Winckelmann's papers kept by, 225

Mytton, "Mr", 181

Nairne, David, 34

Nelli, Pietro, 40

Nettuno (Italy): landscapes from palaces at, 100; Philip von Stosch with Alessandro Albani at, 84

Newburgh, Charlotte, Countess of (wife of Charles Radcliffe): 86; daughters of, 86, 144

Newcastle, Duke of, Secretary of State: antiquarian tastes, 75; payments to Philip von Stosch neglected by, 50–1, 63–4, 75; et passim, 80, 94, 96, 97, 101, 103, 106, 111, 113, 129, 136, 141

Newport, "Mr", 121

Niccolini, Marchese, 153

Noakes, Richard, 181

Nonantola, Abbey of, 75

Norris, William, 197

North, Francis, Lord, 168

Northumberland, Hugh (Smithson), Earl of, later Duke of: 174; works of art for Northumberland House bought for, 162–7, 180

Northumberland House, Strand: demolished, 167; fireplaces from, 167; paintings for, 161–7

Odam, Chevalier Jerome, 67, 68

Orford, Lady, 181

Orléans, Duc d', Regent of France, 27, 44

Orméa, Marquis d', 84, 96, 97, 98

Orsini, Cardinal, see Benedict XIII, Pope

Otway, Colonel, 181

Owls, kept as pets, 78

Pailfield, Amos, 24

Pamphili, Cardinal, 62, 74

Paris, porch of St Sulpice in, 156

Paris, statue of, 157

Parker, John, painter, attempt to replace Mark Parker, 148

Parker, Mark: antiquary, 120, 147; banished from Rome by the Inquisition, 146–8; et passim, 119, 120, 123, 126, 127–8, 141, 142

Parma, Dowager Duchess of, rumour of marriage with Old Pretender and portraits of his sons commissioned by, 111

Parma, Duke of, 187

Parnassus, by Mengs, 201, 228

Parody of the School at Athens, by Sir Joshua Reynolds, 25–6

Parsons, J., 197

Pascal Giacinti, 140

Passionei, Cardinal, 194

Passports, difficulty of obtaining, 25, 129, 130, 183

Patch, Thomas, painter: banished from Rome, 172–3; caricature group by, 173

Paterson, James, waistcoat obtained for, 150

Paulucci, Cardinal, 76, 77, 82

Pembroke, Thomas, Earl of, 52

Pennant brothers, 181

Phelps, Major Richard, 25, 204, 205

Philip V of Spain: 43, 114; sale of statues, etc., to, 75

Pico della Mirandola, Cardinal, 27

Piranesi, Jean Batiste, engraving of Villa Albani by, 203

Pitt, William, 183-4

Poland, Cardinal Gianfrancesco Albani, "Protector" of, 22

Polignac, Cardinal, French Ambassador in Rome: 64, 82, 85, 87; Protector for the Pretender, 77; relations with Jacobites, 102

Portocarero, Cardinal, 137

Posi, Paul, 170

Potenza, Countess, and her daughter - in - law, dressing-gowns made for, 199

Pozzi, painter, 162

Pozzo, Cassiano dal, collection of drawings, 39, 184

Ptolemy, statue of, 157

Quadruple Alliance, The, 30, 44, 55

Quarelli, secretary to Alessandro Albani, 119, 218, 224

Radcliffe, Charles: 86, 96, 103, 141, 144; execution of, 112; step-daughters of, 86, 144

Radcliffe, Edward, Earl of Derwentwater, 86

Radcliffe, William, 86

Raphael: *Assembly of the Gods* by, 162, 166; *Marriage of Cupid and Psyche* by, 166; *School of Athens* by, 164, 166, 167

Read, Catherine, 40, 160

Rebellion of 1715, 27, 86

Rebellion of 1745, 84, 112, 132-3, 144, 185

Renaudot, Eusébe, orientalist, 51

Reni, Guido, *Aurora* by, 162, 165, 166

Reynolds, Sir Joshua, 25-6

Rice, "Mr", 134

Richardson, "Mr", 181

Richecourt, Count, 125

Ripperda, Duke of, 82

Rivera, Count, 100, 129

Rizzi (or Ricci): Domenico Francesco, British Consul at Papal Court, 22; appointment not confirmed, 23

Robinson, Sir Thomas, Secretary of State, 23, 149

Rochester, Bishop of, *see* Bradford

Rochford, William, Earl of, cutting of jessamine obtained for, 150

Romano, Guilio, *Feasts of the Gods* by, 162

Rome: Alessandro Albani buried beneath Church of St Sebastian, 235; Cupola of St Peter's illuminated, 234. *See also* Muti Palace

Rosa, Lopez, 153

Roseberry, Neil, 3rd Earl of, 181

Rospigliosi, Villa, copy of painting in, for Northumberland House, 162-7

Rossi, Jerome, engraver, 40

Rotá, Abbé Antonio, 96, 97

Rowley, Admiral, 133

Roxburgh, John, 3rd Duke of, 181

Rupert, Prince, and Margaret Hughes, 156

Russel, James, 188

Russia, Tsar of, 29

Sabatini, Marcantonio, papal antiquary, 38

St Aignan, Duc de, French Ambassador in Rome, 98, 100
St Leger, Hayes (later Lord Doneraile), indiscretions of, in Rome, 145–7
St Odil, Baron, 228
St Saphorin, British Minister at Vienna: 62; on Alessandro Albani, 41, 42, 44, 45, 46, 47, 69; on Pretender's marriage, 35
Saterno, Cardinal, 74
Schmettau, Baron von, Prussian Ambassador, 51, 54
Schott, Carl, Imperial Antiquarian, 49
Scotland: rebellion of 1715, 27, 86; rebellion of 1745, 84, 112, 132–133, 144, 185; rising in 1719, 36
Scott, Captain, 120
Sebright, Sir Thomas, 134
Semple, "Mr", 103
Septimius Severus, bust of, 93
Servandoni, John Jerome, 156
Seven Years War, 144, 167, 175, 180
Shelburne, William, Earl of (later Marquess of Lansdowne), Secretary of State, 232
Shuttleworth, Thomas, arrest of, 134
Sinzendorff, Comte de, 42, 47, 48
Sixtus V, Pope, treasure of, 77–8
Skelton, John, painter, 186, 188
Skinner, Brinley, British Consul at Leghorn, 23, 69, 71, 80, 81, 84, 101, 103, 104; accounts and financial difficulties of, 101, 104
Smith, . . ., Consul at Venice, 221
Smythe, "Mr", 181
Soriano, Prince, marriage of, 134–135, 137; birth of heir to, 136
Spada, Cardinal, 74
Spence, Joseph, 112, 113, 162
Spencer, Georgiana, Lady; alabaster vase given to, 208–9; visit to Rome, 208–9

Spinelli, Cardinal Riviera, 27
Spinola, Governor of Rome, 85
Staffarda, Abbey of, 83
Stanhope, James, 1st Earl, Secretary of State, 41–2, 46, 160
Statues: prohibition of export from Rome, 151–2; restoration of, 155, 159
Stephenson, "Mr", 181
Sterne, Laurence, 232
Stolberg, Princess Louisa, married to Young Pretender, 218
Stone, cure for the, 160
Stosch, Baron Philip von: antiquarian tastes, 12, 39, 49–55, 57–61, 93, 123, 126, 189; appointed by British Government to report on Stuarts in Rome, 12, 13, 15, 61–2, 63 et seq.; appointed Royal Antiquarian to Augustus II, 56, 57; Atlas compiled by, 60–1, 64, 193; attack on coachman of, 78; attempt on life of, and departure from Rome, 87–90, 102–3, 107–8; biographical details, 49–50; catalogue of collection of gems, 193, 194–5; death of, 90, 190–2; dispersal of collections of, 193–4; financial difficulties, 50–1, 56–61, 63–4, 70, 71–2, 78, 82, 85, 188; friendship with Alessandro Albani, 64–5, 82–4, 92, 123, 154, 188; friendship with Bubb Dodington, 94–95; friendship with Dr Bentley, 52–3, 81; friendship with Franz Fagel, 51, 59, 60–1, 64; friendship with Lord Carteret, 53, 59, and employed by, 62, 63 et seq.; gem said to have been swallowed by, 54, 61; Gemmae Antiquae Caelatae by: 52, 55, 68; in Dresden, 56–7; in Holland,

57; invited to Congress of Cambrai, 56; journey to Italy, 54, 60, and to Vienna, 55; meetings with Cardinal Alberoni, 52; memorial inscription prepared by Academy of Cortona, 55; owls and cats kept as pets by, 78, 150; patronised by Clement XI, 54-5, 57; pseudonym "John Walton" used by, 12, 63, 69, 149; referred to as "Cyclops," 54; removal to Florence, 87, 90, 111, 188, and threatened with banishment from, 189; visit to England, 52; will of, 50, 192; William Duckett befriended by, 70-1; *et passim*, 100, 101, 104, 110, 113, 117, 120, 132, 140, 141, 147, 155, 177, 215, 221

Stosch, Henry von, 63
Stosch, Ludwig von, 55
Strange, Robert, engraver: 11, 25, 181, 185-8; wife of, 185
Strauffen, von, Papal Antiquary, 152
Strozzi, Duke, 206, 207
Stuart, Henry, Cardinal, *see* Henry Stuart
Stuart, "Mr", 181
Syon House, 167, 201

Tassie, James and William, 194
Tencin, Cardinal: 100; nephew of, 114
Thomson, . . ., and the "Charitable Corporation", 98
Thun, Count de, Bishop of Gurk, 118, 119, 120, 122, 123
Tivoli: 172; Villa d'Este dismantled, 159
Tivoli, Bishop of, 172-3
Tolomei, Cardinal, 74
Torlonia, Prince, Villa Albani bought by, 202

Towneley, Francis, execution of, 141
Towneley, John, 141, 142
Townshend, Captain, 161
Townshend, Lord, Secretary of State, 48, 62
Treaty of Aix-la-Chapelle (Peace Treaty), 136, 144
Treby, "Mr", 134
Triple Alliance, The, 27, 44
Turnbull, "Mr", 134
Tyndale, T., 197

Unigenitus, Bull, 43, 45
Urbino (Italy), ducal palace at, 32, 38
Ursins, Princesse des: 68, 70; dressing set bequeathed to Pretender by, 70
Utrecht, Peace of, 28, 43

Valenti, Cardinal, Secretary of State: export of statues prohibited by, 151-3; "present" given to, 153
Vane, "Mr", 181
Vatican, student-artists working at, 164
Velletri, campaign of, 222
Venice, paintings in Palazzo Labia, 167
Venus, bought for Duke of York, 221
Venuti, Abbate, Papal Antiquary, statues examined by, 152
Versailles: bust in Museum, 40; visited by Philip von Stosch, 54
Verschaffelt, Peter, sculptor, 156
Victor Amadeus II, Duke of Savoy, Prince of Piedmont, King of Sicily: 28, 29, 43; King of Sardinia, 28, 35-6, 48, 83, 92, 95, 115; meeting with James Stuart, 29

Victoria and Albert Museum, 167

Vierpyle, Simon, sculptor, 170–1

Villettes, Arthur: 97, 98, 100, 121, 140; fan procured for, 123

Waagen, Dr Gustav, cited, 165–6

Wachtendonck, . . ., von, 111

Wackerbarth-Salmour, Count, Saxon Minister in Rome, 88

Wade, Marshal, 132

Waldegrave, James, Lord, Ambassador in Paris, 96

Walkinshaw, Clementina, 218

Walpole, Horace: correspondence with Horace Mann, 15, 50, 54, 120, 130, 137–8, 178, 186, 189, 195; meeting with Alessandro Albani, 16, 100; on Northumberland House gallery, 166–167; reference to Philip von Stosch, 88, 90; sculptured eagle procured for, 129, 161

Walpole, Horatio, 1st Lord, British Ambassador in Paris, 79, 141

Walpole, Horatio, son of Horatio, 1st Lord, 134

Walpole, Sir Robert: busts given to, 93; vase given to, by Philip von Stosch, 93

Walton, John, pseudonym of Philip von Stosch, q.v.

War of the Austrian Succession, 24, 25, 114 et seq., 144

War of the Polish Succession, 96, 103

War, Seven Years, 25, 144, 167, 175, 180

War of the Spanish Succession, 28, 43

Ward, "Mr", 26

Werpup, Baron, 234

Wescombe, Mrs, 104

West, Benjamin, 39, 41, 182

Whiston, William, 52

Whithed, . . ., visit to Rome, 128, 129, 131

Wilkes, John, visit to Rome, 209–211

William Augustus, Duke of Cumberland, 24, 132

William Henry, Duke of Gloucester, visit to Rome, 223, 233

Willoughby, . . ., financed by James Stuart to go to "Muscovy", 82

Wilson, Richard, painter, 171–2

Wilton, Joseph, sculptor, 155, 169, 170, 187

Winchilsea, Earl of, 52

Winckelmann, Abbé Johann Joachim: curator of Alessandro Albani's library, 194–5; elected Hon. Fellow of Society of Antiquaries, 196; description of Cardinal Albani's Villa promised to Society by, 16, 196; murder of, 16, 224; Philip von Stosch's collection of gems catalogued by, 193, 194–5; portrait of, 224, 225; will of, 224; et passim, 11, 12, 15, 39, 41, 179, 187, 189, 207, 210, 211, 227

"Windham, Chevalier", 181

Windsor (Berks.): collection of drawings at, 185; statues by Francavilla at, 161

Wood, Robert, Under-Secretary of State, 25, 26

Woodfall, . . ., and smallpox inoculation, 181

Wright, Denys, 71, 96, 103

Wright, Fortunatus, 161